Gellinek
Going Dutch – Gone American

Christian Gellinek

Going Dutch – Gone American

Germans Settling North America

Jack mit allen guten Wünschen für Dich und Deine Familie

July 2003

Aschendorff Münster

Printed with the kind support of
Carl-Toepfer-Stiftung, Hamburg, Germany

© 2003 Aschendorff Verlag GmbH & Co. KG, Münster

Das Werk ist urheberrechtlich geschützt. Die dadurch begründeten Rechte, insbesondere die der Überset-
zung, des Nachdrucks, der Entnahme von Abbildungen, der Funksendung, der Wiedergabe auf foto-
mechanischem oder ähnlichem Wege und der Speicherung in Datenverarbeitungsanlagen bleiben, auch
bei nur auszugsweiser Verwertung, vorbehalten. Die Vergütungsansprüche des § 54, Abs. 2, UrhG,
werden durch die Verwertungsgesellschaft Wort wahrgenommen.

Druck: Druckhaus Aschendorff, Münster, 2003
Gedruckt auf säurefreiem, alterungsbeständigem Papier ∞

ISBN 3-402-05182-6

This Book is dedicated to my teacher of Comparative Anthropology
at Yale Law School from 1961 to 1963

F. S. C. Northrop (1893–1992)

Sterling Professor of Philosophy and Law, author of the benchmark for
comparative philosophy, *Philosophical Anthropology and Practical Politics*

This Book has two mottoes which bifurcate as the topic's divining rod

The first motto is by GERTRUDE STEIN [1874–1946], a Pennsylvania-born woman of letters, raised in California, and expatriate resident of Europe after 1903:

> "In the United States there is more space
> where nobody is than where anybody is.
> That is what makes America what it is."[1]

The second motto has to do with the German immigration. It is borrowed from a book by THEODOR FONTANE [1819–1898], a Brandenburg-born writer, and a critic of Prussia. An old German woman, whose grandchildren have emigrated to Anmerica is speaking in her dialect of Low German:

> ["Dröwen in Amirika. Doa verstoahn set.
> Un worümm? Wiehl se watt hebben.
> Un woa se watt hebben, doa künn se ook wat.
> Und ick woll, ick wihr ook all doa.
> Joa, min Seel, un et kümmt ook noch so.
> Man blot, dat man ihrst röwer wihr."][2]

> "Over there in America! There they have the know.
> And why? Everyone possesses something.
> And where they own something, they can get ahead.
> And I'd wish I was there.
> Yea, upon my soul, I'm going to get there yet.
> If only one had made it to over there."

---

[1] "The Geographical History of America", 1936.
[2] Spreewaldwanderung [1882] *Sämtliche Werke* [NFA], vol. 12 (Munich 1960) 12: 37. Translation is mine.

PREFACE

Two major interests of the long-time scholar in the field of German Studies Christian Gellinek are here combined: history of the German immigration to North America and philology. In his numerous other volumes published over a span of thirty-five years, Prof. Gellinek has explored the complex history of the migration of German-speaking people to the "New World" as well as topics in the history of the German language. His interests in both reach back to early periods. In the case of language studies, he has concerned himself especially with the Medieval and early modern periods, thus acquiring considerable knowledge about many aspects of language usage and terminology for those periods.

Similarly, Prof. Gellinek's extensive research in early emigration, more accurately general migration of German-speaking people during early periods, has given him insights into aspects of complex patterns of movement by migrating people. It is in the combination of these two areas of knowledge that *Going Dutch* makes its contribution to German-American Studies and to the history of language.

It is important to realize the extent of German trade and movement of people within the restricted boundaries of North Central Europe as well as the involvement of German speakers of various dialects in the trade of other nations, particularly Holland in the early period. This led to very early involvement of Germans in the New World with concomitant linguistic implications. Northern Germans in particular were present in the Dutch settling of the Hudson River area.

The relationship to the English is discussed based on the Low German term *Jantje* (*Kleinhans*, common person). The word was transformed in the course of political and social events. Thus Prof. Gellinek proceeds to narrate the migratory and linguistic movements of German immigrants through the long period of German immigration to the New World. Much of the story is in language, the words acquired by the surrounding linguistic environment and even more so in place names.

While the methodological path may appear meandering, it in fact sets up the background for examining aspects of both colonial and post-colonial American history. As becomes clear in the story of the dollar, the restrictive British colonial monetary policy caused in a convoluted pattern the adoption of the free-wheeling maritime *thaler*. This is then followed back to the Central European less restricted, even chaotic monetary situation. The book moves in this fashion through many aspects of American cultural history relating it back to the influence of German-speaking Central Europeans, their cultural background and migration.

Considerable original materials in addition to past and current research are reflected in this study. Topics and concepts are drawn across a wide range of materials. A reflection on Alexis de Toqueville and Gottfried Duden and their contrasting intellectual approaches to the new American republic shows how both had incomplete, but from their won perspectives accurate views of American life, de Toqueville more optimistic and Duden more skeptical. Prof. Gellinek's excursus on these seminal characters fits

VII

into a patchwork of analysis that is unified in the whole. This fits also a style of writing that does not eschew the colloquial or direct language when a point is to be made.

What is further unique in this book is how smaller details of life and language are teased out of broader contexts and examined for what may be learned that is new or that throws a different light on events that are taken for granted. The early period is clearly Prof. Gellinek's forte, and it is here that much is to be learned that was previously ignored or inadequately explored. This is not to say that the attempt was made to be exhaustive, but rather to present insights, new ways of looking at accepted facts, and, in so doing, influence the direction of scholarship while at the same time providing an interesting story for anyone interested in the German influence on the New World from its early colonial period on.

The German-American story is one that has many facets, a lot of which have yet to be explored. Prof. Gellinek in tying up some of the loose ends of his years of scholarship has elucidated more of these facets and pointed out others yet to be examined. Thus we are well served.

Giles R. Hoyt
Max Kade German-American Research and Resource Center
Indiana University Purdue University Indianapolis

TABLE OF CONTENTS

Introduction XI

PART ONE
PRE-EMIGRATION AND TRANSPORTATION:
From Prelude to Surviving, Peopling and Serving 1
    Chapter 1   Shipbuilding in Lübeck 5
    Chapter 2   Sequestering ships 10
    Chapter 3   Transportation of Cohort Germans by the
                    Dutch Merchant fleet to New Amsterdam 14
    Chapter 4   New Amsterdam changing to New York 19
    Chapter 5   The Yankee vs. the Yorker type 21

PART TWO
FORMATION HISTORY:
Fragments of Freedom Combined 25
    Chapter 1   The spread of the *dollar* as specie 25
    Chapter 2   Libel or freedom of the press as token of democracy 29
    Chapter 3   1803: The Louisiana Sale and Purchase and its
                    repercussions on German mass immigration from
                    1804–1861; "cohort" settling of the wilderness 34
    Chapter 4   The yarn spinner Gottfried Duden vs.
                    Alexis de Tocqueville's Democracy 38
    Chapter 5   The years 1848–1864; the paradigm of the *Deitch*
                    company; the Mason-Dixon line; the strengthening of
                    Northern power and the expansion of the US stature 45

PART THREE
FOUNDING HISTORY:
Rural and Urban Co-founded Settlement Places 53
    Chapter 1   The naming process of places in America 53
    Chapter 2   A list of co-founded places in the British and French
                    provinces of North America [Canada] 58
    Chapter 3   A list of co-founded places in 18th–19th century US history .. 70
                    A. *Extended North* 73
                    B. *Extended South* 94
                    C. *Extended Atlantic* 107
                    D. *The West* 127
                    E. *Pacific Coast* 133
    Chapter 4   Comparative results and hindsight perspectives
                    on the co-founding processes 138
                    A. US 138

	B. Canada	146
	C. A comparison of name losses in Canada and the US	149
Chapter 5	The differences	155

PART FOUR
ASSIMILATION AND ACCULTURATION PROBLEMS:
Language as deconstructing resource...161

Chapter 1	From 1st generation primary German speaking to 2nd generation English speaking	161
Chapter 2	German Bibles as pillars of resistance in North America	164
Chapter 3	Pennsylvania Dutch, a German American Dialect	166
Chapter 4	The "Dutch Uncle" Humor, or *Galgenhumor,* and its critics	170
	A. Washington Irving	175
	B. Thomas Chandler Haliburton	179
	C. Mark Twain	185
Chapter 5	Residues of spoken dialect in controlled acculturation literature	190

PART FIVE
THE GOING DUTCH:
Balancing the FOUR PARTS: debit-credit Germany-US
and Canada: GONE AMERICAN 191

Chapter 1	German law of emigration background	193
Chapter 2	Canada-US acculturation contrasts	195
Chapter 3	The ethno-nationalist American and Canadian models	198
Chapter 4	The price of the bargain: who was *going Dutch*?	201
Chapter 5	*Americana Teutonicae: E Pluribus Duo; A Mari Usque Ad Mare*	203

PART SIX
BIBLIOGRAPHICAL DATA...205

Chapter 1	Glossary of terms used in this book	205
Chapter 2	German American and German-Canadian bibliography	207
	A. Place name sources bibligraphy	207
	B. German American and Canadian bibliography: secondary literature	208
	C. Further background secondary literature	210
Chapter 3	References on state place names	211
Chapter 4	Statistical data	214
Chapter 5	Letter by F. S. C. Northrop to the author, dated 1960	220

The Author 222

INTRODUCTION

Intercontinental immigration of people is responsible for a tension with the inhabitants who moved earlier and who had become settlers in America. If the country sending emigrants is bigger than the receiving one, the tension may be greater than when the receiving country is larger. Whenever a minority of a different culture joins a majority living somewhere else, the tension between them sooner or later will become political. Whether the interests of the newcomers or the requirements of the previous inhabitants will prevail, depends on many factors. Since the prior residents already posses a visible culture, and the newcomers import a competing one, a battle for predominance, or failing that, for conformity to the ways of the majority by the minority sets in: *E pluribus unum*.

Germans made up a large part of the immigrants to the USA and were generally upstanding capable citizens who assimilated quickly while making major contributions to the American and Canadian culture. Having lived both in Canada for five years and the US for twenty-four years, I made many observations. I collected them either in my mind or on paper over the years. Here I try to give due credit to the cooperation between German immigrants and American immigrants of the main cultural heritage, who had arrived earlier. I am going to focus on the process of co-founding America, a thinly populated continent.

Nowadays the US has three to four times as many inhabitants as Germany. But the US population surpassed the fifty million only in the eighteen-eighties, and thus overtook the Germans statistically 275 years after the first settlers arrived. Given the large numbers of German immigrants to America, close to seven million, it has remained a mystery why Germans "disappeared" so fast as an immigrant group in the mainstream. In my opinion, the "push"-"pull" model– the push away from the Old Country and the "pull" toward the new one does not fully explain this phenomenon.

The method pursued here will try to balance a viable economic explanation with a more behaviorally oriented outlook. Although it follows up on individual decisions of families, it tries to expand anthropologically in the adjacent field of "perceptual" geography.[3] My account will not fall victim to the fallacy of unwarranted philiopiety to the "fatherland", but rather take a posture of gratitude toward the US.'s and Canada's majority cultures.

My parameters are geographically defined. I will focus my investigation on a particular group of *landsmen* whose perceptions I still share to some extent, the North West Germans. I try to define their accomplishments as cooperative or cohort undertakings and tie them to the many places in North America they (co)founded. They applied themselves as co-founders of a great many places in America and Canada. What became of these places furbishes my main inquiry. I also try to prove

---

[3] Jürgen Bähr, Christoph Jentsch, Wolfgang Kuls, *Bevölkerungsgeographie*. Berlin W. de Gruyter 1992, p.539 ff.

that only upstanding capable citizens can plot, found and people so many places without the support of the old country or any preference given them by their new government, as these immigrants did.

My task ahead, as Bernard Bailyn noted, is "full of strange complexities" and of "unresolved problems",[4] which are methodologically difficult to resolve. Yet no task is ever totally resolved. The approach will be four-pronged: nautical (PART ONE),[5] geographical (PART TWO), topographical (PART THREE), and perceptual-linguistic (PART FOUR).

The method owes basic ideas to the late Yale professor F. S. C. Northrop's epistemology. He wanted me to write on a dissertation topic set aside for me in 1961 (see his appendixed letter in PART SIX chapter 5). Since it was a comparative topic, it was not accepted by the Yale Law School, nor, for that matter, by the Yale Graduate School. After a four decade long detour, this topic, whose relevance always stayed in the back of my mind, has finally been taken up here.

For the purpose of clarity I organized the census areas in the order that they spread to the west and south, as far as that was possible. I also introduced a nomenclature of my own. Furthermore, each place's history, if the community cared to present it on the internet, was traced, identified and transcribed from "digital-neighbors" website or from "canstat.ca". Final comparative results will be presented in table form in PART THREE and PART SIX.

Before World War One Joseph Och wrote a Freiburg dissertation which he published in Ohio.[6] I had, of course, expected that these 1,110 places, Och enumerated in 1913, would have almost entirely disappeared, or diminished to at least half their former number, buried by the dust of adverse times. Concerning the first one thousand cities investigated, there is a loss, due to name changes or depletion of residents (up to becoming an empty ghost town) of no more than 13% on average. For political reasons millions of German Americans and German-Canadians changed their German names to assimilative sounding Anglo names, and hence greatly decreased the number of German name entries in the telephone books. The majority of place names I followed in my state-by-state and province-by-province tracer samples survived in both countries surprisingly well. In fact, the amazing result of my final compilation came to a tally of some 30 % higher in 1990 than the 1910 US census had suggested for the period of a hundred years ago. This is only partly due to the subsequent inclusion of more Western States, and the general tendency of the regions to become more densely populated. This kind of "surplus" was not reached in the Canadian compilation. Instead their place names suffered a considerable loss, except in the Province of Ontario.

[4]*From Protestant Peasants to Jewish Intellectuals. The Germans in the Peopling of America.* Oxford Berg 1986.

[5]I thank the staff of the Deutsches Schiffahrtsmuseum Bremerhaven for their help.

[6]*Der Deutschamerikanische Farmer. Sein Anteil an der Eroberung und Kolonisation der Bundesdomäne der Vereinigten Staaten besonders in den Nord Centralstaaten ... Eine statistische und und volkswirtschaftliche Untersuchung.* Ohio Waisenfreund. Columbus, Ohio o.J.

One would underestimate the phenomenon of mass immigration, if one neglected Alexis de Tocqueville's *Democracy in America*.[7] He rightly assumed that enlightenment and virtue come forth and spread with *local* communities, making a township into an individual entity with a future, and not only with a present to get through. Whether a place's name was derived from a transplanted German, or borrowed from the English countryside, it did not matter. Even if public wrath, fanned by "hang the Kaiser" paroles, temporarily demanded the censure of many despised German things, it did not stamp out *all* German place names. There never was a decree issued by the capital of a state or even the Washington federal government to rescind German place names across the board. In other words, the dimension of serving future generations (of a potentially renewed or even increasing German immigration) made an attitude of discretion and retention possible. Communal American self-government kept its own more peaceful future in mind and not only the hostile present. Surprisingly, in this way, irrational elements were subjected to checks and balances in the long run.

In keeping with the municipal role of an enlightened individual place "entity," the US censuses prescribe cooperation and voluntary compliance. Which ever way one does identify him- or herself for the census bureau, having or not having e.g. German or German-American ancestors, the data given are counted. If a person does not wish to divulge his real ancestry, his or her heritage remains unaccounted for, and is thus tacitly changing the data corpus by omission. I found that very hard to understand in the late fifties when I came to North America for the first time. Now I have no problem with it.

Beginning in 1821, American immigration officials started to include ethnic references in their counting, and added apples to apples, when comparing English, Scottish, Welsh, Irish, Hessian, Prussian, Pomeranian, or Westphalian, and pears to pears, as they did after 1934, when they listed British, German, Austrian, Italian, Hungarian, or Pole. For decades upon landing in Canada or the US this writer was both personally irritated yet historically impressed by the piercing border guard question: "Where were you born?" It reminded the landed immigrant each time of the triumph of the *jus soli* (the law of soil) over the *jus sanguinis* (the law of blood) principle, which after 1934 the National Socialist government reversed in its German passport entries.

Ethnicity is but a small rung on the ladder to successful citizenship, with enlightened selfishness being a higher one, and intelligent cohortiveness, in my opinion, being the highest one on a nation's long founding ladder. We will vicariously step on it during this narration until we reach a bifurcation between Canada and the US, leading to a parting of the ways in respect to immigration and settlement. *Immigration to North America helped to bring permanency to the new order of democracy.* Ethnicity wanders into the background, as soon as one's conformity is apparent and accepted. Born Americans become the judge in this regard. Once ethnicity has shifted, in some ways

[7]*DA* 1, 4 The Township as an Individual Entity; Michael Hereth, *Tocqueville: Zur Einführung.* Junius 2001, p. 43-47.

relaxed into a changed over identity family members become de-ethnicized at asynchronic speed; one sooner, the other later, a few not at all. The self within the family becomes both the theater and the courtroom judge in that regard. The process should neither be undervalued nor overestimated. Accordingly, my FIFTH PART chapters are brief ones, and form an anticlimax to the preceding four PARTS. This is my point of view. I hope to have demonstrated it methodically in readable fashion. It is my hope that many a reader may find the "German" hometown of his or her forebears in America.

PART ONE

PRE-EMIGRATION AND TRANSPORTATION:

From Prelude to Surviving, Peopling and Serving

We need to understand why the German Empire did not have a centrally controlled imperial navy. Instead there was a special association, called the German *Hanse*. It was an alliance of profit oriented businessmen and not a hierarchically structured union of cities. Commercial traders formed their patriarchal union in order to better take advantage of their business ventures abroad. Thus their enterprise is aptly and customarily referred to as the "League of the Hanse".[1] During the 18th century the term Hanseatic League arose, just when the use of the term Dutch (=*Deutsch*) for Germans was beginning to recede in its usage abroad. Only born Germans could become members. Their bond was referred to as the *dudesche hanse*. I consider the members as a group of *cohort* Germans, for they were cooperative among themselves and selfish to outsiders at the same time, that is, they were coherent. The spirit of this cohortiveness is well expressed by the motto on the gate to the City of Lübeck, the major trading center of the Hanse: *concordia domu foris pax*, which means: concord on the home front, peace abroad.

The Hanse's influence spread far and wide. The entire sphere of influence, an ellipsoid area, stretched upright at a 45 degree angle from Belgium to East Prussia. It measured at its peak more than 1,100 miles from the tip of Finland to west of the Zuiderzee in the Netherlands. That comes close to the distance from Chicago to Denver, and it was reached at the second half of the 15th century. Other towns and cities could declare themselves members. At its peak the Hanse numbered 70 sizeable and 130 smaller towns. They could excuse themselves from participating at meetings called *Hansetag* or be excluded, if in arrears. They conversed in Low(er) German called *Nieder-* or *Plattdeutsch,* which was also spoken in the 16th century Netherland. This commercial league lasted for 600 years, and its language survived in Lübeck, Schleswig-Holstein, Mecklenburg-Vorpommern, Iowa and Saskatchewan, as we shall see.

At first sight, the Hanse seems to have little to do with immigration, if this phenomenon is seen apart from trading, and irrespective of passing on special trading skills over several generations of outstanding families.[2] During the 16th century the financial situation of German commercial firms was quite prosperous. Their standing was recognized at home and abroad, and so their credit was mostly solid. As exporters of masts, pitch, tarpaulin, wire, beer, wheat, and even weapons the Hanse cohorts

---

[1] Rolf Hammel-Kiesow, *Die Hanse.* C. H. Beck. Wissen. Munich 2000., Heinz Stoob, *Die Hanse.* Verlag Styria. Köln 1995.

[2] Cf. Richard Dawkins, *The Selfish Gene.* Oxford 1976. The German Rororo 2001 translation "egoistisch" is off center, and should read "selbstsüchtig" or "selbstbewußt".

were ready to finance adventurous undertakings. The risks for such shipments and sharing in the responsibility for claims, if their ships were lost with their cargo, were high, the potential gains higher.

Lübeck as head of this alliance of traders had become recognized as first among equals, ever since its burghers had gained the status of a Free Imperial City in 1226 for this Baltic harbor town. Because Lübeck lay East of the Öresund, the passage between Denmark and Sweden, the English trading societies referred to these hansards as "Easterlings" (or in Latin documents as *sterlingi*). A pound of exact weight was called a pound sterling since the Middle Ages.

These Easterlings had a peculiarity: their monopolies were upheld against their former competitors in England for a while, e.g. by bringing their own scales. Similar, but not quite as advantageous settlements were founded in Spain and Portugal. They competed for the same European business ventures by peaceful means as the rest. Their best trading vehicle was the hanse *koggen* or cog, used for hauling cargo on the Baltic Sea.

This structural openness for business at home and privileged closedness abroad can only be explained by the absence of a hereditary upper-class in the city government, as well as the absence of noble families within the city. In fact most influential Lübeckers were immigrants from other parts of Northwest Germany. Until today, a native Hanseat – in Lübeck, Hamburg or Bremen – in all likelihood is not ennobled in the Southern German sense as in the cities of Mainz, Nürnberg or Augsburg.

The commercial firm of the Augsburg Welsers chartered hanseatic ships or hulks from Lübeck, manned them with Northern German (Dutch) and Holland sailors, Portuguese *pilotas*, and loaded them with beer kegs and cargo on the Baltic coast. They sailed to the so-called "Spanish Main" (coast) and colonized a territory called "Little Venice" or (Venetiola/Venezuela). Their enterprise lasted from 1528-1556. At its end even a secret marriage between the second son of the Emperor Charles V, archduke Ferdinand, to Philippine Welser in 1557 as consolation prize for her father's, Bartolomäus Welser's, disastrous financial losses, did not stave off bankruptcy.[3] To understand this maritime traffic we have to know that this temporary "conquest" was undertaken on orders of this powerful emperor, in whose territory "the sun never set". He legalized an unhampered commercial naval traffic to and from the Caribbean to northern South America. Outgoing ships had to be registered in Lisbon, but sailors from all walks of life could be hired without much administrative red tape.

The German population was steeply growing in the 16th century. Consequently there was a huge interior migration going on inside the Empire usually toward the richer coastal areas, and also into the Holland provinces, which were part of the Empire at that time. This population pressure was acerbated by the obligation of young "German" craftsmen to go on the road (*auf die Walz*) for three to five or even more years. It is assumed that tens of thousands of neo-sailors ploughed the high seas on

---

[3]Ed.s, E. Schmitt, K. v. Hutten, *Das Gold der Neuen Welt. Die Papiere des Welser-Konquistadors und Generalkapitäns von Venezuela, Philipp von Hutten*. Hildburghausen 1996.

all sorts of boats. Since the provinces of the Netherlands had only a fraction of the Empire's inhabitants, their commercial fleet was perennially short on sailors and cannoneers. Above all the Hanse, as their English competitor the Royal navy, was tired of having to rent foreign-built ships, and were in dire need of boatmen, gunners, sail makers, wood cutters, ship carpenters, cordwainers, ropers and herring salters.

It was the Netherlanders who had discovered the new sea routes to the islands off the northern coast of South America, the "Spanish Main" in 1526. Charles V first dated by *cedula* the right to settle this area to his Spanish subjects; then he extended it to his Italian, Holland and his "German" subjects. The purpose was clearly the search for silver and gold and the professional sifting of these precious metals for the crown.[4] Mines were set up, but they were worked underground not by the Spaniards, nor the Hollanders, nor the "Dutch", but rather by black slaves, cruelly imported from Africa on the same ships. Only the mining superiors and the essayers were German. Bartholomäus Welser's principal helpers were Heinrich Gessler, Peter Markus, Heinrich Sailer, Heinrich Ehinger, Nikolaus Federmann, Georg Hohermuth, Jabob Reinboldt, Jabob Rentz, Ambrosius Talfinger and Garcia de Lerma. These men became ruined in this trade and died as paupers. The most illustrious one was the humanist Ulrich von Hutten's nephew, Philipp von Hutten, who died, murdered in 1546.

Over four-thousand slaves died from malnutrition and exhaustion. Three hundred other European settlers died also. But for a while Venezuela belonged to the South German banking house of the Welsers rather than to the Spanish-Hapsburg crown. By 1534 at least 14 boats (if not twice that many) were lost at sea. Only one tiny reminder on an old map, the name "Vogel Eilant" south of St. Lucia exists. The trouble was that if a wreck occurred, god's will was supposed to be at work. The fate of a shipwreck and its drowned souls was not subject to litigation in a naval court.[5]

Although we do not know the names of these Hanse ships and thus must leave them nameless, the hulks' seaworthiness to South America and back was proven. They were rugged works of craftsmanship, almost exemplary for the art of shipbuilding at that time. Their sturdiness could withstand the stress of a transatlantic crossing or two. Thus the first main conclusion we may draw is this: the ships that made it to Venezuela, as they had made it to Portuguese Goa in East India thirty years earlier, may not have been very manoeuvrable. Thus they may have made nice targets for English cannoneers on the ocean. If anything, the superior armament of the developing royal navy and not the discovery of America as such contributed to the trouble the League of the Hanse had and would have again on the Atlantic. Due to the Lübeck contour's fear of being overtaken, they were even forced to sail west of Ireland to reach Lisbon, a route the Great Spanish Armada took around England in 1588 as well.

What their convoys were lacking was not seaworthiness, sturdiness, or even cooperation of the crew, but something else. The daring or transatlantic spirit of naval

[4]Walter Grosshaupt, *Der Venezuela-Vertrag der Welser. Scripta Mercatura.* 24. Jahrgang 1992, p. 1-35.

[5]Katharina Schaal, *Schiffbruch in der Rechtssprechung des Lübecker Rats im Spätmittelalter. ZVLGA* 70, 1990, 71-101.

and nautical enterprise was strangely lacking. Their captains, no-instrument sailors[6] to begin with, were not encouraged or even covered by any real indemnity, as English sea captains were. They could not secretly rely on English freebooters's letters, ("*Kaperbriefe*"), which the English Merchant Adventurers possessed. No privateering guarantee was given them. No Queen Elizabeth was their gracious but greedy sovereign and co-sponsor. German emperors were, to put it crudely, Jesuit-educated landlubbers by comparison. They encouraged their North-western subjects to trade with Spain and Portugal rather than to defeat them in the plain peace of daylight, as the English could and would, given the opportunity.

The German 16th century overseas business ended catastrophically and brought commercial havoc. The anticipated huge profits did not materialize. Whereas ironically King Edward IV was brought back to England on Hanse ships, King Henry VIII bought Hanse ships and had them rebuilt and refurbished and loaded with sharp-shooting cannons. He also rescinded Hanse privileges as much as possible. Queen Elizabeth I had Hanse ships sequestered or simply taken over by her best men on sea. On the Atlantic the Hanse hulks formed an entrepreneurial and not a navigational rearguard.[7] No colony such as New Netherland, New France, New Spain, New Sweden or New England welcomed their landing for supplies and support as a New Germany colony would, had it existed on the continent of North America.

---

[6] Joachim Rheticus, *Corographia tewsch*. 1541, rp. ed. F. Hipler ... 1876, p. 140.
[7] T. H. Lloyd, *England and the German Hanse ... 1157-1611*. Cambridge U. P. 1991.

Chapter 1
Shipbuilding in Lübeck

From around the early 16th century the newly launched type of seaworthy hulk contained a structural innovation. It was first documented by an engraving in a Venice shipyard. It was called "carrack" (High German *Karacke*, Low(er) German *Kraeck*). They were no longer "clinkered" on the outside like shingles with hidden nails, but they were constructed from the keel inside up to the outside. The keel/broadside dimensions were changed in favor of an overall length, giving it a "caravelle" and codfish-like appearance. The elongation made a three-mast ship construction possible. These carracks were mainly built *craweel* for sailing against the wind. A good captain and his experienced crew could attack in a new fashion: a convoy could swarm in a line of battle around a hapless enemy in a synchronized letter-eight formation, with a few branders pushing through the middle. Carracks could more fully inflate with a mix of triangular and square-rigged sails and were then unmatched at their speed.

The Hanse shipyards, most of them concentrated in Lübeck, built nine ships in a normal year.[8] Their shipwrights participated in these fundamental innovations. But contrary to the English and Holland convoys the Lübecker were not permitted to sail all year around. The Northern German sailing season began at Marymas (February 2) – still celebrated by the burning of wooden sun wheeled beacons [*beeke brennen:* on the Friesian Island of Sylt] today - and ended on Michaelmas (September 21). In exceptional cases, which were subject to a council resolution, it could be extended to St. Martin's Day (November 11). Trading in the non-sailing 'holy season' was forbidden as well. The break of four months and a few days proved to be very costly and made contract keeping difficult.

Each Hanse captain stood alone against adverse elements on the sea, in foreign harbors, and close to tricky beacons, against better guns, all at his own risk. He was supposed to know when the extra cargo had to go overboard in a heavy storm. He carried, as Low(er) German speaking skippers say, "*die vulle mascopei*" [losing his last shirt], for all or part of the boat. He could be a freighter also, or have cargo loaded in some one else's behalf. Then his loss would be prorated, and he could be brought to court.

The upper echelon of his crew were also part-shareholding shippers, or they held a part (percentage) of the cargo or a loading space square part, similar to a church pew for rent. That explains the spiritual connection of the Christian seafarer to the church calendar carving out and rounding off a shortened year in the name of Captain Christ. After a year and a day (*jar und dag*) the claim went under and became null and void.

Ordinarily a Hanse ship did not carry many guns, certainly not more than were required for self-defense. So a small convoy could be taken over by a brasher sea hero with sharper appetites. But the heart of the trouble lay somewhere else. Only a captain regretted the takeover, the loss of his ship and the command on the high sea or ashore. The crew, more often than not, welcomed the takeover, a pay hike to ten shillings a

---

[8]Karl-Friedrich Olechnowitz, *Der Schiffbau der hansischen Spätzeit*. Böhlau Weimar 1960.

month, better life protection, more and healthier food (including beer[9]), even if it meant serving under the flag of St. George. The Dutch West India Company payed similar wages in guilders. The Hanse did not have a flag of its own in the first place. So the dominant perspective of the Hanse shippers themselves was not national, but bound to the Christian life cycle.

Of the roughly two hundred Hanse ships, which existed around 1560, no more than fifty vessels, according to Philippe Dollinger[10] could carry a very heavy load ("lasts"), of which some were purchased on orders of King Henry VIII by one or two English Brotherhoods, who would rebuild and outfit them from keel to topsail. The English were always on the lookout for transatlantic- worthy Hanse ships. A careful look at table 1 will prove that point. This topic will also be taken up later. In any case, the ones built by the Hanse, particularly if they could load silver, were welcome prey in the North Atlantic and English channel during the second half of the 16th century.

Table 1

	Ship Type	Rig/Tunnage	Flag/Charter	Dep./Destinat	Category	
	Kogge COG	1 Mast	Hanseatic	Baltic	Freighter	
	Hulk HULK	2-3 Mast	Hans/Holland.	N.S./Atlantic	Freighter	
	Carrack CAR	3 Mast	French/Engl.	Atlantic	Gunfreighter	
	Galeon GAL	4 Mast	Spanish	Atlantic	Battleship	
	Caravel CRAV	3-4 Mast	Engl./French	Atlantic	Transporter	
	Fluite FLUI	3 Mast	Hollandic	Atlantic	Fr./Transporter	

Year / Nr.	Name	Rig/Tunnage	Flag	Dep./Interim	Fate	Cap./ Passeng.
1529 / 1	Conception		ESP	Venezuela	safe arrival	Gessler
until / 2	Sta. Maria Reg.		ESP	Venezuela	safe arrival	Ehinger
1556 / 3	Sta. Maria Concep		ESP	Venezuela	safe arrival	Ph.v.Hutten
1534ff. / 4-8	5 boats		LÜB	Lübeck	shipwreck	lost
1534 / 9	Hanseatic	HUL	LÜB	Venezuela	shipwrecck	lost
1544 / 10	Jesus Lübeck	CAR 1700 t.	ENG	Atlantic	return Eng	Fr. Drake
1568 / 10	Jesus Lübeck	27brassguns	ENG	Mexico	Slave trade	W. Hawkins
1569 / 11	Judith	CAR	ENG	Carribean	Slave trade	W. Hawkins
1570 / 12	Adler Hamburg	HUL	HBG	North Sea	cargo/loss	capture
1570 / 13	Adler Lübeck	4 M HUL	LÜB	North Sea	cargo/loss	capture
1571 / 14	Dragon	HUL	LÜB/ENG	North Sea	sold to	Sweden
1571 15-21	T Transporter	HUL	CATH.LEAG.	Lepanto Batt.	troops	D.J. D'Austria
1571 / 21	Swan	50 tons	LÜB/ENG	North Sea	taken over	crew included

[9]Konrad Pilgrim, "Der Durst auf den Weltmeeren,"*GWU* 19 (1968) 683-696.
[10]*Die Hanse.* 4th ed. Stuttgart 1989. Originally translated from the French in 1964.

Year / Nr.	Name	Rig. Tunnage	Flag	Dep./Interim	Fate	Cap./ Passeng.
1572 / 22	Pascha/Pasco	70 tons	TURK/ENG	Lepanto battle	small boat	pressed
[1577] / 23	Pelic.Gold.Hind	3 M 120 t,	ENG	La Rochelle	circumnavig.	Drake
1582 / 24	Leicester	GAL 400 t.	ENG	Southampton	battles	Fenton
1582 / 25	Hanseatic	HUL	HAN	Falmouth	taken by	Lady Killigrew
1583 / 26	Delight	HUL	ENG	Norumbega	taken from	capt. Clarke
1585 / 27-31	Hanseatic	HUL.S	LÜB	North Sea	sequestered	London
1587 / 32	Eliz.Bonavent	HUL	LÜB ?	North Sea	purchased	London
1587 / 33	Mary Rose	HUL	LÜB ?	North Sea	purchased	London
1588 / 34-39	E. Transp.s	HUL	LÜB	Atlantic	pressed	freighting
1588 / 40-44	Sp. Transp.s	HUL	LÜB	Atlantic	pressed	freightiung
1588 / 45	Falcon Mayor	CAR	ESP	England	shipwrecked	Armada
1588 / 45	Großer Falke	ditto	HANS LEAG	Baltic	captured	saved
1588 / 46	GranGrifon	CAR	ESP	England	shipwrecked	Armada
1588 / 46	Großer Greif	ditto	ROSTOK	Baltic	captured	Engl. Cap.
1588 / 47-51	No names	HUL.S	ESP	England	shipwrecked	Armada
1589 / 52-63	Hanseatic	CAR	POM/LÜB	Atlantic	taken	Drake
1589 / 64	Hanseatic	CAR	HBG	North Sea	captured	saved
1590 / 65-69	Pomeranian	CAR	HAN	harbor	sequestered	London order
1591 / 70-73	Hanseatic	CAR	LÜB	harbor	sequestered	London order
1591 / 74-79	Hanseatic	CAR	HAN	before Cadiz	captured	Drake
1593 / 80	Bremer	CAR	BRE	North Sea	captured	London order
1593 / 81	Rostocker	CAR	ROS	North Sea	captured	London order
1595 / 82-84	Lübecker	CAR	LÜB	North Sea	captured	London order
1602 / 85	Blaue Taube	CAR	HBG	North Sea	delivered by	Kap. Holste
1602 / 86	Halber Mond	CAR	HBG	North Sea	delivered by	Kap. Balhorn
1602/3 / 87	Half Moon	CAR	LÜB	Hamburg	takeover by	cap. Hudson
1602/3 / 88	Gold.Anker	CAR	HBG	North Sea	delivered by	Kap. Meinßen
1620 / 89	EngelGabriel	CAR	LÜB	North Sea	stranded	Grohte-fedder
[1629]	Mayflower II	CRAV	ENG	Atlantic	landed safely	[Plym. Rock]
1627-32 90ff.	Hans.Flotilla	CRAV.S	GERMANY	Baltic	sequestered	[Wallenstein]
1629 / 102	Herkules	CAR	LÜB	North Sea	banware seq.	[Hollandic]
1638 / 103-112	Medit. Fleet	COG.S	LÜB	Mediterran	pirated by	[Corsairs]
1639 /113-122	Hanseatic	CRAV	HANS LEAG	Sp. Harbor	pressed	[Madrid]
1639 /123-125	Hanseatic	CRAV	HANS LEAG	New Guinea	pirated by	[Brandenbg.]

| Sum of total | Loss: | 125-200 ships | | | | |

Year / Nr.	Name	Rig/Tunnage	Charter Co.	Ocean	Passengers	Dep./Dest.
[1630] / 1	Eendracht 1	FLUI	D.West India	Atlantic	15 German p.	Adam/ Nadam
1639 / 2	Harinck	FLUI	D.West India	Atlantic	7 German p.	Adam/ NAdam
1641 / 3	Koning David	FLUI	D.West India	Atlantic	17 German p.	Adam/ NAdam
1642 / 4	Houttuin	FLUI	D.West India	Atlantic	x German p.	Adam/ NAdam
1643 / 5	Swan	FLUI	SWED	Atlantic	x German p.	Stock./ Delaw.
1650 / 6	Kattan	FLUI	SWED	Atlantic	? German p.	Stock./ Delaw.
1657 / 7	Draetvat	FLUI	D.West India	Atlantic	x German p.	Adam/ NAdam
1657 / 8	St.JanBaptist	FLUI	D.West India	Atlantic	9 German p.	Adam/ NAdam
1658 / 9	Bruinvis	FLUI	D.West India	Atlantic	33 German p.	Adam/ NAdam
1659 / 10	Trouw 1	FLUI	D.West India	Atlantic	98 German p.	Adam/ NAdam
1659 / 11	Moesman 1	FLUI	D.West India	Atlantic	23 German p.	Adam/ NAdam
1660 / 12	Bonte Koe 1	FLUI	D.West India	Atlantic	79 German p.	Adam/ NAdam
1660 / 13	Moesman 2	FLUI	D.West India	Atlantic	32 German p.	Adam/ NAdam
1660 / 14	VerguldeOtter	FLUI	D.West India	Atlantic	52 German p.	Adam/ NAdam
1661 / 15	De Trouw 2	FLUI	D.West India	Atlantic	27 German p.	Adam/ NAdam
1661 / 16	St.JanBap.2	FLUI	D.West India	Atlantic	38 German p.	Adam/ NAdam
1661 / 17	Hoop 1	FLUI	D.West India	Atlantic	x German p.	Adam/ NAdam
1661 / 18	Gulden Arent	FLUI	D.West India	Atlantic	5 German p.	Adam/ NAdam
1661 / 19	VerguldBever	FLUI	D.West India	Atlantic	51 German p.	Adam/ NAdam
1662 / 20	Trouw 3	FLUI	D.West India	Atlantic	27 German p.	Adam/ NAdam
1662 / 21	Hoop 2	FLUI	D.West India	Atlantic	72 German p.	Adam/ NAdam
1662 / 22	Vos	FLUI	D.West India	Atlantic	x German p.	Adam/ NAdam
1663 / 23	Roosebom	FLUI	D.West India	Atlantic	71 German p.	Adam/ NAdam
1663 / 24	Bonte Koe 2	FLUI	D.West India	Atlantic	x German p.	Adam/ NAdam
1664 / 25	Stettin	FLUI	Dutch charter	Atlantic	52 German p.	Stettin/ Nadam
1664 / 26	Trouw 4	FLUI	D.West India	Atlantic	17 German p.	Adam/ NAdam
1664 / 27	Eendracht 2	FLUI	D.West India	Atlantic	38 German p.	Adam/ Nadam
1664 / 28	GekruisteHart	FLUI	D.West India	Atlantic	8 German p.	Adam/ NAdam

1664 British	Takeover	N.Adam named	New York	with 1,500	inhabitants	
Capacity of	1,037 pass.	or 80%	loaded with	German	passengers	
1748-1754	English	ship transport	with 2,390	German	passengers	
	departure	Rotterdam	134 times	destination	Philadelphia	121 times
		London	34 times		New York	20 times
		Hamburg	11 times		Charleston	10 times
1748-1754	(figures	based on	A. Brinck	1993]		
1760-1775	12,000 p.	A. Brinck	S. Wokeck	1993/1983	Philadelphia	88 times

What would the sailing route back from Venezuela be? The heavy boats could not sail straight back to Europe, but had to take a break at a "refresher" station in North America, to cauterize, get water, food, (biscuits and *ersatz* beer, often made from pine cones) and get repairs done. The captain could be mistaken by the refresher station's friendliness or hostility. Although the Emperor took a pro-Spanish position, German Hanse cities' boats were welcomed lukewarmly as competitors in Spanish or Portuguese harbors. If it wasn't for speaking Low(er) German, the crew would not have gotten along too well in New England harbors. In the New Netherland's ports which were governed from abroad, they might be admitted more readily.

Considering his options, a Welser financed Hanse captain would likely try a clandestine stopover and refresher break in a no-man's-land that was just becoming the "English Main".[11] It might be his last stopover, and he might have had to choose between a salty grave or an indentured service for his crew, making them, if they survived, involuntary "immigrants" to North America. Let's pretend to take a stopover at such a ghost harbor on the English Main. A place called "Norumbega" near the Penobscot river – spelled in a dozen different ways – was used as a refresher "station" by Simon Ferdinando, John Walker and Francis Drake.[12] My assumption that Hanse ships used it at that time to refresh too is based on the fate of Drake's own Hanse ship, which has a history of its own, now to be told.

[11]Spelled Mayne. The US state name Maine is not a derivative of the French province, as is mistakenly assumed by *Harms Erdkunde* Band VII. Paul List Verlag Munich 1970, p. 183.

[12]Benjamin F. De Costa, *Maine. A Bibliography of its History*, II (1977); and Drake's map shown in Magdalen's College, Cambridge, England, and on plate LIII of Peter Wood's German trl. of *Abenteuer der Karibik* (1992) p. 90. See also James A. Williamson, *The Age of Drake*. London 1946.

Chapter 2
Sequestering Ships

A Lübeck shipwright company built a great carrack before 1540. Fittingly for a dowager of the sea she was baptised the *Jesus von Lübeck*. By those standards her large dimensions measured as follows: she weighed 1700 tons without guns and load, was 100 ft. in length (twice overall), 50 ft. in width, had four masts and 27 guns (one ton each). It was Lübeck's greatest carrack at that time, built in a three-deck modern caravelle style, for which the King of France and the King of England bid. According to the law of the Hanse city, a sale abroad of a ship had to be approved by the senate (a kind of early export permission). Prior to that date of 15 November 1544 it is listed on the ship rolls of the English navy. Nine months later the *Jhesus of Lubeke* fought against the French at Shoreham. In 1546 the English artillery officer, A. Anthony, drew a picture of this flagship on King Henry VIII's ship roll. It is shown from the starboard side next to an identical but slightly smaller looking Hanse ship called "Paluncey". They can still be seen as a wall map and part of Pepys Collection at Magdalen's College in Cambridge, England. Both have the characteristic Hanse ship 'castled' bow and stern.[13]

In 1558, the Jhesus of Lubeke was as approaching twenty years of age supposed to be dry-docked. Instead she was reprieved for her sturdy build. In 1563-65 she was chartered to Lord Dudley. In 1564 valued at £ 2000, she was provided with 11 more brass guns. In 1567 John Hawkins, during his third expedition to Africa and the West Indies, handed over command of this flagship to the experienced hands of young Francis Drake (1541-1596).

Now we can pick up the yarn of our main thread: this ship from Northwestern Germany was bought together with a crew of 300 mariners who were mostly Low(er) German speaking boatmen who thus understood basic English commands. By this time as an English expeditionary flagship of a six carracks convoy, the *Jesus* had 200 more men aboard than usual, English, German, Holland, and Portuguese. Under deck it brought slaves from Guinea to the West Indies as well, and, not always fortunately, silver from Venezuela to England. The profit margin hovered around 60%.

The *Jhesus* was taken from the English while a seemingly hospitable but really treacherous drinking celebration went on with the Spanish host in the harbor called San Juan de Ulua in Mexico in 1568. The crew which constantly had to be replenished because of scurvy, now had to fight for their lives in a land battle, which they were not used to. All but two ships were burnt in the harbor. Because of this loss the English navy had to be rapidly built up to about a hundred ships for England's protection, after their number had gone down considerably at the end of Queen Mary's rule. While the English Tudor navy could not compare to the Hanse "fleet" in number, the Elizabethan

---

[13]Michael Lewis, "The Guns of the Jesus of Lubeck", and "Fresh Light on San Juan de Ulua", *The Mariner's Mirror*, 22 (1936) p. 324-345, and 23 (1937) p. 295-315; Karl Reinhardt, "Karacke Jesus von Lübeck", *Verein für Lübeckische Geschichte und Altertumskunde* 31 (1949) S. 79-110. Friedrich Lütge, *Die wirtschaftliche Lage vor dem Ausbruch des 30 jährigen Kriegs*. Darmstadt 1977.

navy began to surpass them. Not only was the balance redrawn, German Hanse ships were not needed any more to fill the ranks of that newly outfitted English navy by purchases from abroad. The navy's most accurately firing guns could hit targets at up to 360 ft. distance.

During takeovers of Hanse ships by Hawkins or Drake, some of the "enemy" crew either drowned, if accidentally shipwrecked, or they were saved more often and turned into neo-English colonial seamen. Drake alone is known to have lost several thousand mariners, albeit few ships, if any; but between 1500 and 2000 Northwestern cohort Germans during such takeovers remained unaccounted for.[14] The crews taken over by Hawkins and Drake again and again amounted to numbers higher than their own English seamen initially taken aboard in Plymouth. We have reasons to assume that some of them made it safely on land in Maine, as it is called now, or where ever the refresher station was. The American coast then called the "English Main" was long and not yet populated by white settlers. According to my figures published five years ago[15] the involuntary migration to "Maine" must have ended just a generation before the voluntary one started. In any case more Hanse ships did not return when the preparations for war in the defense of English ships began in earnest. The battle planning of the royal English navy against the royal Spanish navy was on. Both were fully independent in their own ship building programs. But both sides needed more ships and equipment than they could build or buy to create a GREAT ARMADA. The League of the Hanse was unfortunate in having to provide more ships and manpower to both sides, and thus lost her last chance of building up a commercial fleet of her own which could defend her against freebooting English convoys.

We now have to turn our attention to Table 1 which reflects ship movements of a peculiar kind. We may register a gradual change of hands first after these ships' safe arrival, then a doubtful arrival, then to a fair sale, to sequestering, and finally rude takeover from German to English command by English captains in times of undeclared war. This list shows that sudden change of command could take place almost anywhere from Portsmouth to Venezuela, or at a refresher station in Norumbega. One English freebooting ship could take on two to three cohort *craeks*. An English convoy under Drake could take up to twelve. In a different source related both by Williamson and Mattingly, we even read of 60 Hanse ships being taken before the estuary of the river Tejo on the Portuguese coast. They ascribe the taking of the 12 Hanse ships, we listed under 1591, to Lord Cumberland. Both the *Adler von Hamburg* and the *Adler von Lübeck* were almost as large and sea-worthy as the *Jhesus of Lubeke*, still they were "raped". Their fate was not due to their ill construction, or their slowing sturdiness, but had to do with the crew's lack of spark and intuitive courage. What can a captain achieve if he knows his crew admire "Franz Draek",[16] as if he was one of their own notorious men?

---

[14]Garrett Mattingly, *Die Armada*. Serie Piper Verlag 1988, wondered why no German scholar ever researched these losses of ships and men.

[15]*"Those Damn' Dutch,"* trading officep. 93.

[16]Walter Biggs, trl., *Relation oder Beschreibung der Rheiß ... durch Franciscum Drack*. Cologne

Furthermore we find Hanse main ships, geared and rigged for battle, as well as transport hulks, won by prince Don Juan d'Austria at the Battle of Lepanto in 1572, in Malta and elsewhere in the Mediterranean. But an even wider eye opener can be found in the literature about the Battle of the GREAT ARMADA in 1588. We hear of the former Hanseships *Falcon Mayor* (=*Großer Falke*) and another flagship *Gran Grifon* (= *Großer Greif* from Rostock) fighting for the Spanish and sinking. The Spanish Armada also witnessed the shipwrecking of many accompanying Hanse transporter hulks. At the same time such Hanse hulks which had been pressed into English service fought on the winning side also. After the English victory, sequestering of innocent Hanse ships became the order of the day in the time period from 1589 to 1595. In 1598 the Hanse trading office in London, the famous *Staalhof*, on English orders had to be closed.

By around 1600 the English fleet had about 450 ships, while the Hanse fleet numbered only slightly more than half that much. The serial ship building Netherlanders were still ahead of the others. But they also became the leading charters until 1648. Their main harbors were Amsterdam and the German Friesian semi-republic of Emden which they had occupied. But the final insult against heavily laden Hanse ships came from the Brandenburg "corsairs", who started to participate in these raids off the coast of Africa. During the Thirty Years War neither the Catholic League's general Wallenstein nor the protestant Swedish King Gustaf Adolf Wasa paid for their sequestered Hanse ships, some of which may have been identical. If most of these ships had been built on credit, the shipwright companies would be near bankruptcy. And yet the irony of it all, the *Jhesus* survived 24 years of stressful service in the royal navy and was not sunk. How many Hanse ships were taken over? We could document 125 Hanse ships in Table 4, but there were probably twice as many taken over in all. Calculated on the basis of available ship building data, more than twenty years of steady shipbuilding was taken advantage of by unfriendly competitors. These Hanse ships netted high profits for English, Dutch, Spanish, and to some extent even French Huguenot businessmen.

Another severe setback was the lack of accounting by double bookkeeping in Lübeck, Hamburg, and Bremen shipping companies. With international trade the Venetian Republic had introduced double bookkeeping showing activa and passiva in a comparable balance.[17] Both the House of the Welser and the Hanse did not introduce this system. Therefore, they could not accurately check out their real losses. On balance we may say: there was a gradual decline, but not a sudden downfall. The destruction of their ships was less of a danger than the loss by clandestine or public takeover. This way, the profits were reaped by the competition. The secondary benefactors were clearly the Netherlandic West India Company and the private charter

1589. For a colored depiction of "borrowed" Hanseships see *America de Bry 1590-1634*, ed. Gereon Sievernich. Casablanca Berlin New York 1990.

[17]Lucia Paciolis, *Summa de Arithmetica: De computis et scripturis*. Venice 1494; Henning Ghetelen from Lübeck Low(er) German trl. of Fra Canzano da Montalboddo, *Newe unbekanthe Landte und ein nevve weldte*. Nuremberg: Johann Stüchß 1508.

companies. Cohort seamen were taken over with their ships with the captains removed by the English in large numbers. The crew sailed on under a foreign flag. This way they took on a different economic function. They became well-paid loan workers; their ships chance-chartered freighters and transporters. Slow organisational changes in shipbuilding history were more relevant than technical innovations. The Hanse's organisational framework was too slow to respond and thus in the long run became underdeveloped, which supports Douglas North's nobel prize winning economic theories from 1993[18]. Part and parcel of the problem was the social and economic decline of the German seaman's professional standing. The English seaman's reputation, on the other hand, was steadily rising at the same time. The Northern German captain by himself was too closely allied with the interests of his freighting company, and thus gave up his ship without too much of a struggle, for he could not really command his crew to fight for king and country. The Hapsburg Emperor was almost a foreigner to the Lübekers, and a cohesive country did not exist.

A cohortively organized "brotherhood" like the Hanse League with a dwindling number of ships, a company without maritime planning, without a fleet, without a common flag, cannot compete commercially on the oceans. You cannot colonize without a commercial fleet at your disposal for lack of organized transportation. The ships did not return to their home harbor often enough, a few sailors may have been lucky to come back home at all. What kind of a homeland would that have been? The Swedes and Poles were coming to the Baltic coast; the Netherlanders to Amsterdam, their island of Texel, and to Emden; Anhalt-Zerbst to the Friesian Jever, and the States of Brandenburg-Prussia were spreading rapidly as well. The Lower Saxon Imperial Circle (*Niedersächsischer Reichskreis*) became poor. Denmark not only levied a toll on the passage through the Öresund, but tried to impose a tariff on the German Elbe traffic as well. The adhesion of the members to the Holy Roman Empire of the German Nation fell apart. The Hanse towns in their selfishness tried to survive as best they could under these adverse political circumstances.

---

[18] *Geldumlauf, Währungssystem und Zahlungsverkehr in Nordwesteuropa 1300–1800. Beiträge zur Geldgeschichte der späten Hansezeit. QDHG Neue Folge, XXXV.* Böhlau 1989.

Chapter 3
Transportation of Cohort Germans by the Dutch Merchant Fleet
to New Amsterdam

The cohort Germans, which we prefer to call "Dutch" because they were designated by North Americans as *Deutsche* well into the late 18th, even early 19th centuries, had to pay a fee in advance of the passage or get indentured. They were carried by the Dutch West India Company (VWC) on ships called *fluites* such as are listed in Table 1 , second part. These ships were smaller than the *Jhesus*. Instead of 400 slaves, packed into C or D decks, 50–100 immigrant passengers were placed on B or C decks. We noted that 40–100 souls were carried by these boat types to New Amsterdam, whereas bigger built English ships, still starting their trips from Rotterdam, carried 200–400 souls one hundred years later.

In 1664, the year of the takeover of New Amsterdam and New Netherland, no shot was fired by the English fleet. They simply anchored threateningly close and put up an ultimatum to the burghers. During the last shipping season before this power change 1663/64 the docked Dutch ships had delivered German-Dutch passengers to the tune of 10% of New Amsterdam's population of 1500 inhabitants. Some of these ships had crossed the Atlantic two to three times between 1659 and 1664. It is not exactly known how many of these passengers stayed in the city and how many moved up the Hudson valley or to what was later to be called East New Jersey.

Joyce D. Goodfriend[19] in her very thorough and sophisticated study lists only 10% of these passengers arriving in New Amsterdam between 1639 and 1664. The others, in her opinion, must have moved on or were omitted from her count for unknown reasons. Although her book contains several brilliant deliberations on Dutch, English, and Black ethnic groups, she fails to distinguish between Netherlanders (mostly Hollanders) and German "Dutch", a differentiation also not drawn by Stephanie Bernardo.[20] How can one explore the meaning of ethnicity, and then register these two important groups as one and the same? These remarks are not made to denigrate this otherwise utterly enlightening and richly documented study of colonial social history. Prof. Goodfriend's point that a melting of the three principal ethnic groups the English, Hollanders, and German, did not take place in New Amsterdam and New York[e], is only partially correct. Intermarriage between Low(er) German speaking *Deutsch* and Dutch speaking Netherlanders were frequently concluded. The first recorded marriage in New Amsterdam is such an intermarriage between Egbert van Borsum born at Emden and Annetje Hendricks from Amsterdam in 1639. They were blessed with four healthy sons, Herman, Cornelis, Henry the hatter, and Tyman. There were many such church concluded marriages to follow, usually registered in the Dutch Reformed Church. I do not understand what is meant by "social identity"? I would have preferred

---

[19]*Before the Melting Pot: Society and Culture in Colonial New York City, 1664–1730*. Princeton U. P. 1992.

[20]*The Ethnic Almanac*. Doubleday & Co. Garden City, N. y. 1981. See also E. B. Green and V. D. Harrington, *American Population Before the Federal Census of 1790*. N. Y. 1932 rp. 1966.

to call that phenomenon "social standing." If that standing was in balance, intermarriages could take place. Here again the Low(er) German speaking German cohort groups could not have had much trouble to understand and speakDutch, being so similarly spoken in the 17th century. There were no "nationalities" existing at that time, as several American writers assume. On the contrary, some 30,000 Lutherans lived and worshiped in 1664 Amsterdam not as foreigners, but as residents, according to Philip von Zesen, who became an (honorary) citizen of Amsterdam himself.[21] Why should a few of them not have migrated with or without Amsterdamers on to New Amsterdam? That would have been highly improbable. I like her term "cohort", but not in connection with a "conquest" There never was a conquest either by the Hollanders, nor by the English until and during the takeover of 1664. Both takeovers were achieved by peaceful means. And one must not forget that at the Conference of 1667 the Netherlanders got Surinam, a part of Guiana, in exchange for their loss. Thecooperation we argue for in our study lasted only while a clan, a family, or a firm could pay its bills. It is not a social, but an economic designation.

Goodfriend's Fourth Chapter unfolds the occupations pursued in New Amsterdam and New York[e] and their ethnic composition. She repeatedly sweeps the Northwest Germans under the rug. But their share of the inhabitants amounted really to 25%. Goodfriend's shortcuts inflate the Netherlandic statistics and keep them artificially high but keep the English numbers artificially low. In the year 1695 she (p. 69) asserts that 65% of the labor force, that is manual "laborers", were Hollanders. What were all the many Lutheran craftsmen doing in New York[e]? They did not live on welfare.

In 1683 New York[e] was divided into wards. In these wards, not ethnic, but political distinctions mattered and were catered to which called for contributions for favors. How could a large city by those old colonial standards be headed by a Palatine-American Lieutenant Governor for almost two years, such as Jacob Leisler (1640-1691) if he did not have the majority of votes in these wards? The tally coming from the corner of a certain ethnic "identity" would not have delivered nearly enough votes. Neither did he go Hollandic (called "batavianizing") to marry his bride Aeltje Tymans, except for spelling his name Leyslaer during the last five years of his life, nor did he "anglicize" to make shady land deals or maritime slave tradings. His tax reform policy may have hit rich city merchants harder than ordinary businessmen in his own ward. The noted historian Ronald W. Howard, in his section, Part II, The English Province[1664-1776][22] does not dissolve the controversy still surrounding Leisler's "Rebellion". He judges him a Calvinist fanatic who feared a Catholic plot in the Colony. Contrary to the Netherlandic Reformed Churches and the French Huguenot Church, the Lutheran Church did not expect their worshippers to persevere in their native tongues. Seen in this perspective Lt. Gov. Leisler's tax reform plan may have amounted more to a levelling than to arebellion. And the charge that he could not write or speak

[21]*Europas Erster Baedeker Filip von Zesens Amsterdam 1664.* Ed. C. Gellinek, *Culture of European Cities*, vol. 2. P. Lang N. Y. Bern Frankfurt am Main 1988 p. 300.

[22]Milton M. Klein, ed., *The Empire State. A History of New York*. Cornell U. P. 2001, pp. 126-129; Charles H. McCormick, *Leisler's Rebellion*. New York 1989.

proper English was far-fetched. Leisler had polemicized against trading with slaves. That made his rival, the richest man of New York, Fredryck Flypse (or Philipse) his sworn enemy. Flypse's advantage was that as a Friesian he hailed from the European Atlantic Northwestern seacoast and could speak English flawlessly. Leisler had no such luck with his High German Palatine accent. Except for this high-pitched éclat, ending in Leisler's conviction, hanging, and quartering, the cooperation between the various New Yorkers outweighed the clashes in the long run.

In my listing of the earliest 200 German-*Deutsch* immigrants of New Amsterdam 75% of these families came from north of the Benrath line, where one said "Appel" instead of "Apfel", and spoke Low German. In Table 2 a list of basic English words will be compared to their Friesian, Low and High German equivalents irrespective of the required capitalization of nouns:

Table 2

English	Friesian	Low German	High German
apple	appel	appel	apfel
brother	brother	broder	bruder
day	dei	dag	tag
father	feder	fadder	vater
good	god	god	gut
he	hi	he	er
ic [Old Engl.]	ek	ik	ich
leather	ledder	ledder	leder
little	litik	lütt	klein
love	liava	lewe	liebe
man, men	man, mon	man, men	mann, männer
make	makia	maken	machen
milk	melok	melk	milch
mother	moder	moder	mutter
open	epen	open	offen
run	renna	rönnen	rennen
sheep	skep	shap	schaf
smoke	smokia	schmöken	rauchen
tell	tella	(ver)tellen	(er)zählen
this	thit	dit	dies
we	wi	wi	wir

It follows from this Table that those immigrants who spoke with soundshifted High German phonetics as in column 4 had more trouble to speak and understand English than the other two groups. The original advantage of the speakers as in columns 2 and 3 with their way of articulating without a sound shift similar to English is to be correlated with at least the passive capability of speaking or understanding both

Netherlandic (which some of them knew from Olde Amsterdam) on arrival and English soon after arrival. Not by coincidence some of the 17th century Northwestern German immigrants to New Amsterdam hailed from well-known Hanse towns, above all Lübeck, Hamburg, and Bremen. By comparison a great disadvantage would be suffered by the non-Northwesterners, the "strangely" speaking Palatines, who as a large down-trodden group arrived two generations later than the above passengers.

These and other formerly outstanding Hanseatic towns ceased to assemble in a *Tohopesate* (Hanse town diet) just about the time when these towns were left by the earliest emigrant families documented in town records for the first time. We shall show the correlation in

Table 3

(last participation at a Hanseatic Diet):			(Year first emigrants left that city):
1. order city	Lübeck	(1669)	1642 (P. Jordaensen)
2. order city	Bremen	(1669)	1638 (Jan Dircksen)
2. order city	Hamburg	(1669)	1641 (A. Pietersen)
1. order city	Braunschweig	(1669)	1648 (P. Tönies)
1. order city	Danzig	(1669)	1652 (M. Reifferding)
2. order city	Münster	(1619)	1661 (W. Wesselsen)
2. order city	Lüneburg	(1629)	1658 (C. Bleyers)
2. order city	Osnabrück	(1619)	1639 (J. Hendricksen)
2. order city	Königsberg	(1579)	1643 (Peter Collet)
2. order city	Magdeburg	(1629)	1638 (Dr. H. Kierstede)
no Hanse city	Hannover		1648 (Caspar Steinmetz)

Three generations later in Queen Anne's reign, on top of being extremely poor, the next wave of Palatines spoke as wide apart from English as could be imagined, although they belonged to the same family branch of West Germanic speakers as did English, Low German, and Friesian speakers. I will treat the Palatines and their troubles further below in chapter 5.

Here I consider the immigrants arriving as cohorts from the Hanse territory north of the dividing line running from Düsseldorf-Benrath all the way up to the former Danzig, These people, after they had undergone an interior migration to the new economic capital of the Western world, Amsterdam, went on to New Amsterdam, which compared to Old Amsterdam was just a fisher village at that time. Their successful members may have intermarried as often as possible in the Old Country so that they made the linguistic and cultural switch to a new cohort before leaving or at the latest in New Amsterdam. But their self-interests and goals were the same. In the beginning (until 1664) both young Northwestern Germans and Englishmen and

Scotsmen competed for the favors of the ruling burghers of New Amsterdam and their daughters' hands. The tabling of these mostly Northwestern German settlers in New Amsterdam (1630-1664) shows top-heavy traits, going together with goal-oriented selfishness: only 22% belonged to the helper category; 48% to the principal professions such as merchant, tavern keeper, baker, carpenter, smith, miller, shoemaker, cooper, tailor and others; 30% fall under the heading of elite professions, government official, sea captain, director, physician, attorney, schoolmaster, clergyman, and others.[23]

The Northwesterners brought along a very influential minority, the Friesians. There are Dutch or Western Friesians and German or Eastern Friesians. They were neighbours in the territory of Lower Saxony, as it is now called. In 1667 the West Friesian territory became semi-dependent on the Netherlands, the East Friesian on Denmark. Promptly the Danish government barred toll-free traffic on the German river Elbe by building a new town "Glückstadt"and collected toll. Near the estuaries "Friesia" was an undefined territory inhabited by seafarers, sea robbers, pirates and traders, who only talked when they had to, but acted swiftly. Their principal towns were Leer, Emden, Norden, Jever, and Aurich where many of the first settlers of New Amsterdam hailed from. They spoke a West Germanic language which was, as we saw, even closer to English than Low German. They understood and conversed also in Low(er) German and of course had little trouble in basic English. Characteristic for the influence of Friesian is the first person pronoun *ek*, both represented by this spelling in the Hudson Valley and in Cape Dutch.[24]They came over in sufficiently strong numbers to found the Saturday vegetable market of New Amsterdam in 1656. One of their famous words, used for legal reasons for a ten-to-fourteen year old youngster (kid laborer) is *"boi"*. English "boy" besides "guy" and a few other "New Yorkisms" may go back to early Friesian influence. In any case the clubs of the New York area formed by North Friesian islanders from Sylt, Föhr, and Amrum, from where young men have traditionally emigrated to the States, are still going strong in contemporary New York City after three hundred fifty years of cohort service.

[23]*"Those Damn' Dutch"*, p. 50f., 96-101.

[24]See Charles T. Gehring, *The Dutch Language in Colonial New York* ... UMI Dissertation . Ann Arbor, MI 1973, p. 30ff.; Fritz Ponelis, *The Development of Afrikaans...* P. Lang Berne 1993, p. 195ff.

Chapter 4
New Amsterdam changing to New York

Colonel Richard Nicolls who commanded the English expeditionary fleet and military occupation force became the first English deputy governor of the province. He reorganized the government of the areas surrounding the city first. Outside many more Englishmen had settled than inside the city. Inside the town limits he proceeded with caution, but as vigorously and tactfully as the situation allowed. After the takeover of New Amsterdam by the English he hesitated nine months before he substituted English equivalencies for existing town offices such as sheriffs, board of aldermen, and mayor. In a sense the takeover was comparable to that of a Hanse ship. Under this new English management the Dutch inhabitants, who had grudgingly attached their former loyalty to the Dutch West India Company, openly sided with the English colonial masters and secretly even welcomed them. For the new regime meant better working conditions for most families.

After a short undramatic relapse to Netherlandic power and an interlude of 16 months in 1673/74, the Colony became English permanently. Fort Frederick Henry became Fort James, New Amsterdam was renamed New York in honor of the Duke of York, King James's brother and successor, the designation New Nederland yielded to New England. It did not merely stay just another commercial investment, but developed to a colonial empire with a potential entitling it to special considerations from London. We must however recognize how small this enterprise still was in 1678. Only three ocean worthy sailing ships, seven boats, and eight sloops were registered in New York harbor.[25] This small commercial fleet grew only very slowly. But as the sailing ships turned around a second time and back to Europe with exported goods such as tobacco or cotton, so they brought back young Englishmen, whose immigrant numbers did not abate. At the end of the 17th century, the small English community in New York Town consisted mainly of newcomers, not cohorts.[26] For, as Goodfriend asserted, given the high rate of turnover the English town population failed to grow substantially. However this loss of membership was eagerly replenished by newcomers from other countries such as the German territories, particularly after the repossession by the end of the Dutch interval in 1674. The English share of all newcomers, according to Goodfriend, was not higher than 10%. From this time onward we not only mark the change in the spelling of the town's new title but that of last names as well. From 1664-74 the town spelled New Yorke, afterwards New York without the -e.. Gradually immigrants independent of the English crown and the small military garrison, and the civil administration sought prospects of their own. One category was notably absent at that time: the indentured English male servant. Typically, Englishmen with prospects married native Dutch women of the second (cohort) generation. Finally an Anglican Church was built and gave spiritual as well as secular haven "to the most

[25]Thomas A. Janvier, *In Old New York*. N. Y. Harper & Brothers 1894, p. 25.
[26]Goodfriend, p. 52.

heterogeneous and the least rooted group" of the emerging "city", the Englishman. Usually, they became the enterprising merchants on a slightly smaller scale than the cohort Hollanders who established ties and a reputation of their own. The influx by the English did not necessarily lead to an automatic reallocation of economic power, but more of prestige.

Chapter 5
The Yankee vs. the Yorker type

After an outbreak of small pox and a subsequent grave epidemic of yellow fever[27] in the Colony of New York during the first decade of the 18th century a load of 3,500 semi-skilled mostly protestant and very exhausted Palatine family members came over on a "stipend" of Queen Anne. Upon arrival they needed 250 coffins which were paid for by the government. That seemingly generous royal gesture notwithstanding, an influx of some further 8,500 South German family members of the same ilk had arrived. Only a fraction remained in New York, but many came back from the surrounding lands of New York later. The reason was that these German immigrants could not become citizens. Why? They could not own property, since they had no church to affiliate with. And since they could not express their concerns in English collectively they could not settle anywhere permanently.[28]

Compared to these large numbers of south western German immigrants, the Palatines, made settled Americans in New York and English newcomers with a naval background in N. Y. harbor feel crowded. A tension developed. The other newcomers tried to outdo these tough, itinerant, and non-settled rivals who hovered on the low end of the social totem pole for jobs. Who were these people? According to my own figures in *"Those Damn' Dutch"*, more than 20% of all "Dutch-German" (*Deutsche*) first or christian names (also in Dutch spelling) were baptised Jan (or Hans, Johann, Hannes, etc.) in the territory of New York during the first half of the 18th century. Even 8% of all German surnames were Jan-derived as well. Jan is the Low German and Hollandic way of spelling John. The English diminutive was Johnny, in Hollandic *"Jantje,"* but *"Janke"* in Low German. An ENCYCLOPEDIA BRITANNICA article advances a military origin of this only slightly slurring term of the nickname *"yankee".* The OXFORD ENGLISH DICTIONARY wavers between an Indian origin and a Dutch "conjecture."[29]

The milieu in which the word "yankee" appeared in New Amsterdam was military, and more specifically naval. Precisely in this milieu the Palatine Germans, who appeared differently from their Northwest German cohort cousins, cut out a poor figure. Yet in this surrounding these strange newcomers had to work: and unfittingly in British run naval stores.[30] In harbor quarters shipyard helpers, canvassers, sail makers, salters and fishmongers, and market trade helpers for low wages were urgently needed, Commands were given them by first-class mates or petty-officers of

---

[27]John Duffy, *Epidemics in Colonial America*. Baton Rouge 1953.

[28]Henry Z. Jones, Jr., *The Palatine Families of New York ... in 1710* . Universal City, CA 1985. A. G. Roeber, *Palatines, Liberty, and Property: German Lutherans in Colonial British Americ a* Baltimore 1991.

[29]Vol. XXIII, p. 877, entry "Yankee", is signed by the late anthropologist at the University of London, M. M. Douglas; OED, 2nd ed., 1989, vol. XX, p. 692.

[30]Walter A. Knittle, *Early Eighteenth Century Palatine Emigration: A British government Redemptioner Project to Manufacture Naval Stores*. Philadelphia 1936.

the British merchant navy. Their language originally could not have been better than of a go-in-between "caterwauling" while praising their petty wares at dumping prices. Originally then a slightly contemptuous coloration of the term "yankee" (*Yänke*), derived from "*Deutsch*" Janke with an audible e. It is also different and obviously distinguishable from the higher echeloned Hollandic "*Jantje*". As soon as it was contrasted with "Yorker" it became more descriptive than acerbic, as the Encyclopedia articles allow. Yankee as a free-floating nickname used perhaps as early as the middle of the 17th century became descriptive of the New Netherlander, allied with the Northwestern German, turned New Englander onrushing to New York from the East, either from the Connecticut-held Long Island, or from Albany down the Hudson Valley before the end of that century. The earliest literary proof that the meaning is really "Little John" comes from an epithalamium (a so-called *Mengelgedicht*) by a Dutch lawyer employed by the Dutch East India Company in Capetown, dated 1672

"Kryght groot en *kleinhans* licht sijn deel"
(Important people and *krethi* & *plethi* easily get their share [of the wedding dinner])[31]

Lifted from the Old Testament background of 2. Samuel 15:18, the implication of the New York meaning is someone who is very eager, but not in cool Yorker style, a successful, but itinerant, not a settled businessman. The paired (important vs. not too important) Yorker-Yankee contrast designates ways of conducting business, the former medium to large in a store, the latter small, selling harbor merchandise, the former depositing money on a counter, the latter horse-back riding with a wicker basket and wheeler-dealing. Then the original background disappeared from memory. The New Englander was American, no longer English, the *Deutsch* sounding yankee was also a bit Low German, but that trait was fading. Rather it had an admixture (*Mengel*) of Hollandic or Friesian in its background. It took three generations to breed a new type yarn-spinning American trader. We recognize the (New) Yorker harbor milieu in which the nickname yankee surfaced for High German *Kleinhans* in Low German *Jantje*. Eventually the British began using it in a different fashion for all Eastern Americans. American citizens, on the other hand, used "yankee" for not-so-British New Englanders such as "Connecticut Yankee", later on in "damned yankee", or "German yankee" in 19th century Illinois. A two tier yankee nickname was attached to the "Forty-Eighter" regiments from Missouri, who donned the blue coat and fought as "Yankee Dutchmen" for the preservation of the Union.

That the term "yankee" was picked up in the Low(er) Dutch-German version by English sailors need not surprise us, if we realize that the European "German" States had more than ten times as many inhabitants as The Netherlands before 1600 and still five times as many around 1700. The Thirty Years War had decimated "Germany" as a parcelled whole, but had spared Danzig, Breslau, and the Hanse cities Hamburg and

---

[31]Gerrit Komrij, *Die Afrikaanse Poesie*. Bert Bakker Amsterdam 1999, p. 17, 1096f. See also Grimms *Deutsches Wörterbuch*, vol. 5 (1873) column 1110 for entry "*Kleinhans*".

Bremen. The relatively rapid acceptance of the poor yankee by genuine Netherlandic gentlemen (i. e. non-yankees) became normal. During the 18th century this type naval-stuff trader operating outside clans and cohort families must have become the first genuinely blended American, talking persuasive basic English of the Northwestern newcomer color, stereotyping its speaker for successful itinerant trade.

"Oh, the profit were unutterable, especially when a handsome young merchant
Bears the pack himself." (Sir Walter Scott, *Kennilworth*)

Therefore I disavow the origin of yankee as an inner-Dutch polemical word which I had argued for, unbeknownst to me supported by the Random House Dictionary article at that time, which identified "Yankee" as a Connecticut Yankee.[32] The term itself became detached from its self-conscious "identity" tag. A Yankee as a type became a successful early proto-American.

---

[32]"*Damn' Dutch*", Jan Kees = Yankee, RHD ed. 1967; this speculation had been followed by Stephanie Bernardo. *The Ethnic Almanac*, p. 154.

PART TWO

FORMATION HISTORY

Fragments of Freedom Combined

Chapter 1
The spread of the dollar as specie

American history was formed foremost by the forces of democracy, the freedom of the press, and last not least by the might of the dollar. Does the spread of this currency have something to do with the spread of democracy and immigration history? We shall see. Trading skills, credit worthiness and accurate bookkeeping in colonial New York stores could not overcome the most pressing problem, a currency could have: a dryness of specie. Ever since 1695 the treasury in London had forbidden the exporting of sterling silver coins to her American colonies.

England had an acute shortage of currency herself. Since the country did not have natural, let alone profitable, silver mines on the Island and the famous mines in *Joachimsthal* (Bohemia) and in Freiberg (Saxonia) had become depleted by the middle of the 16th century, English explorations overseas became necessary. Both her trading partners and clandestine enemies, France and Spain, had declared bankruptcy in 1557. England wanted to forego such a dilemma. The King authoritatively denied the colonists the value of higher monetary denominations. But he could not deny them the basic commodity exchange value. His underlying "reasoning" was faulty.

Compared to England's restrictive monetary policy matters were uncontrolled in "Germany". The territory where the Hapsburg imperial mint had a control of – for convenience's sake referred to as Germany – was partitioned into two spheres of influence, one, the north-northwestern territory above the Benrath Line, where the thaler (spelled *daller* in Low(er) German) was the principal monetary unit and two, south of it, the gulden or *guilder* area. After a short interval of non-recognition,[1] the Lübeck thaler[2] was coined officially and widely accepted. In 1566 this currency was recognized as second imperial currency and valuta. In these northwestern imperial territories some sixty mints coined thalers ideally minted at 894.5 "fine"/28.8 grams of silver.[3] This northern silver currency was more closely allied with the Reformation leaning electors and the Hanse towns, the gulden currency with the Catholic Hapsburg controlled countries. A dynastic connection between Spain and the Austrian ruling

---

[1] H. Hornhagen, "Der Handel des Lübecker Kaufmanns Johan Glandorfs," *VGHst Lübeck*. Reihe 55, vol. 12. 1985, p. 187.

[2] First mentioned as *"daller"* in Bugenhagen's 1488 Church School Education treatise (Lübecker *Kirchenordnung*).

[3] Wolfgang Heß und Dietrich Klose, *Vom Thaler zum Dollar 1486-1986. Staatliche Münzsammlung München*. München 1986, p. 63.

25

house of Hapsburg was functioning at least temporarily so that the new overseas mining profited both leading European countries for the time being.

Since the Netherlands dominated the spice trade with India, and thanks to the efforts of the Dutch East India Company which filled her coffers at home in Amsterdam, England if she didn't want to be left out frantically had to look elsewhere for mining prospects. A man only known as Daniel, a mining engineer from Freiberg who had trained prospective miners in England before, sailed with Sir Henry Gilbert to Bonavista, Newfoundland, where he worked as an essayer for a season. Sir Gilbert's sister ship, on which large samples hoarded by Daniel were sailing back apparently sank in a gale not too far from the coast. Since German miners were considered the leading technicians by the middle of that century, German miners were called over by Queen Elizabeth to train English miners-to-be and essayers, before they were to be sent over to North America again. Sir Walter Raleigh, a half brother of Gilbert, sent his captain Richard Grenville over to the area of Cape Hatteras in the future North Carolina. The Jewish German specialist and mine director, a gentleman called Joachim Gans from Prague, was the chief engineer of that expedition.[4] All these efforts came by and large to nothing. Then it was decided that it was much more lucrative to catch and sequester the silver or silver coins laden Spanish galleons filled with *pesos*. Poorly coined, half coined or roughly minted or even cut the wrong way, they could be reminted, restamped or recoined and used for currency, instead of the Spaniards paying back their debt to England. The English could make booty quickly and repay their debt the easy way.

The so-called "ship pieces of eight reals" (*reales de a ocho*) became the source of a highly profitable freebooting. We already know the heroic seamen: Hawkins, Drake and younger cruisers. As soon as the *pesos* were reminted or recoined they were considered on a par with Hanse German *dallers*, Spanish *dolera* or Italian *tallera*. They were equally desirable in England, on the European continent, and on the eastern seaboard of North America. The reason was simple to understand: despite their rough and often unround appearance (due to sometimes cutting octagonally), their silver content and weight was genuine, often surfed by German mining and coinage engineers in Potosi, Bolivia, and edged by the sign of the royal (hence Real) Spanish mint. The *dollar* is not pronounced the Spanish way, but the Low(er) German, or "Dutch" way with an open a, and the double l is Low(er) German as well. It needs to be stressed and repeated that the term was not coined from the High German *Thaler*, not from the Dutch *daelder* (at 1 ½ guilders), but from the Low(er) German *daller*. According to Hans Nussbaum[5] the London foreign exchange dealers introduced this spelling in Boston, in New Amsterdam and finally in London itself. With the reader's permission it needs to be repeated: the dollar at the time of the change from the 16th to the 17th century could have been minted or weighted in Bolivia, taken over by Drake, recoined abroad, apparently sometimes even aboard, outranking the pound sterling, the

[4]Gary C. Grassl, "German Mineral specialists in Elizabethan England and Early English America," *Yearbook of German-American Studies*, vol. 31, 1996, p. 45-61.

[5]*A History of the Dollar*, first ed. 1944, p. 10; 2nd ed. 1958.

guilder, as well as the *"Reichsthaler."* Via Emden, Friesland, it spread even into the Netherlands, where the crafty *mijnheers* coined fake dollars of the same weight, happily landlubbing and circulating as if they were genuine.[6] It could of course not displace the native guilder *(florin)*. But in North America the dollar dislodged tobacco, molasses, rum, dried fish, or cotton as means of payment. Its amazing history is of vital concern to immigration research, for ironically, by background, the dollar is a genuine "immigrant" currency.

The fairly surprising result within the framework of our study: the freewheeling maritime dollar with this peculiar piratical background became a currency, an immigrant specie and valuta, one might say, with a Low(er) German derived protestant name, in a sense just another American-English nickname for a *thaler*. It pushed and was pulled, it was popular and independent more than a hundred years before it became US currency for gaining the US monetary independence from Europe. During the interval the paper dollar notes created havoc, but that is a different story. By circulation it lead to the introduction of the real American-coined Treasury dollar in 1792, after the Spanish milled dollar-peso had been sliced into decimal cents in 1785. Until today you may call a cent a penny. Canada had a polyglot monetary system until 1867, which we need not follow up here.

Suffice it to add on the more anecdotal level that neither the "Pillars of Hercules", as on the peso, nor the letter S through the letter U gave rise to the $ sign, but really the letter 8 struck over the letter P standing for *peso*. The dollars ran away from their moving mints as fast as they could, for they were too good to be true, so that by 1805 they were minted out of silver no more.[7]

Whereas William Penn had travelled throughout "Germany" in 1682 to extend an invitation to members of persecuted protestant religious denominations to come to his new colony, Pennsylvania, the 1740 Act of Parliament allowed "foreign" protestants (including those from the Palatinate again) to settle anywhere in the English colonies of North America. This place was planned, above denominational struggles, as a "city of brotherly love", tolerating all kinds of currencies.

These Germans constituted the third such group after the one to Pennsylvania which landed in 1683ff., and to New Bern, North Carolina in 1712, soon to be scattered all the way up to the Hudson Valley, N. Y. Then, Benjamin Franklin in Philadelphia moved away from his positive assessment of these new co-citizens of 1752, and the following years, for they were less educated and "not used to freedom".[8] After the end of the Seven Year War the fear of English Americans of a French-

---

[6]Philip L. Mossman, *Money of the American Colonies and Confederation. A Numismatic, Economic and Historical Correlation.* Numismatic Studies Nr. 20. The Ametrican Numismatic Society. New York 1993, p. 64.

[7]*Vom Thaler zum Dollar*, p. 202. A small-scale native silver coin minting on a German rocker press (*"Taschenwerk"*) operated in Boston, MA, from 1652-1690; see ed. John Kleeberg, *Money of Pre-Federal America.* A. Numismatic Society. New York 1992, p. 6-7.

[8]*The Papers of Benjamin Franklin*, vol. 4, p. 483f., letter to Peter Collinson. For the exceptional J. Leisler see above.

"German"-American alliance, for instance in Illinois, gradually subsided. So the immigration could be continued unimpeded. Men and women played their individual role in business and family, and fulfilled their cohort tasks. The Yorker may have held his nose up a little bit on the Yankee who nevertheless laughingly often guessed things right. The future of the roving dollar was assured everywhere.

Chapter 2
Libel or freedom of the press as token of democracy

Perhaps no other not-yet-Yorker was more typical for becoming a "German" Yankee by tough-mindedness and stamina than a printer by the name of John Peter Zenger (1697-1746) for demonstration purposes. I became familiar with his life and his courage in an odd way. I had bought a withdrawn book from the Harold B. Lee Library at Brigham Young University. The title, Anna Zenger: Mother of Freedom, intrigued me. In this age of cold-nosed deconstruction the main caption of the publisher, Farrar & Straus, non-plussed me even more:

"In this novelized biography of a colorful figure in a romantic period of American history (the author) Kent Cooper suggests a solution to a mystery that is more than two hundred years old. Who wrote the articles in the New York Weekly Journal which resulted in the trial in 1734 of John Peter Zenger for seditious libel of the governor of the Colony of New York?"

Cooper, a former Associated Press director, wanted to bring recognition to Anna Zenger, the printer`s wife, as the first woman newspaper editor in the American colonies, and thus describe and praise one of the unsung heroines of American newspaper history. I read the whole book with a mental reservation until I reached the author`s Note in the end. The whole hypothesis rested on the assumption that Anna née Moul(in) was a young American of Dutch extraction and belonged to the freeman`s class, with a highly educated lawyer father in her background. This is where she was supposed to have picked up her writing skill. Otherwise how could she edit so brilliantly?

The New York Dutch Reformed Church Book entered under the date of Sept. 11, 1722 her marriage to John Pieter Zenger. Cooper had deciphered the accompanying note, given in Dutch, that the couple, John as well as Anna, hailed from "High Germany". Cooper commented: "This surely is an error. Zenger was a Palatinate, while Anna was Dutch."[9] It escaped Cooper that "Palatinate" stood for Southwest German, and Dutch in that context meant *Deutsch*. Church records are seldom falsified.

Anna Catharina Maul, the daughter of Johannes Maul and Anna J. Theiss was baptized in Hohenroth near Driedorf (Herborn) on Jan. 24, 1698. Her father petitioned to emigrate with his family of seven from Nassau-Dillenburg in 1709. They took a boat from Rotterdam to England and were en route for 6 months, and finally arrived in New York in Apr. 1711 as one family of 3,500 Palatines, We know that the queen had allowed such a settlement in her colony. Upon arrival Anna was 13.[10] So she did not grow up as a native. Dutch and English were foreign languages for her. She could not have learned about constitutional problems, freedom of the press without study. Her

---

[9]Kent Cooper, Anna Zenger: *Mother of Freedom*. New York 1946, p. 330. This book triggered another fiction for juveniles by Thomas Galt, *John Peter Zenger: Fighter for Freedom* N. Y. 1951.

[10]Henry Z. Jones, JR. *The Palatine Families of New York 1710*. vol. 1 and 2. Universal City, CA 1985, p. 600-606, 793, 1124.

famous "Dutch" father dwelling in New York arrived as a middle-aged German in that city. We do not know his profession. Down the drain goes Cooper`s daring hypothesis.

The New York Weekly Journal has the style and betrays the mentality of the eighteenth-century legally trained student of political philosophy and the legal language of the day, a kind of American counterpart of the contemporary London Journal.[11] Thus the literary genius ascribed by Cooper to Anna Zenger is fictional.

The reason why the choice journalist, Kent Cooper, invented a "mother of freedom" on the loving side of the printer, Mr. Zenger, was to fill a vacuum of reputation. He took his cue from the fact that Mr. Zenger had been looked at or even been defamed by other writers as the "proprietor of a second-class printing shop", "who never became a refined practitioner, for one reason, because his grasp of the English language remained defective...".[12] In fact, he has "often been slighted and disesteemed".[13] Or: "Peter Zenger may have gone to jail for any number of reasons – devotion to an ideal, Teutonic stubbornness, some odd quirk of character, or what-you-will."[14] Before we examine the controversial Palatine a bit more closely, we can retort with an authoritative description of Governor Cosby`s command of the English language: "His spelling and his grammar were often at fault."[15] If an Irishman without too much polish can be appointed by London, after he had failed in Minorca to a governorship abroad, why cannot a self-made German-American businessman become a bona fide popular printer of repute?

Zenger`s claim to fame rests on the freedom of the press trial at the Supreme Court of the Province of New York, in which the jury acquitted him of the charge of seditiously libeling the government of governor William Cosby. His acquittal in August, 1735, is attributed to the reputation of his brilliant defense lawyer from Philadelphia, Andrew Hamilton, an eighty year old Scotsman, whom Zenger had heard argue a famous case while he himself resided there. The verdict of not having libeled the government seditiously stands as the first trumpet of American Independence. Who really was Zenger? Was he a "German" yankee?

Johann Peter Sänger was born in the *Oberpfalz* (Upper Palatinate) near the Rhine in 1697. He came over with his parents and two siblings in 1710 on one of these six-

---

[11]Vincent Buranelli, "The Myth of Anna Zenger," *The William and Mary Quarterly,* Third Series, vol. XIII, 1956, p. 157-168, *165.*

[12]Vincent Buranelli, ed., *The Trial of Peter Zenger*. N. Y. University Press 1957, p. 4. This study is dependent on Livingston Rutherford, *John Peter Zenger, His Press, his Trial and a Bibliography of Zenger Imprints*. New York 1904. Short modern appraisals playing down Zenger`s significance are Thomas P. Slaughter, "John Peter Zenger," *Dictionary of Library Biography (DBL)* vol. 24, 1984, p. 380-382; Mary Sue F. Poole, "John Peter Zenger," *DLB*, vol. 43, 1985, p. 474-480. Stanley Nider Katz, ed. *A Brief Narrative of the Case and Trial of John Peter Zenger* ... Harvard U.P. 1963; revised ed. 1972, was unavailable to me.

[13]Sanford H. Cobb, *The Story of the Palatines. An Episode of Colonial History.* 1897. A Heritage Classic. Rp. 1988, p. 138.

[14]V. Buranelli, "The Myth of Anna Zenger", loc. citat., p. 161.

[15]James Grant Wilson, *The Memorial History of the City of New York*, vol. II. N. Y. History Company 1892, p. 218.

months boat trips to New York, during which his father died. He belonged to one of 3,500 Palatine families "invited" by the English royal patroness, the benefactor of their freedom, to settle in New York, New Jersey, or Pennsylvania.[16] In 1711 he was indentured with the printer William Bradford (who hailed from Leistershire, England) for eight years, and as a printer's devil learned the art and mystery of printing from the bottom up.[17]

After the end of his long toil with the king's printer he became a journeyman. But the modern interpreters forget to mention that he enjoyed a position of trust at an early age, which he lost due to circumstances: he was a collector of sundry public taxes and was in arrears his enemies said, not honestly.[18] "He was prosecuted, having no means to liquidate the debt, he left the city. He afterwards applied to the Assembly for leave to do public printing enough to discharge the debt, but was refused. "[19] Obviously then he was not treated fairly. He may have thought he had left New York for good. He went to Philadelphia, married Anna White, with whom he had a son, and moved on to Maryland, where he became a citizen, and a printer of colonial laws and proceedings. If he had not been widowed early in life, he might have staid further south, but as it was, he came back, even briefly worked for William Bradford again, but finally set up his own shop, becoming a rival to his former master in 1726.

In 1730 he printed the first arithmetic book ever published in New York written in the Dutch language. He was trilingual and could typeset in German, English and Dutch. He frequented the Dutch Reformed Church because of his wife, and even played the organ there.

As a former German he was leaning toward the Dutch Yorkers, and called his middle name Pieter.[20] His bride Anna C. now spelled her maiden name Moul, a phonetic concession to the Dutch sound of German "au". After they were married in 1722, Zenger was naturalized on July 6, 1723. He was made a freeman printer on Sept. 10, 1723. By that time his youthful perpetration at least on the surface seemed forgotten.

[16]Researched thoroughly by Allen Knittle, *Early Eighteenth Century Palatine Emigration.* Baltimore 1965, with exact appendixes; and by Henry Z. Jones, JR. *The Palatine Families of New York 1710.* II vol.s. Universal City, CA 1985. The former counts more than 3,500 families, the latter ca. 8,500 persons. We don't know how many died on the high sea, but 250 coffins had to be paid for by public funds for worn out arrivees. Orphans were regularly separated from sisters or brothers.

[17]Buranelli, *The Trial*, also declares Anna, his wife, "a native of Holland". But then, even prof. Joyce D. Goodfriend, *New York before the Melting Pot.* Princeton University Press 1992, mingles Hollandic and *Deutsch* consistently. See above PART ONE chapter 3.

[18]James Grant Wilson, *The Memorial History of the City of New York.* N. Y. History Company. vol. II 1892, p. 226.

[19]Doc. History N. Y. IV. 1042, *N. Y. Assembly Journal*, I 627, 636, quoted in Martha A. Lamb, *History of the City of New York*, vol. I. N. Y. 1877. She is the only early commentator, who grants Zenger having had professional "talent" (p. 548).

[20]The Z is a Hollandic spelling of the S in his last name, Sänger is Zanger, the e being a concession to the former Umlaut ä in his native name. Remember, he was a thirteen year old half-orphan when the Sänger family arrived in New York. Upon arrival they were spelled the Dutch way.

In November 1733 he started a newspaper, the New York Weekly Journal, having what we would call a "Whig" party slant in hindsight. Zenger, who was not a journalist but a printer drew the attention of writers with a sharp pen. The most famous among them was probably James Alexander, heir to the Scottish title of Earl of Stirling, by profession a lawyer, who turned this paper into an opposition paper which caught on and became popular. Since the imbuing strife broke out over the governor's artificially bloated salary demands, the governor became the butt of jokes and was regularly lampooned. Since he had a small character and no self-critical sense of humor-- Cosby had to leave his last position as governor of Minorca under the cloud of a bribery charge-- the crisis was on. The opponents to governor Cosby assailed the right to print a song, poking fun on his style of governing New Yorkers. The text began:

> We are the lads who dare resist
> all autocratic power.
> If you`d help come on enlist
> this is the fateful hour.
> In freedom`s cause we`ll take our stand
> And that`s because we love this land
> > With a Fa la la la.   *and ended*:

> Pour the wine and fill the cup.
> Down it without a care.
> Cosby knows the jig is up;
> Vict`ry is in the air.
> So here`s a health unto the best
> And let the devil take the rest!
> > With a Fa la la la.

Another number resorted to verse of which two lines are enough to get the drift:

> Cosby, the mild, the happy, good and great,
> The strongest guard of our little state ...

Somehow Zenger's old enemies high and low remembered that the printer had been run out of the city before, and tried to break his will and have him divulge the men behind the noms de plume "Cato", "Philo-Patriae, "Thomas Standby" or else. Four particularly offensive issues of the journal were ordered to be publicly burned. Nobody was willing to do this, except a wretched black slave who had no choice in the matter. In the absence of the magistrate only a sheriff was present at the burning.[21]

---

[21]Comparatively, no honest carpenter was willing to produce a ladder on which the provisional governor of New York, Jacob Leisler (1640-1691), also a palatinate was to step up to be hanged for alleged treason in March, 1691. During his trial his opponent, the Dutch millionaire, Fr. Philipse, poked fun about his German accent, just as his relative, Adolphe Philipse, the supreme court justice, poked fun on Zenger during the trial in 1735. Could this be a mere coincidence?

Zenger, because he couldn't pay the excessively high bail of 400, was thrown into jail, serving a nine months' imprisonment and was shut in tightly. No lawyer was allowed to see him, no ink and pen was permitted. But after a week he could whisper his instructions through a chink or hole in the door. The upshot: his newspaper, the *New York Weekly Journal*, continued to appear, his wife with the help of his friends substituting for the jailed printer.

A great victory for freedom of expression occurred at the end of this trial. The jury was persuaded by the famous Philadelphia attorney, Andrew Hamilton, to pass their verdict not only on matters of fact, but on matters of law. This outcome was helped along by Zenger's persistence, by his bold, discreet and tenacious behavior in jail, and also by his courageous wife at home and in the Zenger print shop, where she held up the flag. The principle behind it is that truth could not be libelous, much less seditious.

This printer had labored hard as an immigrant entrepreneur making his enterprise the business of the people of New York City. The yoke of the government, packed on his shoulders, galled him and weighed heavily on him. It is to his credit that with the help of the ablest lawyer and other outstanding intellectual friends, he threw that yoke off. In that sense the printer was an early Yankee *and* Yorker. In fact we think he may have been a forerunner of later revolutionaries. For a resistance to a particular governor could lead to resistance to the king's administration in America, and ultimately to the crown itself. Ironically the king spoke with an undesirable foreign accent as well, and hailed from the same country. John Peter Zenger was more than a portent.

It is to his credit as a German immigrant having become an American patriot that Zenger rose from editor of a press to arbiter and keeper of its freedom. This thought was most succinctly expressed in the November 12, 1733 number of his own Journal:

> "The liberty of the press is a subject of the greatest importance,
> and in which every individual is as much concerned
> as he is in any other part of liberty."

Research on heritage and "yankeeship" can be tricky. Often one single fundamental misunderstanding, e.g. what the meaning of *Dutch* is in New York, can lead to unwarranted conclusions. It is a pity that no picture of Johann Peter Sänger alias John Pieter Zenger or of Anna Zenger née Maul or Moul, his heroic wife, survived. Zenger is more than just a footnote in the history of American journalism. Zenger helped that henceforth reporting was to be based on the freedom of thought, the ultimate pillar of public liberty then and now. True Yankee grit.

Chapter 3
1803: The "Louisiana" Sale and Purchase and its repercussions on
German mass immigration from 1804-1861;
"cohort" settling of the wilderness

It would have been much clearer from a historical point of view and for political scientists not to speak of the "Louisiana" Territorial Purchase by the U.S. government from France, but of the "Mississippi" Purchase leading to the actual sale and tranfer in 1803. The Territory of Louisiana to which France held title, originally included the entire valley of the Mississippi-Missouri. By having it retro ceded by Spain to France, Napoleon hoped to claim the entire exploration title again in his hand, before he could sell it to the US government. At the heart of the matter figured the freedom of navigation on North America's big dividing and at the same time connecting river, and the right of stapling, depositing and exchanging wares at its mouth, New Orleans. This guarantee by Spain made the virgin lands on both banks of the navigable river – all the way up to the future "Canada", which Simon Fraser crossed all the way to the Pacific coast for the first time – most valuable, particularly from a continental point of view, and could therefore not be left in the hands of a weak state here and in Europe, Spain, nor of a stronger one abroad, France, but demanded payment for further trade concessions from either government by the United States.

Two developments "peaked": Napoleon suddenly realized he could not hold the larger Louisiana against Britain, and likely lose it without the benefit of compensation. The secretary of state, James Madison, was aware that Ohio was only the first of several states from the Northwest Territories (the northern part of the greater Louisiana) to join the Union in 1803. Napoleon with the clairvoyance of a "Corsican Yankee" calculated that he would get a considerable amount of money (as it turned out, 60 million livres) for something he held only on a thin straw, legally perhaps, but by no means militarily, let alone administratively. He needed extra money for his expensive coronation to Emperor of the French.

President Thomas Jefferson could not legally prevail at the negotiating table in Paris and prove his constitutional authority, without the Senate's prior consent, to geostrategically double the size of his country. It was troublesome enough to play out his shrewd and patient competency as a diplomat while obtaining the Senate's subsequent sanction. Not many people realize that Merriwether Lewis and William Clark explored the New West after the Purchase, from 1803-1806, to the mouth of the Columbia river and back. Clark subsequently became the territorial governor of Missouri from 1813 to 1820, and superintendent of Indian affairs at St. Louis, a year after Missouri had been granted statehood.

This immense territory, "Greater Louisiana," was subsequently carved into (Little) Louisiana, Missouri, Arkansas, Iowa, North and South Dakota, Nebraska, and Oklahoma in their entirety, and most of Kansas, Colorado, Wyoming, Montana and

34

Minnesota. Millions of people had to be either invited by propaganda, *Reiselektüre*,[22] or chain letters, to come and settle as farmers and become citizens. All this was very unregulated and open-ended. People, particularly if they weren't French Catholics, and could capably help themselves, felt welcomed by this opportunity of a life time and assimilate through hard, independent work. Soon afterwards these settlement areas were considered "poor man's paradise" (Julius Fröbel).

Jefferson also was shrewd enough to realize that such an impending mass immigration required a migration-friendly policy, and that in this way, good predominantly Republican-leaning future citizens would come and stay, masses of voters-to-be would press his Whig adversaries to the wall.[23] Before the onrush set in, there were no more than 50,000 people living in Greater Louisiana. During the following decades literally millions of new American migrants and immigrants from abroad rushed forward and streamed into the North West Central and the South West Central regions. In these territories, certainly at the beginning of this period, land at 3 ½ cents an acre could be purchased. The Louisiana/Mississippi Purchase did not alter the direction of the new North American expansion, but strengthened and accelerated it by shortening the time frame of settlement. It was paid for by ready government funds, not by borrowed money or a tax increase[24] during the end of the silver dollar era.

This compact advance went straight west: Ohio (a state in 1803); Indiana (1816); Illinois (1818); Missouri (1821); and south: Louisiana (1812); Mississippi (1817); Alabama (1819). The "rest", actually 2/3 of the loot, stayed "unorganized" for a couple of decades. From the Congress of Vienna (1815) to the German Freedom Rise (1848), according to the census (1800 to 1850), authenticated by Wilbur Zelinsky, and repeated as fact by the editors of the *Kolloquiumsbeiträge der Technischen Universität Dresden*[25] more than 1.6 million "Germans" came to settle predominantly in these virgin territories. Heinz Kloss documents the order and sequence of these settlement phases thusly: first, and logically so, arrival in Ohio (1800), then Indiana (1810), Illinois (1820), Missouri (1820), Michigan (1830), Iowa (1840), Minnesota (1859), and Kansas (1850).[26] These settlers, mostly farmers and craftsmen,[27] cleared, made land

[22]P. J. Brenner, *Reisen in die Neue Welt. Die Erfahrung Nordamerikas in deutschen Reise- und Auswanderungsberichten des 19. Jahrhunderts*. Tübingen 1991.

[23]Otto Vossler, *Die Amerikanischen Revolutionsideale in ihrem Verhältnis zu den Europäischen*. R. Oldenbourg Verlag München und Berlin 1929, p. 162.

[24]Merrill D. Peterson, *Thomas Jefferson and the New Nation: A Biography*. New York Oxford 1970, pp. 746-768.

[25]*Deutsche in Amerika: Die Einwanderung im Kartenbild*. Institut für Karthographie. Dresden 1994, p. 17; see also final grid in PART SIX table 9.

[26]*Atlas der im 19. und frühen 20. Jahrhundert entstandenen deutschen Siedlungen in USA. Atlas of the 19th and early 20th Century German-American Settlements*. N. G. Elwert Verlag Marburg 1974, p. 8ff.

[27]Joseph Och, *Der Deutschamerikanische Farmer ... Eine statistische und volkswirtschaftliche Untersuchung*. Columbus, Ohio 1913.

35

arable, and adapted their ploughing skill to the prevailing conditions. Their neighbors were either Americans, or other immigrants from the Old Country or from England, Scotland, Ireland, Scandinavia or the Netherlands, or elsewhere. In any case, under these aboriginal conditions, cooperation with neighbors and cohortiveness (equidistant sharing) among themselves was called for. If lacking the chances for survival decreased.

According to my statistical comparisons the trend that much more than half of these newcomers to the United States so far hailed from Northern and Northwestern "Germany" continued to hold true for the North Central States in the 19th century as well. Although the internal geographic localization of the emigration associations *(Auswanderungsvereine)* was equal from the Northern half (17) and the South (also 17),[28] and directed also toward the cities, where more help was required. These settlers came from a country, where there were twice as many cities in North Germany than in South Germany, according to Keyser-Stoob, *Städtebücher*. In a kind of reverse trend to the above statement the more thinly peopled North and Northwest Germany, north of the Benrath Line, was more depopulated by this mass emigration in the first half of the 19th century than the German South. That was particularly true of Mecklenburg, Pomerania and Holstein in the North. They suffered proportionately a higher loss of skilled farmers and less than skilled farm workers. On the opposite end of the scale is Bavaria which suffered the smallest loss.

Apart from these statistics it is of course more difficult to ascertain these immigrants' influx into the big North American cities. This was done very well by Paul Rossnagel, on whose's 1928 figures, the last ones which are comparatively reliable in this respect, our expanding calculations are based. (See PART SIX Table 9). But if one separates the names German settlers gave their places, these two separating spheres of influence, Northern versus Southern, normally conformed to this distinctions, normally adhered to: descriptive, possessive-commemorative, and a few shift names. When the "German" place names, used in their co-founded North West Central states municipalities, villages, towns or cities, are added, the Northern German name sphere encompassed 65%, the Southern German 35%. That does not always implicate a direct heritage of a particular town in the North or the South of the Old Country, but that obviously could happen often enough.

Perhaps during no other period than during the first decades of the 19th century may we register that the whole of North America was the "product" of an ongoing transformation to an arable landscape. The Louisiana Purchase proved its value several times over being a vast stretch of land requiring the freedom of navigation on the rivers and of trekking over land. Both these ideas of actual striving for self-sufficiency and unimpeded transportation came to fruition. Nowhere can the natural world and the human neighborhood interact better than on water, and upon arrival at one's destination, on farmland with cattle breeding, husbandry, sowing and ripening, creating

---

[28]Stefan von Senger und Etterlin, *Neu-Deutschland in Nordamerika. Massenauswan-derung, nationale Gruppenansiedlungen und liberale Kolonialbewegung.* Nomos Universi-tätsschriften Geschichte Band 5. Baden-Baden 1991, Anlagen 1 und 2, pp. 459-463.

and repairing tools, and exchanging the use of farm machinery among cooperative neighbors.

Chapter 4
The yarn spinner Gottfried Duden
vs. Alexis de Tocqueville's Democracy

We now have to look into an emigration alarmist's arguments. The Rhenish-Prussian lawyer Gottfried Duden (1789-1856), the author of a notoriously famous *Report on a Journey (1829)*, an inflammatory piece of pro-emigration literature for Germans, surprisingly also locked horns with the Norman-French aristocratic lawyer Alexis De Tocqueville's (1805-1859) *Democracy in America, part I* of 1835, an internationally famous political classic of lasting endurance, which we came across before.

Although they seem worlds apart, the latter's appearance enticed Duden, after his return from Missouri, to publish the first negative German review in book-length format on Tocqueville's work, in 1837, coupled with a shift of opinion about his own prior book. How can one be a gentleman farmer in Missouri, an emigrant counsellor on a large scale reneging on his former enthusiasm for immigration to the US all within a time span of less than a decade?

Since Duden could not extinguish the feverish emigration wildfire of the 1830s, he had ignited by his first edition of 1829,[29] and strengthened by his second edition of 1833, he not only misunderstood Tocqueville's *Democray in America* as a prime witness to political science (predicting future triumphs and problems in the U.S.), but accused himself of having naively painted too rosy a picture of the likely success *German* agricultural immigrants would meet in Missouri and elsewhere in the U.S. But had he not farmed in Missouri before he wrote? Did he not report as a man of experience and as a gentleman? We need to unravel these contradictions.

Duden's own husbandry experience as an erstwhile "Latin" farmer (who knew his Cicero) near the Missouri River west of St. Louis from 1824 to 1827, gained with the help of his neighbor, who happened to be Daniel Boone's son, had taught him a life-long lesson, applying to every would-be emigrant to America: mosquito bites!

---

[29] Full title: *Bericht über eine Reise nach den westlichen Staaten Nordamerikd's*
und einen mehrjährigen Aufenthalt am Missouri (in den Jahren 1824, 25, 26 unde 1827),
in Bezug auf Auswanderung und Ueberbevölkerung ... dargestellt
a) in einer Sammlung von Briefen,
b) in einer besonderen Abhandlung über den politischen Zustand der nordamerikanischen Freistaaten, und
c) in einem rathgebenden Nachtrage für auswandernde deutsche Ackerwirthe und diejenigen, welche auf Handelsunternehmungen denken,
von Gottfried Duden. [XVI plus 244 S.]
Gedruckt zu Elberfeld im Jahre 1829 bei Sam. Lucas, auf Kosten des Verfassers. 1 ½ Rthlr.
Rp. bei Scheitlin u. Zollikofer. St. Gallen. Switzerland 1833; 2nd and 3rd rp. Eduard Weber Bonn, 1834, 1835.

Translated into American English by James Goodrich et alii as *Report on a Journey to the Western States of North America and the Stay of Several Years along the Missouri*. University of Missouri Press. Columbia, MO 1980.

Rarely does it happen that a well-known travel author prepared himself so thoroughly about his topic, an "empty" foreign country's possibilities in comparison to his native country's overpopulation. He recommended a mass emigration to a much praised foreign country such as the United States, in which he had worked, in the eighteen twenties. Gottfried Duden was the son of a wealthy Remscheid pharmacist, who had studied law at several German universities and had become a judge when the Napoleonic wars spread turmoil into the Rhineland. He decided to quit the legal service and to investigate first hand, where German families, willing to change countries, could carve out a better life for themselves. Together with a friend he travelled to Missouri during the last year of President Monroe's and the first two years of president John Quincy Adams's government (1824-1827). He bought a farm in Warren county three years after the territory had turned State. He was one of those farmers who but had not many practical skills. In the year 1825 he began to arrange for a "Duden" settlement called "Dutzow", managed by "Baron" J. W. von Bock who hailed from the Berlin area, and a "Lake Creek" settlement, managed by Friedrich Münch of the Giessen (in Hessia) area. Some seven years later that part of Missouri was densely populated. One generation after Duden's stay the area of the lower Missouri numbered a great many German-American inhabitants.

Duden's arrival occurred some three years after the cession of the formerly Indian territory to the U.S. It was not only arable land but good for cattle grazing as well. Moreover it was especially beautiful, and as such was praised by the prophet of the Latter-day Saints, Joseph Smith jr., who moved through there with his so-called "Camp of Zion" trek on June 14, 1834. In his *History of the Church*,[30] he dubbed it "the delightful regions of this goodly land – the heritage of the children of God". Temporarily it served a group of Mormons as resting ground.

Leaving his friend Ludwig Eversmann in charge of his farm, Duden returned to Germany and took up his writing again.[31] Back among his friends he collected his many letters he had written to them while in America, and edited the ones fitting his purposes. His trip had carried him from Rotterdam to Baltimore, Pennsylvania, Ohio, Cincinnati, Louisville, St. Louis and Missouri (letters 1-14). His stay in Missouri and the agricultural problems during the settling process filled letters 15-34. His return journey was dealt with in letters 34-36. This letter collection covered the time period of May 1824 to June 1827. After he had condensed as well as expanded his consecutive narrative frame into 36 sections (pages 1-274), he followed these up by a treatise on the Nature of the North American Free States (*Freistaaten*) with reference to mass emigration of German agriculturists and would-be farmers in North America (pages 275-348).

This Duden *Report* on his special journey of a three year duration climaxed in a rather exuberant praise of the opportunities, prospective settlers of education, training

---

[30]Vol. I, chapter 16, p. 197.

[31]Begun by *Ueber die wesentlichen Verschiedenheiten der Staaten und die Strebungen der menschlichen Natur*. Cologne 1822. Rp Eduard Weber Bonn 1835.

and means would find in Missouri. It sparked a fire of an emigration fever, so that http://www.usmo.com/ history/duden.html got carried away into maintaining: "this is why today people of German heritage make up the second largest ethnic group in the United States."

Walter D. Kamphoefner[32], well grounded in social research, more realistically speaks of "The Significance of Chain Migration in the Immigrant Experience" to Missouri, an insight which earlier writers[33] had touched upon in their prior analyses of Gottfried Duden's original *Report*.

Now, was Duden a "dream spinner" who cut his own yarn opportunistically when he did some public breast-beating accusing himself eight years after its first publication? Claiming he had not meant to let down daring young emigrants, he nevertheless annexed a "Reconsideration" to his reprint of 1837 which is both peculiar and not well-known at all. First of all and surprisingly, he republished his otherwise unchanged *Report* together with a book-length review of Alexis de Tocqueville's *Die nordamerikanische Demokratie* in a one-two sequence in the same book[34] Immigration lay outside Tocqueville's scope of inquiry and Duden himself had not really advocated any unconsidered or ill-planned emigration (*"leichtsinniges Auswandern"*) in the first place, although he had been ambiguous about it.[35]

Duden gave his reconsideration a strange third-person title, which in English reads like this: Duden's "Self-Accusation" about the demerits of his American Journey Report, as a warning against further spur-of-the moment resolutions to immigrate to North America. Then he shifts into an odd first-person continuation in an appeal to examine himself and gauge his own competence or fitness for becoming an immigrant. It reminds one vaguely of the Canadian immigration self-administered point system. Duden then condemns himself that his Journey Report could have been misleading to superficial readers (*"Halbleser"*), whoever they might be.

According to his own estimate a "strongly built" immigrant needed at least *Rthlr.* 1,000.- plus passage fare and travel money to his place of destination. The better-offs (*"Honoratioren"* and "Latin" farmers like himself) needed at least four times that much

---

[32]*The Westfalians from Germany to Missouri.* Princeton U. P. 1987.

[33]Gustav Körner, "Beleuchtung des Duden'schen Berichts über die Westlichen Staaten ... "(1834), in: *Deutsch-Amerikanische Geschichtsblätter*, XVI (1916) 280-333; see also Mack Walker, *Germany and the Emigration 1816–1885.* Harvard U. P. Cambridge 1964, p. 257.

[34]*Die nordamerikanische Demokratie und das v. Tocqueville'sche Werk*
darüber*, als Zeichen des Zustandes der theoretischen Politik.
Nebst einer Aeußerung über Chevalier's nordamerikanische Briefe ...
* actually only about Book I of 1835
von Gottfried Duden. [the fourth review in German, first in book format]
Duden's S e l b s t = A n k l a g e wegen seines amerikanischen Reiseberichtes,
zur Warnung vor fernerm leichtsinnigen Auswandern.
Bonn, bei Eduard Weber. 1837. [104 S.] Rp. 1843.
[348pp.] Gedruckt bei Carl Georgi.

[35]This is why Theodor Eschenburg, *Alexis de Tocqueville Werke und Briefe*, ed. by J. P. Mayer et alii. Rp. dtv 6163. Munich 1976, thought of Duden as confused (*"wirr"*).

money, he estimated. In fact, did he not advise to use slaves rather than white workers for hire? He did since he had the border state of Missouri in his mind (p. 88).

He vaguely hinted at a founding of a colonial township (*"Pflanzstadt"*) for German culture in the Western parts of North America. More to the point he stated also that with the help of at least two slaves and plenty of children of one's own, a couple could live the carefree life with a success rate "six times" that in Germany (*sic*, p. 237). Here at the very latest we have proof that Dr. jur. G. Duden was a dream spinner who did not tell it as it was and as he himself had experienced.

Apparently quite a few unsuccessful emigrants wrote accusing or condemning letters to Duden's book distributor in Bonn without realizing that he "gave up his office" as "*Justizrat*" to publish apologies of emigration to North America "at his own expense" (so p. 95), "barely covering his costs". One reader had written from Pittsburgh, Pennsylvania, on 16 July 1833 that Duden had made a hefty profit as a Missouri farmland dealer of acreage near the river. Finally Duden's arrogance is unleashed in a key passage on p. 96:

> "Since the immigration process increased and swelled so enormeously, one had to be watchful of a variety of riff-raff, such as one barely runs into at itinerant fairs in Europe. Do such people think of anything else but filling their stomachs and roam the markets?"

The rest of the reconsideration is essentially a tirade against the stupidity of his fellow man, who dared to try what Duden while he was a younger man himself had tried under personally much more favourable circumstances.

The fact remains, a year after Gottfried Duden's death back in Germany, more than 38,000 Germans had settled in the area of the lower Missouri, and hundreds of thousands elsewhere in North America.

Duden's trconsideration did not change many people's minds. The German mass – chain and individual – emigration to the Western States of North America continued to grow unabatedly. Instead of carrying mere ten thousands, the stream swelled even more and reached dimensions of over a million during the following decades of the nineteenth century. No area reflected the policies of daring, dismissal, retrial, fulfilment or failure more sharply than the spreading of democracy not only in America, but also as a mass phenomenon and as a part of a massive "levelling" emigration to the US and Canada throughout the nineteenth century.

While Duden committed his about-face on his own prior writing, he felt, he could not ignore Tocqueville. Technically Duden could neither neglect Tocqueville's *De la Démocratie en Amérique* nor, since he didn't, immediately follow his reconsideration piece with a negative review of Tocqueville's master treatise on democracy. But he could *reverse* the process and start with a review and then renege. He blamed some of his own misunderstandings on a limpid translation into German, such as the one he used. The first part of 1835 that Duden had in front of him to review, made his review the fourth, but first negatively written one in German.

Duden split his lengthy review in eight sections without understanding Tocqueville's main premises. At the outset he needed to concede Tocqueville's high esteem and reputation among intellectuals, which amounted to a strong positive public echo and an assured acclaim of his work. And as a kind of *captatio benevolentiae* in reverse, Duden granted that his own Journey Report had only received "an unwanted notoriety" by comparison. So was he jumping the bandwagon from the rear end?

He felt an urge as "a fellow expert" (p. 1) to use Tocqueville's work and borrow from it as springboard for putting a few feathers into his Missouri farmer's cap. He regretted, of course, in another *captatio benevolentiae* to have had to dissect the well-meaning arguments of a young, popular French aristocrat, who he says will ignore his (Duden's) criticism altogether. (p. 2) That did not prevent Duden from pushing, in his following Introduction, the indelicate hope that some glitter may fall on and spread over the shrunken reputation of his own books (p. 4). He wanted to use his lengthy review of V plus 83 pages (*sic*) to win further acclaim for his own literary ambitious views, concerning the insight into "what it really looks like in North America", rather than merely speculate about it theoretically, as does Tocqueville, and then arrive at "brilliant aphorisms" only. These shallow arguments are quite superficial.

Duden's main criticism aims at Tocqueville's key notion, "*moeurs*", which the most modern translator, Harvey Mansfield, keeps partly untranslated as Latinate English "*mores*". This term does not pass muster with Duden. Nor does Duden recognize the notion of "equality" in its Tocquevillean tension with "freedom" as a political factor to compare to. The main problem with Duden is, he thinks additively, Tocqueville dialectically. Duden does not accept the linking processes from points of departure. Duden admonishes that most of the "*mores*" configurations have existed already in Tacitus's *Germania*. As in Germany, Duden wants to distinguish between the upper classes and ordinary citizens. He thinks that inequality distinguishes them clearly by birth right and heredity. In this respect the two lawyers thought similarly. However, emotionally Tocqueville did not hail democracy's coming, while Duden did not appreciate it intellectually. Still, Tocqueville's thinking became a helpmate of the democratization process. Duden's did not.

Both the analysis of hope by Alexis de Tocqueville and the analysis of mass misery by Karl Marx seemed to favor the trial and error process of migration to greener pastures. Ultimately the practical answer, life in unfettered freedom with all its inherent risks, the duty toward oneself called for leaving a country whose imperial chancellor, a few decades later, blocked democracy from taking root and grow.. This corollary was unforeseen by Tocqueville and Duden.

Equality, if denied you in your native village, fathoms a rebellious streak in stronger than average characters to leave and shift for themselves elsewhere, perhaps on a thinly peopled terrain which was at least theoretically guaranteeing equality. Actually one could in political reality strive toward the fulfilment of the U.S. constitutional promise of inherent equality.

Germans were unequal before the law at home for the duration of their nineteenth-century life, and did not become equal under the law until after they had assumed citizenship in the U.S. Ironically Tocqueville equipped with a crystal-clear mind does not speak about that as lying outside his topic, whereas the suspicion-minded Duden with all his doctrinaire subterfuges does have more than a calcified opinion about these processes, if only he would not have oscillated so much. Democracy is a steamroller, and requires sweat. And if you can't stand the heat, get out of the democracy cooking kitchen. There is no total equality or inequality among arriving first-generation immigrants. Rather there is supply and demand instead. The inequality of one's tasks, one's scope of action, and one's will to achieve it, is just as important as constitutional equality. These are not two separate apples on a plate. What is freedom, if not equality of citizens? In fact, Tocqueville recognizes, perhaps grudgingly only, that democracy craves for the equality in freedom.[36] Although Duden's long review of Tocqueville's Democracy in America did not leave traces in the German *"Kameralwissenschaften"* (a forerunner of political sciences), equality in the process of climbing up the ladder of education was not influenced by either writer. Duden, nevertheless, did not seem to have understood its concepts. The narrowing of the elite to *"Honoratioren"* (the financially secure upper ten), helped by pedigrees and family connections, instead of working for the genuine levelling and ultimately eliminating of crass inequality, as far as possible, was outside Duden's perspective.

For him truth could perpetually be redefined, stretched, analogized, where for Tocqueville truth was something so precious that he didn't like to expose it to the chance of a battle of words, once he found it. For him it was like a light that he was afraid of snuffing out, once he started bandying it about.[37]

Duden's accusation levelled against Tocqueville as a "loquacious talker" and a light-weight opinion linking "word mincer"[38] is preposterously unjustified and untrue. However, neither of the two writers could depict, what it really looked like in North America (in the sense of Rancke). Tocqueville did not, as Duden alleged, write "aphorisms" as a genre in his Democracy in America. The German did not systematize his own approach other than add the assembled more or less factual observations linearly, perhaps somewhat haphazardly. The "dream spinner" Duden not only cut his own yarn in a self-accusing manner, he did not perceive the red herring in the rope of his justly famous competitor's presentation.

I do not want to denigrate Duden overly much, nor do I want to construct an intellectual *voisinage* between these two men. But somehow Duden represents the cantankerous type of German, the well-educated *Spießbürger,* (bourgeois) despite his first-hand American experience and the fact that he commanded a substantial

[36]Alexis de Tocqueville, Discours à lAssemblée Constituante, 12 Sept. 1848, second-hand quotation from Otto Vossler, *Alexis de Tocqueville: Freiheit und Gleichheit.* Frankfurt 1973, p. 256 f.n. 175.

[37]Postume Souvénirs d'Alexis de Tocqueville publié par le Comte de Tocqueville. Paris 1893, quotation and location from Albert Salomon, *Alexis de Tocqueville: Autorität und Freiheit*, Zürich 1935, p. 177.

[38]Gottfried Duden, *Die Nordamerikanische Demokratie und das v. Tocqueville'sche Werk* (1837) p. 3.

independent income. He would never come close to developing into a Yankee type guesser either. For making use of such a gift he did not possess enough humour. Hence I would be surprised if the State of Missouri ever erected a statue in his honour. Who can be remembered as non-shrewd at home and non-innocent abroad equally well at the same time?

Chapter 5
The years 1848-1864; the paradigm of the Deitch Company;
the Mason-Dixon line; the strengthening of the Northern power and the
expansion of the US stature

In the opinion of a keen-sighted immigration critic, Joachim Reppmann,[39] Schleswig-Holstein, different from the failure of the revolutionary attempts taking place in South and Middle Germany, became the only German state which actively rose against the government of its dukedom.[40] In military terms, the Schleswig-Holstein army under the command of a Prussian general was temporarily beaten by the Danish army in 1851. But the Schleswig-Holstein uprising, nevertheless, made it possible that a stream of exiled people and emigrants began to leave "southern Denmark". Thus by an irony of fate these German-speaking inhabitants arrived in Iowa and other western territories as Low German speaking "Danish" subjects.

In the political language of American newspaper editorials these and other "German" refugees of the revolution were referred to as "Forty-Eighters", even if they arrived a few years later than 1848. The earlier wave was subsequently dubbed "the Greys" on account of their accumulated experience, the next wave arriving up to twenty years later "the Greens" being more politically motivated and comparable to greenhorns in the new country. These newcomers were intent upon transferring political as well as pedagogical innovations to America- witness Mrs. Carl Schurz's modern kinder-gartens.[41]

Of the several hundred thousands immigrants leaving for America from their large central European country in the decade of 1848-1858, only a considerably smaller group technically belonged to the "Forty-Eighters".[42] A numerically even smaller group of those hailed from Schleswig-Holstein. Some of these men had fought in the insurrection army and taken up arms against their Danish King. The other more civilian ones have sometimes been referred to as the *"Europamüden"* (Tired of Europe) and others as "Latin farmers". But the majority, particularly from the High German speaking parts, were craftsmen who sought economic security, that is, substantially better paying jobs abroad.

Reppmann demonstrates that the Schleswig-Holstein group of some 10,000 emigrants from the dukedom combined these two motivations. Their economic ambitions could not be satisfied at home, their sympathy for the political protest had gone astray and left little hope for the future. It is true that the Danish King in a gesture of appeasement had proclaimed and issued a general amnesty in 1852. Yet the

---

[39]*"Freiheit, Bildung und Wohlstand für Alle!"* *Schleswig-Holsteinische "Achtundvierziger" in den USA 1847-1860.* Verlag für Amerikanistik Wyk auf Föhr 1994.

[40]W. Carr, *Schleswig-Holstein 1815-48. A Study in National Conflict.* Manchester U. P. 1963. The story was different in Mecklenburg-Strelitz, from where 16,000 emigrants left.

[41]Ed.s Henry Geitz, Jürgen Heideking and Jürgen Herbst. *German Influences on Education in the United States until 1917.* Cambridge, MA 1995.

[42]Ed. Charlotte L. Brancaforte, *The German Forty-Eighters in the United States.* New York 1989.

45

administrative controls and chicaneries, paired with tightening Danish language requirements in the classrooms, the courtrooms, and on the pulpits, (at least on alternating Sundays) lasted "oppressively" until 1864, when the *Bundesexekution*[43] (the federal punitive expedition) to Denmark brought victory to the Prussian-Austrian armies. Had at first the Danish government opposed somewhat the Schleswig-Holsteiners, now in turn the unloved Prussian government subdued the natives with Prussian over-regulations by imposing a different less liberal law system.[44] Consequently, another wave of Schleswig-Holsteiner left for the North West Central States of America in the sixties and seventies of the 19th century.

The farmers and farm hands from Schleswig-Holstein spoke Low German, the former professionals still understood it well. In addition quite a few understood and could manage to converse in Low Danish (*Plattdänisch*, the language of the Southern Jutland's [i.e. North Schleswig's] law). The leading heads and spokesmen of this emigrant group were lawyers and journalists at the same time.

First among them ranked Theodor Olshausen (1802-1869), a former Schleswig-Holstein cabinet minister under Count v. Reventlow. Olshausen was considered a popular tribune both in Kiel and in St. Louis, MO, and became a leader of the Missouri Republican Party. In between he also played a role in Davenport, Iowa. Nikolaus Rusch, a native of Dithmarschen, south of Eiderstedt, was voted into office of Lieutenant Governor of Iowa, as John Rush, in 1859. Reppmann demonstrates how due to an interplay of a reactionary treatment back home, a chain immigration (*Kettenauswanderung*) took place at a feverish pitch coupled with a feeling of "good riddance" on the part of the new German administrative authority. This wave became a mass movement. Among these 2,500 or more "Forty-Eighter" emigrants from Schleswig-Holstein were some outstanding individuals with the special gift and enough enterprise to publish American language newspapers (apart from those in German). Foremost among those was Theodor Olshausen and his younger brother Arthur in St. Louis, the western part of which was almost a German enclave for a while. Their paper in 1851 dealt with agriculture, horticulture, trade unions, and popular hygiene. Furthermore the lawyer and amateur anthropologist Olshausen travelled, wrote and published a book about the Mississippi Valley[45] and about the Mormons as well.[46] He was considered a dangerous liberal on whom a warrant had been set ("*ein steckbrieflich gesuchter ... Verfassungsschwärmer*"). The Olshausen family of his younger brother has produced outstanding scientists in Missouri until today. His other brothers branched and blossomed as famous lawyers in Schleswig-Holstein until today

---

[43] Described in detail by the war correspondent of a famous Berlin newspaper, Theodor Fontane (1819-1898), *Der Schleswig-Holsteinische Krieg im Jahre 1864.*

[44] David A. Jackson, *Theodor Storm. The Life and Works of a Democratic Humanitarian.* Berg Publishing House. Providence, R. I. 1992, p. 129ff. on "Prussianization."

[45] *Das Mississippi-Thal. Der Staat Missouri.* vol. I and II. Kiel 1854.

[46] *Geschichte der Mormonen oder Jüngsten-Tages Heiligen in Nordamerika.* Göttingen Vandenhoeck und Rupprecht 1856. See C. Gellinek, *Avenues Toward Christianity: Mormonism in Comparative Church History.* State University of New York Binghamton 2001. 196 pp.

also. Another famous Forty-eighter was Friedrich Kapp (1824-1884) who became immigration commissioner of New York City, before he returned to Berlin, where he became an MP and a co-founder of the *Deutsche Bank*.

At the outbreak of the Civil War in 1861 twenty-three Northern Union states stood against eleven Southern Confederate states. The two hostile populations measured 22 against 9 million, or not counting the black slaves, 6.5 million southerners. The Union also held a lopsided advantage in their better structured and much more productive industry as well as the double length of their railroad tracks. All the advantages seemed to have been theirs. So why rebel and begin that war of secession in the first place? There was one big exception: the majority of the well-trained US officer corps, including West Pointers, hailed from the South. Strategically superior Southern generals could therefore win battles against superior numbers and fire power from the North half way through the war until about 1864.

Since immigrants had not settled in the South – except Texas, which was a slave state – in great numbers in the 19th century, it becomes clear that many volunteers of the 75,000 per State, president Abraham Lincoln had asked for toward the end of the war, had to be and actually were of German heritage. This fact had a long honorable tradition. The Hessian soldiers had been feared and lured over to the American side with promises of land; president Washington had preferred to surround himself with a "German" bodyguard. His forager general was Heinrich Lutterloh, his army baker general Christopher Ludwig (1720-1801). The training of the fledgling American Army by Friedrich Wilhelm von Steuben 1730-1794) is too well known to be recounted here. Several auxiliary regiments during the War of Independence were commanded by 18th century American generals of German heritage: by major general Johannes [von *or*] de Kalb (1721-1780), Nicholas Herkimer (1728-1777), general Gabriel Hiester, and colonel von Weissenfels, Friedrich von Riedesel, Wilhelm von Knuyphausen, Friedrich Baum. Ironically general Karl Wilhelm "Baron" von Dieskau (1701-1767) was appointed general inspector to the commander-in-chief of the French Army in New France in 1755, because of his intimate knowledge of light artillery, and the high regard he was held in by King Frederick II of Prussia.

I do have spattered information about American officers and men in the War of 1812, as well as the genuinely British part of the fledgling Upper Canada which came forth with brave soldiers fighting over maritime rights, charring the White House and the Ontario Provincial Government house. Since only a quarter of the 80,000 people of Upper Canada of that day were British descended, it follows that "Loyalists" had to participate in the quarrel. The bravery of the combatants seemed to shame the fruitlessness of the struggle. Loyalists and Hessians fought well on both sides. The Tory Loyalists from Upper Canada felt differently about the War than the coastal dwellers, particularly of the fledgling Maritime provinces, where the interest in continued trade outweighed many other considerations of patriotism. In fact many thought that the peace of 1815 "blasted all [their] prospects".[47] How could one be

---

[47]Ed. by Phillip A. Buckner and John G. Reid, *The Atlantic Region to Confederation*. U of Toronto

unloyal to the nation from which both countrymen, not yet Canadians, nor totally materialistic Americans, have descended? Of the forty-five thousand United Empire Loyalists who came from the US, three thousand five hundred were free blacks, who settled in Birchtown, Nova Scotia. At least one quarter to a third of the Loyalists from the US were Germans who had stayed in the Hudson Valley, Pennsylvania and elsewhere. Some of their assets had been confiscated. Accordingly, their sons would not be prepared to fight for Uncle Sam, but preferred the direct "loyalty" to a king who had originated from a Hanoverian line himself. It is probably realistic to assume that at least five thousand bore arms for their newly adopted country. I have not read any adverse comments on their valour while bearing arms for their naturalized country so similar to their former homeland. On which side they fought or refused to engage in war they like the Mennonites were strongly represented among the loyalists, most of them were educated, literate, skilled and often quite talented.[48] The most outstanding individual was perhaps the shipping mogul and steam ocean liner magnate, sir Samuel Cunard, whose grandfather had been born Kuhnert from Pennsylvania. The outstanding military general was Franz von Rottenburg, born in Danzig in 1757, who without being a citizen defended Quebec as "British" commander in 1812. The anomaly soon ended and gave way to the oldest borderline of peace between manifestly befriended countries.

To return to the Civil War (called War of Rebellion nowadays): Minnesota had meanwhile been admitted a free state in 1858, Kansas in 1861, the Dakota and the Colorado Territories also in 1861; Missouri, Kentucky and West Virginia (splitting off from Virginia) were admitted to the Union as "slave states" in 1863. These latter three were slave holding, and yet did not secede from the Union, rather they fought on the side of the North. The North had heritage regiments that were organized in *Landsmannschaften* under such outstanding commanders such as Carl Schurz, (1829-1906), the subsequent secretary of state, and lesser known officers by the names of Blenker, Osterhaus, Steinwehr, Weitzel, Schimmelpfennig, and Wagener. This way the orders could not be misunderstood, and similar men fought shoulder to shoulder. Hundreds of other officers, and probably as many as 200,000 men of the *"Deutsch"* extraction served in the Union's army of more than 900,000 men. Obviously they must have been of tremendous help, instilled with fresh patriotism and valour as they were. This is the story of a suppressed but noble tradition, overlooked in hindsight, that is. Loyalty toward the United States had set in long before in the 18th century and also sporadically to the Colonies in the 17th century.

An anti-tradition of sorts consisted of a much better known attitude of the early Pennsylvania-German settlers who were pacifists for religious reasons and may have belonged to the Amish or the Hutterites. Most of the old-fashioned communities they came from did not play a strong role outside the closed walls of their colony. An anti-

Press 1994, chapter XI War and Peace, p. 241.

[48] J. M. Bumsted, *Understanding the Loyalists*. Sackville 1986; Ann Gorman Condon. *The Loyalists Dream for New Brunswick* . Frederickton 1984. Virginia Easley de Marce. *The Settlement of Former German Auxiliary Forces in Canada after the American Revolution*. Sparta, Wisconsin 1984.

violence, anti-oath-taking tendency was present. Already Benjamin Franklin had sharply polemicized against them in 1753, when he thought that they were "unused to freedom".[49] At the bottom of his grudge lay his unwillingness to accept at face value their attitude not to bear arms on behalf of their naturalized homeland.

It is interesting to point out another fundamental difference: Southerners opposed land giveaways of unsurveyed plots west of the Mississippi to immigrant civilians and to immigrant soldiers. These 160 acre lots could be purchased by them from the government for a nominal fee. These so-called give-aways benefitted foreign born working-class whites who were unlikely to vote slavery. The Missouri senator Thomas Hart had championed the Pre-empting Act in 1841 legitimizing squatting in the wild. President Lincoln signed the Homestead Act in 1862 to the effect that after five years of working on improvements the claimant's land was free and clear. This is the way the demanding life of the tall grass prairie farmer started. From Nebraska to Dakota many "German" farmers tried their luck and met success.

As a consequence to the Civil War the "Mason and Dixon line", which had been drawn from 1763-1766, changed its demarcation line character. The whole line moved south, as it were, from the 40° of Northern Latitude to the 36°30' N. L. as a penalty of war. Thence it marked no longer a historical boundary dispute between Maryland and Pennsylvania, but between free states/slave states state lines. Missouri as a slave state was excepted from this base line, since the dispute had come to an end in Congress over the Compromise Resolution of 1819/20. The line had been marked by the two British astronomers and surveyors Charles Mason (1730-1787) and Jeremiah Dixon (1733-1779) at a length of 316 miles west of the Delaware river during three years. They were helped by the German American David Rittenhouse (1732-1796), according to Benjamin Franklin, the foremost American astronomer (from Germantown, PA), who later on drew the boundaries between New York and Massachusetts, as well as more than half of the original Thirteen Colonies' state boundaries.[50] But the Mason-Dixon line, once it came to be fully extended to the Pacific, popularly became known as the "boundary" between the North and the South. Thus the geographical line took on a political dimension.

This line is just as significant and constitutive in America as the German Benrath line in Germany, which due to its natural historical origin in the Middle Ages ran crooked. The Benrath Line and axis, as we remember, separated not only two territories with ways of phonetically speaking German differently, but gradually came to separate two epistemologies: hanseatic cohesion expressed by non-philosophical practices, non-speculative ways of seeking freedom, the *Olde Germanic Freedom*, if necessary, elsewhere (even abroad). The absence of dialect both in the Northern

---

[49]He was incorrect with respect to two outstanding palatinates, Leisler and Zenger, see f. n. 8 above.

[50]The deputy surveyor of Upper Canada in the 1790s was Joh(an)n Stegmann. Except for Ottawa's subsequent aggrandizement, his divisions still stand. Bytown as Ottawa was then called lay in the judicial district of Lunenburg; see PART FOUR chapter 4.

dialect-free German way of speaking called *"Bühnenaussprache,"* and the American speaking fashion free of dialect is a remarkable coincidence. It follows almost by parallel logic that most of the German immigrants came from their North and mainly settled in the Northern part on top of the Mason-Dixon line. This way they could live among friends, be free-staters (excepting again Missouri!), and work for themselves while they were against slavery.[51] No wonder that there existed a not so popular "German Yankee" as a cliché of a self-sufficient human type in the eyes of the beholding slave owners in the South.

Let us close this section with a personal reminiscence of a presentation given by the Yale Glee Club forty years ago. I only remember these two lines as part of that traditional song:

> "The *Deitsch* Company is the best company
> where ever't came over from Old Germany"

and then some hurrah! hurrah! lalala, ... and background rumbled laughter over "icebine" (*Eisbein*) and lager beer. It is accompanied by a yodel given by the subsequently famous chaplain of Yale College, the Reverend William Sloane Coffin, whom I admired as a preacher at Yale, but who was then a senior Yale undergraduate in the class of '49. Thus we can summarize with a sigh of relief: *Yale yodel-locuta, causa finita.* (When Yale decides, if only by a yodel, the case is closed.)

The *Deitch* or German heritage Companies' celebrated man power, their shooting accuracy and fighting stamina greatly strengthened the cause of the Union, and may have helped tip the scales. In more than one ways did the *Deitch*, and finally the Americans of that Germanic heritage, took their stand at the frontline. They took the same "...increased devotion to that cause" as everybody else. Others sowed and reaped at home as cohort civilian fellows for their own benefit and for the good of the United States.

President Theodore Roosevelt (1858-1919), the great Americanizer, attacked the questionable allegiance – "fifty-fifty Americanism" was his phrase – which permitted certain Americans of German origin to praise German "culture"[52] at the expense of the American civilization under which they lived, during the first decade of the 20th century. Conversely, the prospects of German *Kultur* were sunk briskly, sometimes with the help of some slander, during the two years of neutrality, 1914-1916. On the other hand, there were many loyal German Americans who were drafted and served even during the interim of neutrality. It was during the latter part of the First World War, 1917-1918, that the United States became a major power by European standards. While the US did not give up her neutrality right away but slowly, she did not hasten her entry in the war either.

---

[51] Their palatine brethren had gone on record with the earliest articulated protest against slavery in 1688 in Germantown, PA, founded five years earlier.

[52] A. L. Kroeber and Clyde Kluckhohn, *Culture: A Critical Review of Concepts and Definitions.* Random House New York 1952.

There was debate about the status of Americans of German origin shortly before the outbreak of the war against Germany. But while the loyalty may still have been divided from 1914 to 1916, once the fighting began in France, this controversy died down abroad. According to the military record, the *"Kraut"*[53] fought as bravely and honorably as all the other men called "doughboys" in the expeditionary corps. When it counted, they felt like Americans and repaid the trust put into them. Together with their comrades in France they served their home country. Individual heroism supported by group valour does not require verbal de-ethnicization amidst gun-smoke. You just fight. *E pluribus unum.*[54] By now we hope to have convinced the reader that the majority of German immigrants were upstanding citizens who stood their ground in normalcy and in adversity.

[53]Contrary to popular belief it does not derive from the German army's cabbage dish, *Sauerkraut,* but is much older. The root is Low German *"crewt"* or red river crab, an 18th century Cottbus clothier association's trademark on military uniforms exported in large quantities to North America beginning 1750. By 1830 crewt, pronounced kraut, was used as nickname for the Rostock (Mecklenburg) militiaman decked in blue and some red.

[54]This US motto, as well as the Canadian motto, *A Mari Usque Ad Mare,* use Latin as a patina of respectabiliy, and yet both are Germanic in spirit. The US motto praises the cohort character of the countrymen and areas, the Canadian motto expresses its sovereignty by an old formula expressing the two extreme borders *(hrain)* used first by the *Annolied* in 1050.

PART THREE

FOUNDING HISTORY:

Rural and Urban Co-Founded Settlement Places

Chapter 1
The naming process of places in America

Before we get into into the different settlement areas the reader has to be familiarized with technical terms. Europeans are used to tag place name changes to occupational forces, military governments and take-overs by the victors, after a territory has been separated. This is different in the United States and Canada. In either country place name changes are ongoing even during peace periods all the time. In fact, the business of place naming and name changes is a corollary subject of geography.[1]

The craft of counting and cataloguing place names is referred to as typonomy. Students of American typology are unfortunate in having no genuine rounding off parenthesis that holds this branch of inquiry firmly together. There are too many invisible connections. It may be more than a mere coincidence of curiosity that the nicknames of the two longest and commercially most important rivers in the Old and the New Country are referred to as "Father Rhine" (=*Rhein* river) and "Ol' Man river" (=the Mississippi). Ironically the shorter of the two rivers becomes grandfather to the longer one by comparison, also concerning the settlement of a minority in the new country. Both banks the Mississippi witnessed the co-founding of plenty of places, counting from the estuary of New Orleans in northerly direction, we found surprisingly many "Deutsch" settlements, called Hohensolm, Waldeck, Mannheim, Geismar, Oldenburg. Bingen, Plettenberg, Hamburg, Brunswick, New Hamburg, Tilsit, Altenburg, Bremen, Offenburg, New Hanover, Dutch or South St. Louis, Hamburg again, New Melle, Hamburg a third time, Frankfort, German Valley, Hanover, Steuben, Potsdam, Hanover, Bethel. Remarkably, nineteen out of twenty-five names are Northwestern German in origin. Was it common to have self-repeating names as signs of reorientation elsewhere? It was indeed.[2]

Approximately 175,000 self-repeating place names exist in the present US. according to the National Gazetteer of the U.S.A. The findings were commented for the general reader by George R. Stewart.[3] On the other end of the scale, despite

---

[1]Henry Gannett, *A Guide to the Origin of Place Names in the United States*. 1971. George R. Stewart, *Names on the Land. The Classic Story of American Placenaming*. Lexikos San Francisco 1967 (with an Introduction by Wallace Stegner).

[2]Allan Wolk, *The Naming of America*. Nelson Nashville/New York 1977. Wilbur Zelinsky, *The Cultural Geography of the United States*. Prentice-Hall, Inc. N. J. 1973.

[3]*American Place Names*. Oxford U. P. 1970; Kelsie B. Harder, *Illustrated Dictionary of Place Names in the United States and Canada*. N. Y. 1976; George Henry Armstrong. *The Origin and Meaning of Place Names in Canada.*. McMillan Toronto rp. 1972.

53

persistent myths to the contrary, it has been ascertained that "very few of [American] place terms have derived from the original inhabitants."[4] This is different with rivers and State names.[5] But not all Indian-derived names really are Indian. I can contribute that even fewer Indian names were adopted by German speaking name givers, Conestoga in Lancaster county, PA, being the great exception. A map of 1648 spells Milwaukee "Meleke", seemingly as a French name, but in reality meaning "Little Mill" in Alsatian German. The spelling and meaning of a place name was sometimes so hotly contested that the definitive ruling from Washington, D. C was appealed for.

German as place name giver in America came third after English and French. Catholic French gave names in North America (excluding Quebec) roughly 5,000 times.[6] Apparently, the protestant religion of French Huguenots prevented them from preserving the identity of their few settlements in 18th century Virginia, South Carolina and West Florida. The Mennonites were prolific as name givers both in Pennsylvania, Ontario, Saskatchewan and Manitoba. Some loyalists transferred Mennonite place names to New Brunswick.

At no time, according to my own calculations based on the numbers researched and documented throughout this book, did the German place names surpass two thousand in the US, or three hundred and seventy-five in Canada. These roughly two thousand and four hundred North American place names of German origin can be documented as having been in use in either country for some time. We will see which ones are still in use, and which of the less than say 10% were used repeatedly, such as Hamburg, Bremen, Munster, Brunswick, and Hanover, and why. These names are also found on the disappearance lists of place names as well (see end tables in PART SIX).

We wonder how broad the idea of America in practical terms was to allow for delegating so much freedom of naming to the local level. The nine census areas, East to West, are called: NEW ENGLAND, MIDDLE ATLANTIC, SOUTH ATLANTIC, EAST NORTH CENTRAL, EAST SOUTH CENTRAL, WEST NORTH CENTRAL, WEST SOUTH CENTRAL, MOUNTAIN, and PACIFIC. The people immigrating to the various "census areas" made different use of the majority of available and transferable names. Some of these names sounded outlandishly keen, even poetic, others sober or pedestrian. Many did not stay the same in rural and urban US history. The traditional US Census east-west sequence will be rearranged for and adjusted to our purposes of illustrating the German immigration "push" and "pull" movements. The natural order of the German immigrant influx requires a different sequence, as will be shown later on in this chapter. The cohort immigrant power went slightly different

[4]Ronald L. Baker, ed. *The Study of Place Names*. 1991, p. 46; George Earlie Shankle, *American Nicknames*. 2nd ed. N. Y. 1955. 524 pp.

[5]27 of the 50 states have Indian-derived names. Of the state mottoes 24 are English, 22 Latin, 2 Indian, 1 Greek, 1 French, 1 Spanish – altogether six languages are enlisted. See Isaac Taylor, *Words and Places: Illustrations of History, Ethnology & Geography*. Re-edited with an Introduction by Edward Thomas. E. P. Publications 1978.

[6]Henry G. Bayer, *Romanic Review*. vol. XXI (1930); Walter E. Weidhaas, "German Religious Influences on American Place Names," *American German Review* 23 (1957) 32-34.

ways each time. The EAST NORTH CENTRAL together with the WEST NORTH CENTRAL areas with twelve states will be referred to as "*Extended North*"; the EAST SOUTH CENTRAL and the WEST SOUTH CENTRAL areas with eight states as "*Extended South*." The MIDDLE ATLANTIC, SOUTH ATLANTIC, and NEW ENGLAND areas with eleven states will be referred to as "*Extended Atlantic*"; the eight MOUNTAIN states as "*The West*". The ninth and last census area, PACIFIC, with three states, will be called "*Pacific Coast*." So for convenience's sake the nine census areas are being reduced to five migration rayons. (See Table 4)

Three hundred and eighty municipalities, formerly representing together almost a million inhabitants US wide, and eighty-eight, representing some one hundred thousand residents in Canada, had used up their places' original designative power. In checking the data on digital-neighborhoods, another shrinkage became apparent, one, further disuse since 1980 (partially correcting these older data, partially mirroring new prevalent conditions), and two, engulfment or gobbling up of territory and finally the official annexation by charter rewriting to a larger and likely more suburban or even urban community. The percentage of these losses of about 13% holds only for the first 1,000 places, examined in 18 of the states that have experienced the largest German influx in the US. The overall loss percentage from 1,644 place names climbs to an average of 20% occurring overall in the US from 1913-1990. The figure of the total German Canadian place name loss is 29% occurring from 1867-1996. Still, there are more German place names in use in the US today than there were in 1910.

In looking over these many names, it occurred to me that quite a few of them were sounding odd (from the point of view of the English speaking surrounding), even a bit outworn: take f. i. *Knittel* or *Couts*, or a bizarre designation like *Schoenefuss*, which became Shenevus, NY . How would such a place name be pronounced by residents of the second or the third generation? Was the designation carried in their name still comprehensible to successors or newcomers? Would the information value for the post-founding generation still carry the name significance for them or would the meaning have dissipated and spent itself as outlandish sounding in the long run?

Amazingly and partly contrary to the assessment above, some of the place names that sounded more clearly German and perhaps even moderately provocative, survived. An ordered vote to do away with them after 1916 or after 1941 never became a political reality in the US. Place names such as Berlin or Hamburg were not all exchanged or all renamed, because inside their "walls" a minority of such municipalities still thought that they carried a commemorative value for the majority of the founding and the next generation of Americans, war or no war and corresponding bad feelings. Take for example Berlin and Hamburg. A "punitive" sounding renaming of Berlin, Ontario, to Kitchener in 1915 was not primarily proof of the shedding of a former name identity but of an expression of grown Canadian loyalty by relatives of German-Canadian volunteer soldiers, killed in action in France. Of the 20 Hamburgs most were done away with, but four survived in Iowa, New York, Pennsylvania and Arkansas. Or of the 26 Berlins as a town name three were, for some reason, according to the index of *Geographie der Erde Neue Enzyklopädie 2000*, still found tolerable in

55

Maryland, New Hampshire and Wisconsin. But that is not the whole story. According to "City Information" in *PlacesNamed.com* there are now an excess of 35 Berlins known in twenty-three US states, if all of these website listings are completely reliable. Some of these, I suspect, refer to the same place twice. Could there really be no less than 3 Berlin each in GA, MD, NH, NJ, OH, PA, and WI? Who would have thought so.

I could independently identify barely existing places with very few inhabitants in small rural places that were not listed in Funk & Wagnalls *Hammond World Atlas* of 1980. Since there are no government tregistry offices (*Einwohnermeldeämter*) in the US, the local boards could vote at will. Theoretically at least a traditional name could be reinstated after a cooling-off period. One cannot be sure whether the website is decisive in each and every case. I am not sure in every case what happened, when the original language loyalty had spent itself and had thus withered away, without settling a naming issue in the collective mind for other than tourist attracting reasons.

If, however, an intermingling of an historical association, a geographical reminiscence, and a unequivocal linguistic meaning came together as for example. in "King of Prussia" the inherent commemorative claim had to be extinguished as unpopular. The same would hold true for such names as Schiller, Uhland, or Palatine. Such names usually had to go.[7] Sometimes an amount of an anti-German political expression was enough to make a switch to an English name. This also worked the other way around, f. i. from Rome to Wurtsboro, NY. But the exchange could also take on a diplomatic sounding dimension, witness "Prussia", Sasketchewan, which ironically became "Leader."

Adrian Room in *Placenames of the World* distinguishes several groups of place names which I would prefer to reduce to just three categories: 1. Descriptive-associative: a place inspires the giving of a particular name, and thus creates or recreates an aura with the help of that name, and invites the settlers' affirmation, e. g. Little Rock, Arkansas, or Golden Valley, ND or Pilger, NE. Whoever has seen it, agrees with this name as a good choice. 2. Possessive-Commemorative: the name "baptizes", as it were, a place by giving it a commemorative ring, such as in Columbus or Steubenville, or German Valley, IL Or it suggests a commendatory association such as in Springfield or Bethel. An amount of identification is called for by such names that may wither. If it is overstated or becomes shrill on account of the war tensions, its usefulness ceases. This is not so surprising considering the fact that 80% of all German place names, given in the US, are possessive-commemorative, and climb even higher, to 83%, in Canada. 3. Shift Names: the name given shifts a point of departure as in Missouri City, or Concordia, or Germania for the town of people from Germany. By renaming them in a more Anglo-Saxon fashion, or in a plain political American fashion, the transfer for an existing place name from the Old Country is substituted, because the original one in question has lost prestige or its associative power. This is not to deny that German-American settlers such as Mr. Frank, the founder of

[7]But not for the Huguenot founders of New Palts, N.Y.

Frankfort, Kentucky, became forgotten after one hundred and fifty years. On the other hand, the sausages named Frankfurter may have endeared the name inextricably anyhow, war or no after-war feeling. Interestingly, the prestige of Bismarck carries enough weight for the capital of North Dakota and another city in Missouri to remain named in his honor. Another Bismarck remains hidden in Arkansas as well.

Canadians see in Prince Rupert of Rhine (1619-1682), admiral, proprietor and absentee governor of the biggest land grant ever made in North America [in 1670], called Rupert Land, "exploited" by the cohesive, modern Hanse-style, governed Hudson Bay Company,[8] a royal Stuart Duke of Cumberland; German scholars just Prinz Ruprecht von der Pfalz, the son of the "Winter king" from the House of Pfalz-Simmern. These differences are etched into the Anglo vs. the German approaches toward assessing his life and contributions.[9] The outstanding contribution of this famous bachelor and cavalier was that he was one of the founders of the Royal Society of London.

The measuring stick is rendered by the taken over classical place names, such as f. i. Rome. A brief comparison to the withering of classical place names of towns of the Rome and Athens type in America may be in order. Wilbur Zelinsky, *Exploring the Beloved Country*, has shown that the classical values of colonial name giving American patrons continuously dwindled after 1820 and again after 1890, so that a sizeable percentage of such names disappeared as well. Only Indian-derived place names, and above all, genuine Anglo-Saxon place names, aptly chosen, stay for good. The reason why they do is likely that both these place name types derive from forces not directly connected with the immigration process itself, as Wilbur Zelinsky, Allan Wolk, and R. L. Baker established. It may be surprising for the reader to learn that, according to Stewart as well, one million named places, ever recorded in the US, are no longer in use. A repeat usage is even higher with famous and well known place names, namely as high as twenty times. Now we have come to the point where the co-founded places can be listed, first in Canada, then in the US.

---

[8]Rupert Land was purchased for £ 300,000 by the Dominion of Canada from this Company in 1869; Vitalis Pantenberg, *Abenteuer ohne Waffen. 200 Jahre Hudson Bay Company*. Düsseldorf 1971; E. E. Rich, *Hudson Bay Company*. Three volumes. New York 1971.

[9]Meinrad Schab, *Geschichte der Kurpfalz*. II. vol. Stuttgart 1992; Frank Kitson. *Prince Rupert*. Constable London 1994 based on the research of George Edinger, *Rupert of Rhine: The Pirate Prince*. Hutchinson 1936.

Chapter 2
A list of co-founded places in the British and French provinces of North America [Canada]

According to *The 1996 Corpus Almanac and Canadian Source Book*, 31rst edition, checked against the *Hammond World Atlas* 1980, *The 1996 Statistical Profile of Canadian Communities*, statcan.ca, as well as the *Canadian Postal Directory*

1. Places Named GERMAN, Province of NEWFOUNDLAND and LABRADOR

Daniel's Harbour	-
Schefferville	-
Total	2
poss.-comm.	2

2. Places Named GERMAN, Province of QUEBEC

Bowman	municipalité; pop. 516
Friedrichsburg	-
Frelighsburg	Loyalist founded municipalité; pop. 1,048
Lake Grothe	-
Philippsburg	-
Schefferville	pop. 578
Schwartz	canton Thorne; pop. 397
Stanstaedt	-
Total	8
"South"	3
"North"	4
descript.	1
Poss.-comm.	7

3. Places Named GERMAN, Province of NOVA SCOTIA

[Birchtown	fdd. 1783 by the white British general Samuel Birch for 3,500 black Empire Loyalists]
Clemensport	Loyalist (originally Lutheran) founded village, Church of St. Edward
Creeser Cove	-
East Berlin	Queens, subdivision B; pop. 6,263

Eisner Cove	-
Ellerhouse	-
Gaetz Cove	-
Gottingen	near Lunenburg; no stats given
Hirtle Hill	-
Koch's Point	-
Lantz Siding	-
Lorembec	-
Lunenburg	town; pop. 2,599
Nass Point	-
New Elm (Neu Ulm)	Lunenburg district; pop. 25,949
New Germany	Lunenburg district, contained in above figure
Oxner Cove	-
Rudolf Point	-
Schorle	-
Siemens	-
St. Jacobs	-
Vogler Cove	-
Wentzell Lake	Lunenburg district; see New Elm above
West Berlin	Queens, subdivision B, same as East Berlin figures
Wile Settlement	West Hants municipal district; pop. 13,792
Wittenburg	Colchester, subdivision C; pop. 13,000
Wyse Corner	-

Total	26
"South"	10
"North"	16
descript.	5
poss.-comm.	20

4. Places Named GERMAN, Province of PRINCE EDWARD ISLAND

Marysburg North	-

Total	1

5. Places Named GERMAN, Province of NEW BRUNSWICK

Francfort	fdd, by German Loyalists from the US; -
Germantown	Harvey Parish; pop. 482
Lutz	-

Manzer	in Ste. Mary's Parish; pop. 3,522
Memel	in Hopewell Parish; pop. 812
Newburg	fdd. 1830; Northampton Parish; pop. 1,464
Shepody	Hopewell Parish; pop. 812
St. Martin's	-

Total	8
"South"	3
"North"	4
poss.-comm.	8

6. Places Named GERMAN, Province of ONTARIO

Alsace	found in Nipissing township (=tp.)
Amaliasburgh	settled by German Loyalists in 1784; -
Adolphustown	fdd. in 1783: pop. 946
Alsfeld	Nomanby tp.; pop. 2,678
Arnstein	unorganized at Parry Sound; pop. 3,336
Augusta	fdd. by Paul and Barbara Heck in 1796; pop. 7,626
Baden 1	Wilmot tp.; pop. 13,831
Baden 2	Timiskaming tp.; pop. 3,541
Bamberg	fdd. 1850; in Wellesley tp.; 8,664
Beamsville	in Lincoln town; pop. 18,801
Becher	Sombra tp.; pop. 4,217
Berlin (=Kitchener)	Mennonite founding influence in 1826; German press 1835; *Sängerfest* 1862; (non-Metropolitan part of) city pop. 178,420; noted University
Bismarck	West Lincoln tp.; pop. 11,513
Bowmansville	-
Breslau	Woolwich tp.; pop. 17,325
Brodhagen	Logan tp.; pop. 2,227
Brunner 1	Ellice tp.; pop. 3,137
Brunner 2	Mornington tp.; pop. 3.332
Caistor	fdd. 1778 by John Dochstader; West Lincoln tp.; pop. 11,513
Carlsruhe	Carrick tp.; pop. 2,431
Cassel('s)	Temagami tp.; pop. 871
Casselman	village; pop. 2,877
Cobourg	Agglomeration of 16,027
Cooksville	Mississauga city of half a million inhabitants
Dresden	town, 2,589 inhabitants
Eberts	Chatham tp.; pop. 6,321

Ernesttown	fdd. 1784; -
Falkenburg	Muskoka Lakes tp.; pop. 6,061
Frankfort	-
Fredericksburg	Douglas Parish; pop. 5,666
Freiburg	called Tavistock since 1857; -
Frinkle's Point	(G. Frinkle) George F. the first builder of frame houses in 18th century Upper Canada; -
Glen Becker	Williamsburg tp.; pop. 3,564
Gosfield	fdd.by Kratz in 1782; North G.: 4,768; South G.: 7,650 inhabitants
Hanover	town; pop.. 6,844
Heidelberg 1	Wellesley tp.; pop. 8,644
Heidelberg 2	Woolwich tp.; pop. 17,325
Hespeler	named after William Hespeler, *Branntweinbrennerei* (today Seagram's of Canada); Cambridge county; pop. 101,429
Holstein	Egremont tp.; pop. 2,679
Kingston	(Ft. Kataraqui) fdd. 1783; Agglomeration of 143,416
Kitchener	see Berlin (so named until 1915)
Kleinburg	Vaughn city; pop. 132,549
Klock	Papineau tp.; pop. 973
Krugersdorf	-
Kurtzville	Lutheran congregation 1874; Wallace tp.; pop. 2,350
Lunenburg	Osnabruck tp.; pop. 4,787
Mannheim	fdd. 1850s; Wilmot tp.; pop. 13,831
Marburg	Nanticoke city; pop. 23,485
Marysburg [North]	fdd. 1760; settled by Loyalist Hessians 1785; –
Markham	fdd. 1790 by M. Quantz; "German mills"; highly successful city of 173,383 inhabitants
Metz	West Gerafrata tp.; pop. 3,777
Moltke 1	Carrick tp.; pop. 2,431
Moltke 2	Normanby tp.; pop. 2,678
Munster	Goulbourn tp.; pop.19,267
Munster 2	unorganized Northern part of Sudbury; pop. 7,147
Neustadt	village; pop. 568
New Germany	see Snyder
New Hamburg	Wilmot tp.; pop. 13,831
New Prussia	(Part of the above)
Niagara-on-the-Lake	fdd. 1784 by Peter Lampman; some were *"Plattdeutsch"* speaking; benefactor Sam Zimmermann, had the hanging bridge built by Johann August Roebling, builder of the Brooklyn Bridge, in 1855 (see "Zimmermann" entry below); 1/4 of population by 1870; pop. 13,238

Osnabruck	Loyalist fdd. tp.; named after prince Frederick, bishop of Osnabrück; pop. 4,787
Philipsburg	Loyalist fdd. tp.; first Lutheran pastor in 1843
Rhineland	-
St. Jacob's	-
Schomberg	King tp.; pop. 18,223
Schreiber	tp.; pop. 1,788
Schumacher	Timming city; pop. 47,499
Snyder	part of Oakville town; pop. 128,405
Sophiasburg	settled by German Loyalists in 1784; tp.; pop. 2,283
Spittlers Creek	named after Joseph Spittler who settled here in 1808; -
Strassburg	-
Tondern	Unorganized to Algoma; pop. 7,383
Waldhof	Machin tp.; pop. 1,117
Wallenstein 1	Peel tp.; pop. 4,499
Wallenstein 2	Wellesley tp.; pop. 8,664
Wartburg	settled in 1840s; Lutheran Church 1856; newspaper "Die Wespe" around 1870; Ellice tp.; pop. 3,137
Waterloo	first Mennonites in 1799; fdd. by the Swiss Mennonite in the 1820s, Abraham Erb, with 1,800 Mennonites under the leadership of his brother, Johann E. and a retired Hannoverian officer, Georg Westphal
[Kitchener-Waterloo has 311,000 inhabitants]	
York (Toronto)	"Yonge Street" built to "Richmond Hill", possibly to Lake Simcoe by the Saxon-born Wilhelm von Moll-Berczy's German road gang; M-B was an architect and a famous painter [Toronto has 3.7 million inhabitants today]
Zimmerman	part of Burlington city named after Sam Zimmermann (1815-1857), who financed part of the Welland Canal; one of the richest men in Ontario; Burlington: pop. 136,976

Total	76
"South"	30
"North"	43
descript.	5
poss.-comm.	70
shift names	0

7. Places Named GERMAN, Province of MANITOBA

Tageszeitung, Der Nordwesten, founded 1889; is called *Kanada Kurier* today

Albergthal	-
Alt-Altona	-
Altona	town; pop. 3,286
Bergfeld	-
Berlin	-
Bismark	-
Blumenfeld	Stanley Municipality; pop. 4,616
Blumengart	Rhineland Rural Municipality; pop. 4,204
Blumenhof	-
Blumenhorst	-
Blumenort*	Hanover Municipality; (pop. 9,833)
Blumenstein	-
Edenburg(h)	see Grunthal or Blumenort
Edenthal	-
Edenwold	-
Eichenfeld	-
Friedenfeld	-
Friedensruh	same as Bismark
Friedenthal	-
Friedensfeld	same as Bismark
Friedensthal	fdd. in 1896; -
Gnadenfeld	Mennonites; -
Grossweide	-
Grunfeld	-
Grunthal*	(Blumenort/Grunthal) Hanover Municipality; pop. 9,833
Grunwald	-
Halbstadt	same as Blumengart
Hanover	see Grunthal
Hiebert	-
Hochfeld	same as Blumenfeld
Hochstadt	see Grunthal
Hoffnungsthal	-
Holstein	fdd. 1894; -
Kleefeld	same as Blumenort
Kronsgart	Roland rural Municipality; pop. 984
Kronsthal	-
Neuanlage	-
Neu-Elsass	-
Neuheim	-

Neuhorst	part of Blumengart
Neu-Kronsthal	-
Oldenburg	fdd. 1896; -
Osterwieck	fdd. 1901; -
Rheinfeld	-
Rheinland*	same as Blumengart
Rosenbach	-
Rosenhof(f)	Morris Municipality; pop. 2,816
Rosenort	same as Rosenhoff
Rosenthal	-
St. Boniface	having Belgian roots, this little village of 240 residents in 1871 became part of Winnipeg; German immigrants took over the land , up to 15 Gn churches in W. by 1914; Louis Riel's (1844-1885) birth- and burial place in the St. Boniface Cathedral; a métis, who staged a rebellion, was hanged for high treason , "father of Manitoba"; pop. 618,477
St. Peter	-
Schanzenfeld	see Blumenfeld
Schoendorf	-
Schoenfeld	-
Schoenwiese	see Blumenfeld
Schultz Lake	-
Silberfeld	see Blumenfeld
Sperling	see Rosenhoff
Springstein	Cartier rural Municipality; pop. 3,009
Steinbach	pop. 8,478
Strassburg	-
Thalberg	St. Clement Rural Municipality; pop. 8,516
Tupper	fdd. 1891; -
Waldersee	fdd. 1891 by Germans from Galicia; Glenella Rural Municipality; pop. 555
Waldheim	-
Winkler*	* "Gewanndorf" Mennonite villages; town pop. 7,241
Total	66
"South"	28
"North"	38
descript.	16
poss.-comm.	50
shift names	0

8. Places Named GERMAN, Province of SASKATCHEWAN

Annaheim	village settled by German Catholic pioneers early 1900s; Rural Municipality St. Peter; pop. 214; trailer industry
Barthel	Loon Lake Nr. 561; pop. 881
Berfeld	-
Bergheim	Aberdeen Nr. 373, Rural Municipality (=R. M.); pop. 758
Blumenfeld	-
Blumenheim	Corman Park Nr. 344, R. M. ; pop. 7,152
Blumenort	Lac Pelletier Nr. 107, R. M.; pop. 498
Blumenthal	fdd. by Mennonites 1892; Rosthern Nr. 403; pop. 1,816
Blucher	Blucher Nr. 343, R. M.; pop. 1,155
Bremen	Bayne Nr. 371; pop. 615
Bruno	town; pop. 648
Carlsberg	Chester Nr. 125, R. M.; pop. 521
Colmer	Stanley Nr. 215, R. M.; pop. 696
Ebenezer	village; pop. 166
Edenburg	Aberdeen Nr. 373, R. M.; pop. 758 (Edenwald) Edenwold fdd. 1885 by Danube Swabians; Edenwold Nr.158, R. M.; pop. 2,738
Engelfeld	-
Gartenland	pop. 419
Gleichen	-
Gnadenthal	-
Goerlitz	-
Gorlik	-
Grosswerder	Eye Hill Nr. 382, R. M.; pop. 691
Gruenthal	Rosthern Nr. 403; see Blumenthal
Grunfeld	-
Handel	village; pop. 42
Hartfeld	-
Herbert	fdd. by German speaking Mennonites from Russia, town; pop. 855
Herschel	Mountain View Nr. 318, R. M.; pop. 371
Hirsch	Coalfields Nr. 4, R. M.
Hochfeld/Hochstadt	see Blumenthal
Hoffer	Souris Valley Nr. 7 R. M.; pop. 422
Hoffnungsfeld	-
Hoffnungsthal	fdd. 1891; -
Hohenlohe	fdd. 1855, see Langenburg
Holbein	Shelbrook Nr. 493, R. M.; pop. 1,793
Holdfast	village; pop. 216
Humboldt	Humboldt Nr. 370, R. M.; pop. 960

Jacobsberg	-
Jansen	village; pop. 167
Josephsberg	-
Josephsthal	fdd. 1886; -
Karmelheim	-
Katharinenthal	-
Kendal	village; pop. 98
Kronau	Lajord Nr. 128, R. M.; pop. 1,034
Kronberg	-
Kronsthal	-
Krupp	Happyland Nr. 231, R. M. ; pop. 432
Kuest	Enterprise Nr. 142, R. M.; pop. 265
Landestreu	fdd. 1890; -
Landau	-
Landsheet	-
Landshut	fdd. 1889; -
Langenau	fdd. 1893; -
Langenberg	Lutheran Colony fdd. around 1890
Langenburg	(originally Hohenlohe) fdd. 1885; Nr. 181, R. M.; named after president of the German Colonial League, prince von H.; pop. 768
Leipzig	Reford Nr. 379, R. M.; pop. 367
Lemberg	*Ketten-wanderungs Durchgangs-station;* pop. 335
Liebenthal	Happayland Nr. 231; see Krupp
Luseland	(Luisenland) Progress Nr. 351, R. M.; pop. 377
Mariahilf	-
Marienthal	Cambria Nr. 6, R. M. ; pop. 344
Marysburg	Humboldt Nr. 370, R. M. ; pop. 960
Mozart	Elfros Nr. 307, R. M. ; same as Blumenthal
Muenster	Catholic village; pop. 381
Neuanlage	Rosthern Nr. 403, R. M.; pop. 1,816; same as Blumenthal
Neudorf	fdd. 1890*; Ketten-wanderungs-Durchgangs-station* village; pop. 331
Neuendorf	-
Neuhorst	Corman Park Nr. 344, R. M.; pop. 7,152
Neidpath	Coulee Nr. 136, R. M.; pop. 584
Olgafeld	-
Osler	pop. 618
Osterwick	-
Prussia	now called Leader
Rastatt	-
Rhein	Mennonite settlement; Corman Park Nr. 344, R. M., see Neuhorst

Rheinfeld	Mennonite settlement; Coulee Nr. 136, R. M., see Neidpath
Rheinfelt	-
Rheinland	see Rhein
Rosenbach	see Rheinfeld
Rosenfeld	see Rheinfeld
Rosenthal	-
St. Gregor	village; pop. 128
St. Joseph's	Colony, South Qu'Appelle Nr. 157, R. M.; pop. 1,135
St. Peter's	fdd. by Father Dörfler in 1903; -
St. Walburg	town; pop. 685
Schanzenfeld	-
Schoenfeld	Swift current Nr. 137; pop. 1,547
Schoenwiese	Mennonite settled before 1914; -
Seltz	-
Speyer/Spier	-
Springfield	continues Schoenf(i)eld
Spring Valley	Terrell Nr. 101, R. M.; pop. 343
Strasbourg	(originally Neu Elsass) McKillor Nr. 220; pop. 545
Stornoway	village; pop. 8
Waldeck	village; pop. 335
Waldheim	fdd. 1894; town; pop. 841
Wimmer	Lakeside Nr. 338, R. M.; pop. 523
Wolfsheim	fdd. 1905/06; named after immigration agent, Johann Wolf;
Zehner	Edenwold Nr. 158, see Edenwold; pop. 2,738

Total	100
"South"	48
"North"	52
descript.	11
poss.-comm.	84
shift names	1

9. Places Named GERMAN, Province of ALBERTA

Beisecker	-
Bismarck	-
Bloomsburg	-
Blumenau	Swiss fdd. in 1903; now known as Stettler Town; pop. 5,220
Bruderfeld	fdd. in 1894; -
Bruderheim	fdd. in 1894; town; pop. 1,198

Didsburg	-
Dusseldorf	(Freedom) Barrhead county Nr. 11; pop. 5,870
Ekville	-
Faust	Big Lakes Municipal districs; pop. 5,830
Frankburg	-
Friedensthal	-
Gratz	St. Paul county Nr. 19; pop. 6,335
Heimthal	fdd. 1892; -
Heinsburg	see Gratz
Heisler	village; pop. 195
Herbert	-
Hilda	Cypress Nr. 1 M. D.s; pop. 5,353
Josephsberg	-
Josephsburg	fdd. 1892; -
Kessler	Provost Nr. 5
Lutherhort	fdd. 1892; -
Manola	Barrhead county Nr. 11 M. D.s, see Dusseldorf/Freedom
Mellowdale	German Mennonites settled here in 1908; same as Manola (above)
Nordegg	Clearwater Nr. 99 M. D.s; pop. 2,705, see Kessler
Oberlin	Stettler county Nr. 6, County Municipality; pop. 5,278
Rosenheim	Provost Nr. 52, M. D.s; pop. 2,705, see Kessler
Schuler	see Hilda
Staufer	-
Stettin	La Ste. Anne county M. D.s; pop. 8,737
Stolberg	see Nordegg
Vollmer	-
Waldheim	-
Warburg	village; pop. 549
Wien	-

Total	24
"South"	11
"North"	13
descript.	6
poss.-comm.	18
shift names	0

10. Places Named GERMAN, Province of BRITISH COLUMBIA

Albert Head	Capitol, Subdivision D; pop. 603
Bernhart	-

Engen	Bulkley Nechako, Subdivision A; pop. 6,891
Gotha Point	-
Prince Rupert	City without its Agglomeration; pop. 16,714
Rykerts	Central Kootenay subdivision C; pop. 8,017
Vale	Valemount village; pop. 1,303

Total	7
"South"	1
"North"	5
descript.	3
poss,.comm.	4
shift names	0

Sum Total Ten Provinces of the Commonwealth of CANADA:

German place names	318	100%	in	1996
"Southern"	135	43%[10]	in	1996
"Northern"	176	55%	in	1996
descriptive	42			
possessive-comm.	266			
shift names	1			

Non-German Names used		2%	in	1996 [partially overlapping]
Loss or Disuse of former				
Gn Names	88		32%	since 1867

----

[10]This percentage is higher than the corresponding one in the US. Many German speakers came from Russia and the southeastern or Catholic parts of the Austrian monarchy to western Canada. Therefore, there is no direct parallel to be drawn to the German *Städte* founding distribution into "North" vs. "South".

Chapter 3
A list of co-founded places in 18th and 19th century US history

Traditional US CENSUS AREAS. The arrangement keeps the IX Areas, but also labels these areas, following the German immigration waves and trickles, in *italics* for the purpose of registering sequences followed in this book. The number of co-founded settlements are given in square brackets.

A. *Extended North* [616] 73
    I EAST NORTH CENTRAL... 73
    II WEST NORTH CENTRAL   82

B. *Extended South* [338]... 94
    III EAST SOUTH CENTRAL... 94
    IV WEST SOUTH CENTRAL 99

C. *Extended Atlantic* [486]... 107
    V MIDDLE ATLANTIC... 107
    VI SOUTH ATLANTIC.. 115
    VII NEW ENGLAND... 124

D. *The West* [124] 127
    VIII MOUNTAIN 127

E. *Pacific Coast* [80]... 133
    IX PACIFIC 133

Comparative Results [1,644 plus 20*]... 137

*non-German names

Table 4

I.EAST NORTH CENTRAL		[NORTH]
Ohio	1	
Indiana	2	
Illinois	3	
Michigan	4	
Wisconsin	5	

II. WEST NORTH CENTRAL		[NORTH]
Missouri	6	
Iowa	7	
Minnesota	8	
Kansas	9	
Nebraska	10	
NorthDakota	11	
SouthDakota	12	

III. EAST SOUTH CENTRAL		[SOUTH]
Kentucky	13	
Tennessee	14	
Alabama	15	
Mississippi	16	

IV. WEST SOUTH CENTRAL		[SOUTH]
Louisiana	17	
Arkansas	18	
Texas	19	
Oklahoma	20	

V.MIDDLE ATLANTIC		[ATL. COAST]
Pennsylvania	21	
New York	22	
New Jersey	23	
Delaware	24	

VI. SOUTH ATLANTIC		[ATL. COAST]
Virginia	25	
West Virginia	26	
Maryland	27	
NorthCarolina	28	
SouthCarolina	29	
Georgia	30	
Florida	31	

VII. NEW ENGLAND [ATL. COAST]

Massachusetts	32
Connecticut	33
Rhode Island	34
Maine	35
NewHampshire	36
Vermont	37

VIII. MOUNTAIN [WEST]

Colorado	38
Wyoming	39
Montana	40
Idaho	41
Utah	42
Nevada	43
New Mexico	44
Arizona	45

IX. PACIFIC [PAC. COAST]

California	46
Oregon	47
Washington	48
Alaska	49
Hawaii	50

A. *Extended North*:

I. OH, IN, IL, MI, WI
II. MO, IA, MN, KS, NE, ND, SD

I EAST NORTH CENTRAL

1. Places Named GERMAN, State of OHIO, in 88 counties; and 5000 inhabitants make a city; 1200 place names

Bavaria/New B	pop. 92; 40 Bavarian passengers arrived on the "Duchess d'Orleans" in N. Y. Harbor in 1848 for Bavaria, OH
Berlin	Coblentz county
Berlin Center	Mahoning county, pop. 2,771
Berlin Heights	Erie county, pop. 691
Bethel	Clermont county, pop. 2407, fdd. by O. Denim 1798; "odd that there are not more German names"
Bloomdale	pop. 632
Bloomfield/New B.	pop. 3,393
Bremen	charter drawn up 1832; "The City of Bremen Society" recorded B. as plat 1833; members: Hannoverians and Bavarians
Brinkhaven	pop. 378
Brunswick	area part of the "Connecticut Western Reserve"; A. & J. Freese surveyed it in 1796; German influence in the early 1800s; pop. 34,400
Buchtel	pop. 640
Cincinnati	1rst Gn settler arrived 1788; fdd. as "Losantville" 1788-90; renamed after the military "society of Cincinnati"; "Over-The-Rhine" district fdd. 1802, when C. was incorporated city; John Heckewelder, Moravian preacher; archdiocese; Hamilton cty.; Longfellow called it "the Queen City of the West" in 1830; Marienkirche constructed by architect F. I. Erd 1840 Gn Turnverein fdd. 1848; "deep German heritage"; in 1890: "57% Gn American"; 12 colleges & universities; Greater C. pop. 2 million; city proper 364,000 inhabitants; 38% blacks; abandoned buildings in the subway transit tunnels; 103rd time Gn Day since 1883; Oktoberfest attracts 500,000 annually; the "lingering stigma on all things German" is finally overcome in Cincinnati
Cuyahoga cty.	[county surrounding Cleveland]: "300,000 Americans of German ethnic descent"; 1830 first wave; "played a major role in building Ohio & Erie Canal"; presently 50 German

	clubs in Cleveland, OH; annual Gn American Day celebration, 100 years old tradition; Cuyahoga cty. had 1,412,140 inhabitants in 1990; German Heritage Museum
Cleves	pop. 2,208
Deshler	pop. 1,872
Dresden	pop. 1,581
Frankfort	pop. 3,985
Frederick	Miami county
Fredericksburg	pop. 502
Frederickton	
Fredericktown	laid out in 1807; incorporated 1850, pop. 2,443
Fryburg	
Hanover	fdd. 1801, pop. 803
Hanoverton	pop. 434
Hertzburg	
Kettering	settled 1798; village named Kettering 1952; pop. 62,000
Kunkle	
Landeck	
Leipsic	1. zip code 42602, pop. 2,200; 2 in Putnam cty; 3 in Orange cty.
Mansfield	incorporated 1857, pop. 55,000; branch of Ohio State University; industry
Maria Stein	pop. 2,284
Mechanicsburg	1. zip code 45044; 2. Monroe county; 3. Champaign county
Miller City	pop. 173
Minster	fdd. 1832 by men from southern (catholic) Oldenburg; cholera 1849; pop. 2,650
New Bremen	German Township Trustees, "Bremenfest"; pop. 2.558
New Riegel	pop. 298 (1990)
New Vienna	pop. 2,13
Oberlin	Oberlin college fdd. 1833; first co-ed. college in the US; center for the anti-slavery movement; pop. 8,91
Ottoville	pop. 842
Pyrmont	
Reimersville	
Rossford	pop. 5,61; incorpor. 1939 (?)
Rudolph	pop. 1,37
Sandu(r)sky	
Steubenville	Fort Steuben 1787; incorpor. 1851; pop. 22,25; paper industry 1813-1978
Stryker	pop. 1,68
Vienna	fdd. 1833; scurged by cholera in 1850; 26 abandoned mines; pop. 932 (?)

| West Leipsic | pop. 244 |
| Winesburg | |

Total	53
"South"	14
"North"	38
descriptive	5
poss.-commem.	41
shift names	4

2. Places Named GERMAN, State of INDIANA, in 92 counties, 115 cities

Bingen	fdd. ca. 1835
Blocher	
Bremen	pop. 4,800
Bringhurst	
Crown Point	pop. 16,000
Crumstown	
Decker	fdd. late 1800s
Elberfeld	pop. 635
Elkhart	
Foraker	
Fort Ritner/Fort Wayne German Fest; Our German Heritage	
Frankfort	
Fredericksburg	pop. 1,850
Freelandville	
Friendship	
Fritchton	
Fulda	fdd. 1845, St. Boniface Parish 1847
Gatcher	
Geist	
Hanover	Hanover College fdd. 1827
Heilmann	
Helmsburg	almost a ghost town
Herbst	fdd. 1880; named after August Herbst
Hoagland	
Huntingburg	pop. 5,200
Jasper	pop. 10,000; "reflects the predominantly German heritage"
Kempton	pop. 362
Kitchel	named in 1962
Kouts (= Kautz)	knew 4 flags since 1600s; named after Bernhard Kautz in 1865

Kurtz	
Leipsic	Orange county
Leiters Ford	city
Lippe	Posey county
Mechanicsburg	3 places in Boone, Decatur, Madison counties
Mier	Grant county
Millersburg	6 places, Elkhart, Hamilton, Orange, Warrick counties, and 2 towns, 1, pop. 854
Millhousen	pop. 151
Munster	fdd. 1870; named after Albert Monster; incorp. 1907
New Brunswick	Boone county
New Frankfort	
New Hamburg	
New Harmony	fdd. by Father George Rapp in Posey cty. near the river Wabash 1814; pop. 945 (1980); Historic New Harmony Museum
Oldenburg	fdd. by St. Theresa Hackelmeier, Order of St. Francis, in 1851
Ott	"Ott@Indiana.edu" (has no other entry)
Rossville	pop. 1,175
Santa Claus	Spencer county
St. Meinrad	catholic monastery fdd. by monks from Einsiedeln in the 1850s; Archabbey
St. Wendel	"A Little Germany"
Schererville	fdd. by Nicholas Scherer from Scheren (Saar) in 1866; pop. 30,000
Schley	Spencer county
Schneider	pop. 310
Schnellville	pop. 199
Sedan (2x)	Dubois county; De Kalb county
Shideler	
Stendal	
Steubenville	Steuben county
Teegarden	
Ulm	
Velpen	pop. 393
Vienna	Scott county
Weisburg	Dearborn county
Westphalia	
Zionsville	fdd. by David Hoover in 1830
Total	62
"South"	27

"North"	35
descriptive	11
poss.-commemorative	47
shift names	5

3. Places Named GERMAN, State of ILLLINOIS, in 102 counties

Albers	Clinton county, pop. 1,641 St. Damian Church
Altona	Knox county, pop. 813
Astoria	Fulton county, pop. 2,093; "Underground RR" (slave fugitive help line)
Bartels	
Berlin	pop. ca. 180; 4 churches; 26 Illinois Volonteer Infantry Division, 1861
Bismarck	pop. 1,476
Bremen	Daviess county (one of 23 Bremen)
Brunswick	
Buckner	pop. 478
[Chicago	fdd. by non-Germans; ca. 80,000 German Americans by 1910; otherwise too complex to be included here]
Colb	
Colmar	Mc Donough county
Delhio	
De Kalb	pop. 34,925; settled in 1832; Northern Illinois University, chartered 1895; (24,000 students)
Dieterich	Effingham county, pop. 568
Emden	Logan county, pop. 459
Freeburg	pop. 3,115; platted 1836, German immigration, named after Freiburg (Baden) 1859; "conservative, mostly German community"
Germantown	pop. 1,773
German Valley	pop. 480
Hamburg	pop. 150
Hanover	pop. ca. 908
Hazelhurst	
Hecker	pop. 534
Herscher	pop. 1,278; 3 churches
Hoffmann	Zion Bohnemeier cemetary
Humboldt	pop. 470, named 1891 (one of 34)
Hurst	pop. 842
Kaasbeer	
Karbers Ridge	

77

Kell	pop. ca. 213
Lenzburg	pop. 510
Leonore	pop. ca. 134
Lerna	pop. ca. 301
Lippe	fdd. before 1859
Luther	
Mansfield	pop. ca. 929; 2 churches
Massbach	Jo Daviess county
Millstadt	pop. ca. 2,566; South German inhabitants in 300 families 1860 Census; 7 churches
Mitchellsville Saline county	
Munster	
New Baden	pop. 2,602
New Berlin	Duval county, village, pop. 890
New Hanover	
New Minden	pop. ca. 219
New Munster	
Odin	pop. ca. 1,758
Opheim	
Quincy	
Schaumburg	
Sparland	pop. 1,190
St. Joseph	pop. 2,052
Stoneford	
Strasburg	Shelby county, pop. 758
Teutopolis	"a one-horsed town"; 10 Franciscan friars embarked from Bremen 1858 and founded St. Anthony Friary; fdd. T. in 1875; 65 more friars were exiled in the *Kulturkampf* in 1885; they also fdd. Old Mission Sta. Barbara, CA
Vandalia	old capital of Illinois 1819-1839; fdd. by 300 Hanoverians in 1822. Abraham Lincoln was a state representative here; [relation to steamboat "Vandalia", launched at Buffalo in 1841?]
Vienna	pop. 1,446
West Frankfort	
Total	56
"South"	18
"North"	38
descriptive	11
possess.-comm.	41
shift names	3

4. *Places named GERMAN, State of MICHIGAN, in 83 counties, 265 cities, 1245
   townships*

Alpena	Thunder Bay, Lake Huron; changed name in 1843; organiz. 1857; 1rst (?) Congregational Church in 1862; pop. 11,354; Jesse Besser Museum; industry; college
Altona	Recosta county (one of 14 Altona)
Bach	
Bergland	pop. 618
Bloomingdale	Van Buren county; pop. 503
Brohman	Newaygo county
Brunswick	
Crump	
Decker	fdd. by the Decker family; 19th cent. village; 1rst post office 1899
Deckerville	Sanilac county, pop. 1,015; 4 churches; Historical Museum
Eckerman	pop. 208
Ewein	
Frankenmuth	fdd. in 1845 by 15 "brave Franconian" Germans; "Michigan Little Bavaria
Frankfort	Benzie county, pop. 3.168; six churches; unmanned lighthouse
Frederic	pop. 3,967
Goetzville	(originally named Götze), pop. 123
Hamburg	
Hanover	Jackson county, pop. 481
Herman	
Hermansville	pop. 1,090
Hessel	
Hulbert	
Jacobsville	
Jasper	pop. 1,240
Johannesburg	Otsego county, pop. 2,062
Kinde	Huron county, pop. 1,082
Laingsberg	
Lambertville	Monroe county, pop. 7,959
Leer	
Linden	
Lucas	Missaukee county (one of 29 Lucas US)
Luther	
Minden City	
Metz	Presque Isle county
Munger	pop. 1,898

79

Munith	pop. 3,078
Oberlin	
Pinnebog	
Posen	pop. 263
St. Joseph	on Lake Michigan; discovered by Marquette in 1675; chartered 1891 (St. Joseph is patron saint of Canada) pop. 9,214
Schaffer	
Schoolcraft	platted 1831 in Kalamazoo county; Sch. was a mineralogist; pop. 1,517
Spratt	Alpena county
Stambaugh	pop. 1,281
Stanburg	(originally Starnberg)
Steuben	
Stronach	Manistee county
Vandalia	Cass county, pop. 357
Vogel Center	Missaukee county
Walhalla	Mason county
Wayland	pop. 2,751
Weidman	pop. 696
Webberville	pop. 1,698
Westphalia	pop. 2,099
Winn	
Wisner	
Total	56
"South"	20
"North"	36
descriptive	5
poss.-comm.	47
shift names	3

5. Places Named GERMAN, State of WISCONSIN, in 72 counties, 392 villages

Altoona	fdd. as RR depot 1887, pop. 6,400
Amberg	pop. 917
Berlin	fdd. 1848; daily steamboat trips to Oshkosh,WI 'til 1890; pop. 5.366; former cigar making trade
Bethel	one of 109 B. US wide
Blenker	Wood county
Bloomer	fdd. by a wealthy merchant named Bl.; pop. 3,245 (or 3,085)

Brokaw	pop. 224
Cleghorn	
Conrath	
Crivitz	pop. 996
Deering	former home of Wisconsin Steel til 1980
Dresser	Polk county, pop. 614
Eiche	
Eland	pop. 247
Frederic	pop. 1,124
Friendship	Adams county, pop. 728
Friesland	pop. 271
Germania	fdd. in the 1850s "as a prosperous religious colony" by German settlers; built a dam in 1864
Germantown	incorpor. in 1846; village in 1926; "Old World main street"; 21 churches; *Hessischer Verein*; pop. 13,158
Green Bay	pop. 98,000; home of the Greenbay Packers Football Club; Moravian church
Hager City	pop. 2,075
Hamburg	*"das eisige Hoch im Norden"*; Mennonite background; gingseng root transplant in 1915
Hertel	pop. 110
Holman	
Kellnersville	pop. 350
Kiel	Manitowoc county, pop. 2,910; an UFO sighted in 1965
Knapp	pop. 419
Kohler	Sheboygan county; Sh. Hebrew Cemetery; pop. 1,817
Mellen	pop. 935
Milwaukee	17th cent. Alsatian place named "Little Mill"; settled 1835, incorpor. 1837; fire ravaged 1889; City Hall rebuilt in Flemish Renaissance style 1894; pop. 628,000 metropolitan area; Univ. of WI at Milwaukee; Marquette Univ.; "intellectual capitol of the State"; [Steuben society active until 1935]; *Abendpost und Milwaukee deutsche Zeitung* until 1991, when it absorbed the *Detroit A. P.* Howard L. Conrad, *History of Milwaukee* ... Chicago & N. Y. 1895.
Naugart	Marathon county
New Berlin	pop. 35,000 (see Berlin)
Newcassel	
New Holsten	
Newald	Forest county
Patzau	Douglas county
Pilsen	Marion county
Riplinger	Clark county

Rhinelander	pop. 7,427
Rosendale	pop. 777
Rosenfeld	"Memorial Union Rathskeller"
Rothschild	pop. 4,131; 2 churches
Saxon	pop. 478
Sheboygan	incorpor. 1846; Russlander settlers; Reiboldt & Wolters Shipyard; pop. 52,000; 51 churches; 1 university center; city partnership with Esslingen; a book on German History of Sheboygan
Shulisburg	
Stettin	
Steuben	pop. 161
Stitzer	pop. 469
Vesper	pop. 598
Weyerhaeuser	pop. 283

Total	50
"South"	15
"North"	34
descriptive	14
poss.-comm.	32
shift names	3

I WEST NORTH CENTRAL

6. Places Named GERMAN, State of MISSOURI, in 114 counties; – municipalities

Altenburg	sttld. 1839 by Saxon Lutherans in Perry cty., 1rst post office 1854; pop. 307 Perry cty.; conversion from Gn to English as official language in 1953 (sic!)
Altona	
Augusta	St. Charles county, pop. 263
Berlin	Gentry county, one of 46 Berlins [26 in 1913] US wide
Bethel	Shelby county, west of Hannibal
Bismarck	pop. 1,579
Bremen	fdd. 1850
Brunswick	fdd. in 1820; first German colony arrived 1840/1
Cappeln	place, St. Charles county
De Kalb	Buchanan county, pop.
Concordia	fdd. by the reverend F. J. Blitz, Lafayette county, pop. 2,160

Diehlstadt	pop. 145
Dittmer	(Ozarks) pop. 2,410
Dresden	Pettis county, pop. 463, one of 20 Dresdens [10 in 1913] US wide
Dutchtown	Perry county
Emden	Shelby county, pop. 364
Farber	pop. 418
Frankford	pop. 831
Frederickstown	
Freeburg	Osage county, pop. 446
Friedhelm	
Freistadt	
Frohna	Perry county, pop. 162
Gerster	pop. 40
Gobler	pop. 144
Gorin	(South Gorin). Pop. 130
Hamburg	St. Charles county
Hermann	fdd. 1836-38; 19th cent; winemaking village; "Deutschheim State Historic site"
Hoberg	pop. 62
Holstein	Warren county
Kaiser	pop. 1,213
Kiel	Franklin county
Koenig	Osage county
Lentner	pop. 198
Lohman	pop. 154
Metz	pop. 91
Miller	pop. 753
Minden	
New Frankfort	
New Hamburg	Scott county
New Melle	place fdd. ca. 1838, St. Charles county; German sermons until 1951
New Offenburg	St. Genevieve county
Reger	
Rhineland	pop. 157
Saxenburg	
St. Louis	fdd. 1764 by French fur traders; 1800-1802 French again;The Lewis and Clark expedition began here in 1804; 1rst steamboat 1817; incorporated city in 1822; German mass migration began here 1840ff; in early 1850s city ordinances had to be translated into Gn for their benefit; fire and cholera; "fiercely loyal Gn influence" during Civil

War; RR completed 1874; 1876: 350,000 inhabitants, separation from St. Louis county;1890: 4ʰ largest city [down to 8ᵗʰ in 1940]; the surroundings of St. Louis were sometimes called *"Plattdeutsche Prärie"*. 1904: Fair and Olympics; "Golden Age" 1865-1900; 100 breweries (f.i. Anheuser-Busch); McDonell-Douglas Industries (now Boeing); Metropolitain St. Louis area: 2.6 million inhabitants; city 350.000 inhabitants

Strassburg

Turners — Greene county

Washington — fdd. ca. 1819; "characterized by the Old World charm of the German heritage"; wine country

Wentzville — place, St. Charles county, pop. 5,088; "crossroads of the Nation"

Westphalia — fdd. 1835, pop. 287

Wittenberg — pastor Stephan brought some 700 Lutheran "Stephanites" there in the 1840s; "succumbed to the great flood in 1993"

Total	53
"South"	13
"North"	40
descriptive	12
poss.-commem.	38
shift names	3

7. Places Named German, State of IOWA, in 99 counties and 950 "cities"

Adel — fdd. 1847, Dallas cty., pop. 3,500, brick streets that "connect us to our past"

Allendorf — Osceola county

Altoona — city, pop. 10,345

Cleves — pop. 20 (?)

Coburg — pop. 58 (1990)

Conrad — town, settled by J. W. Conrad in 1853 in Grundy county, pop. 964

Emmetsburg — Palo Alto county, pop. 3,958

Fredric

Fredericksburg — pop. 1,830

Froelich — Clayton county, fdd. by father of John Froelich, threshing tractor (1892) inventor

Fruitland — Muscatine county

Garber — surveyed 1873 by John Garber, pop. 150

German Valley	Cossuth county
Graettinger	
Guttenberg	historic Mississippi river town, settled first in 1673 by the French; German influx started 1843; pop. 2,500
Hamburg	town, pop. 1,248
Hanover	
Hesper	
Holstein	platted in 1882; co-founded by Henry Thielmann, in honor of his homeland, pop. 1,449
Klemme	pop. 587
Knierim	
Koenigsmarck	
Linden	Dallas county, pop. 201
Lohrville	Calhoun county, pop. 453
Lucas	pop. 224
Luther	Boone county, pop. 154
Luxemburg	pop. 257, St. Donatus stone monument for Luxemburg immigrants
Melcher	Marion county, pop. 924
Metz	named after Christian Metz (1794-1867), Iowa pioneer; Jasper county
Meyer	"Shitake mushrooms"
Millersburg	pop. 188
Minden	
Mondamin	Harrison county, settled 1867-68
New Vienna	Dubuque county, pop. 376, St. Boniface Church
Odebolt	fdd. 1877, pop. 1,158, Odebolt Museum
Oelwein	pop. 6,493, Oelwein Area Historicsal Society Museum
Osterdock	pop. 49
Otho	pop. 529
Ottosen	fdd. By Chris Ottensen, grain dealer, 1896; Humboldt county, pop. 72; 2 devastating fires
Rebman	
Reinbeck	pop. 1,605
Rossville	Allamakee county
St. Lucas	pop. 174
Schaller	pop. 768
Schleswig	pop. 851; "strong ties to Schhleswig-Holstein; *Liederkranz*; [Theodor] Storm Lake
Shambaugh	pop. 190
Stanwood	pop. 646
Thornburg	pop. 91
Ulmer	

Westphalia	Fdd. by Catholic Germans in 1872; pop. 144; St. Boniface Church
Yetter	pop. 49
Zwingle	pop. 1,320
Total	52
"South"	17
"North"	35
descriptive	10
poss.-comm.	38
shift names	4

8. *Places Named GERMAN, State of MINNESOTA, in 87 counties, 650 (sic!) cities, 1800 townships*

Adolph	St. Louis county
Becker	Sherburne county, pop. 902
Berta	
Bethel	Anoka county, pop. 394
Bigelow	Nobles county, pop. 231
Bruno	
Brunswick	Kanabec county, (one of 39 Brunswick nation-wide)
Cologne	Carver county, pop. 563
Danube	Renville county, pop. 562
Effie	Itaska county, pop. 130
Ei(t)zen	Houston county, pop. 221
Enfield	Wright county
Erhard	Otter Tail county, pop. 181
Essig	Brown county, pop. 522
Flensburg	Morrison county, pop. 213
Freeburg	Houston county
Friesland	Pine county
Fulda	Murray county, pop. 1,792
Gatzke	Marshall county, pop. 131
Giese	Aitkin county
Greenbush	pop. ca. 800
Hamburg	Carver county, pop. 492
Hanover	Hennepin county, pop. 787
Heidelberg	Le Sueur county, pop. 73
Henning	Otter Tail county, pop. 738
Herman	Grant county, pop. 485
Hermantown	St. Louis conty, pop. 6,761

Hoffman	Grant county, pop. 576
Humboldt	Kittson ccounty, pop. 74
Ihlen	Pipestone county, pop. 101
Jasper	Rock county, pop. 599
Karlstadt	Kittson county, pop. 881
Kiester	Faribault county, pop. 606
Klossner	
Kroschel	Kanebec county
Luxemburg	
Mansfield	
Nassau	Lac qui parle county, pop. 83
New Germany	Carver county, pop. 253
New Ulm	fdd. by Frederick Beinhorn as a *"Turner"* town in 1852-54; peopled by "Wuertemburgers" (Swabians); official Hermann the Cheruscan monument, a replica of the Detmold monument on a smaller scale, erected in the 1880s as "a national symbol" of the "great contribution by Americans of German heritage" passed as a resolution by the 106th Congress ; pop. 14,000; Bavarian-style Heritagefest; Martin Luther College
Odin	Watouwan county, pop. 102
Pietz	
Potsdam	Olmsted county
Rauch	
Redlob	
Remer	Can county, pop. 342
Rosedale	
Roseland	Kandiyohi county
Ross	
St. Joseph	Benedictine Monastary, goes back to 1857 and to settlers from Eichstatt, Bavaria; Stearns county, pop. 3,294 (1990)
St. Kilian	
Saum	
Schley	Can county
Theilmann	
Ulm	see New Ulm
Waldorf	Waseca county, pop. 243
Total	56
"South"	23
"North"	28
descriptive	7
poss.-comm.	43
shift names	4

87

9. Places named GERMAN, State of KANSAS, in 105 counties

Altoona	Wilson county, pop. 469
Arnold	Ness county
Bavaria	Saline county
Bern	Nemaha county, pop. 457; situated on the trail to California
Bison	Rush county, pop. 347
Bremen	Marshall county; fdd, 1869 ?; Farmers Mutual Insurance Co. in 1887; "Ostfriesenspuren"
Buhler	Reno county, pop. 1,277
Clements	Chase county
Deerfield	Kearny county, pop. 677
Dresden	Decatur county, pop. 73
Elbing	Butler county, pop. 184
Elkhart	Morton county, pop. 2,318
Elmdale	Chase county, pop. 83
Fellsburg	Edward county
Frankfort	pop. 927
Frederick	fdd. 1878; "ghost town"; ravaged by repeated fire and tornadoes, pop. 18
Goessel	Marion county, pop. 506; fdd. 1874 by Russlander; Mennonite Heritage Museum
Hanover	Washington county, pop. 696; Pony Express station on the Oregon trail; fdd. by Mennonites in 1857
Harlan	
Heizer	
Hepler	Crawford county, pop. 150
Herkimer	
Hesston	
Hollenberg	Washington county, pop. 28
Humboldt	Allen county, pop. 2,178
Hyner	
Keehl	
Kipp	Saline county
Liebenthal	Rush county, pop. 112
Liberal	pop. 16,573; Sewarde county; fdd. around 1880
Lucas	Russell county, pop. 452
Manter	Stanton county, pop. 354
Marienthal	Wichita county, pop. 154
Milberger	
Munden	Republic county
Odin	
Offerle	Edwards county, pop. 323

Olmitz	pop. 130
Olpe	Lyon county, pop. 431
Olsburg	pop. 192
Overbrook	
Pfeifer	fdd. 1877 by Russlander Germans
Philippsburg	
Rossville	pop. 1,052
St. Francis	fdd. 1885, pop. 1,495; Cheyenne County Museum
St. Joseph	
Schoenchen	
Stuttgart	Phillips county
Traer	
Timken	Rush county, pop. 87
Varner	
Vesper	
Webber	Jewell county, pop. 39
Weir	pop. 730
Westfall	
Westphalia	Anderson county, pop. 152
Winifred	
Yoder	Mennonite founded village in Reno county
Zimmerdale	Harvey county
Zimmerli	
Zurich	Rooks county, pop. 151
Total	61
"South"	20
"North"	41
descriptive	8
poss.-comm.	51
shift names	2

10. Places Named GERMAN, State of NEBRASKA, in 93 counties, 540 municipalities

Beatrice	"Ostfriesensiedlung" in Gage county, pop. 12,496; 5 churches; "a city of factories and homes"
Beemer	Cuming county, pop. 672
Belden	Cedar county, pop. 149
Benkelman	Dundy county, pop. 1,193
Bloomfield	"the busy city"; Knox county, pop. 1,126
Bruno	Butler county, pop. 141
Bruning	Thayer county, pop. 332

Brunswick	Antelope county, pop. 182
Burchard	Pawnee county, pop. 105
Deshler	Thayer county, pop. between 892 and 1,108 (2 website entries differ)
Elkhorn	Douglas county, pop. 1,398
Gehring	
Giltner	Hamilton county, pop. 367
Goehner	(temporarily Gaynor); Seward county, pop. 192
Grand Island	Platte river; on Oregon trail; Low German speaking group fdd. it in 1857; incorporated 1872; sugar beet processing; 86 plants; pop. 44,000
Gross	pop. 7
Haigler	Bundy county, pop. 225
Herman	Washington county, pop. 186
Hickman	fdd. by reverend C. H. Heckman in 1866; incorpor. 1885; pop. 1,081
Holstein	Adams county, pop. 207. Dairy place on the Oregon trail
Humboldt	Richardson county, pop. 1,003
Kramer	Lancaster county, pop. ?; plant nurseries
Little Oldenburg	fdd. by Oldenburgers in 1871; *4. Plattdeutsche Konferenz* Oct. 2001
Martinsburg	pop. 90
Max	Dundy county, pop. 164
Minden	Kearny county, pop. 2,749
Mitchell	Scotts Bluff county, pop. 1,743
Nenzel	pop. 8
Norden	pop. 10
Obert	Cedar county, pop. 39
Oak	Nuckolls county, pop. 68
Pauline	
Pilger	Stanton county, pop. 361
Richland	pop. 96
Ringgold	McPherson county
Roseland	Adams county, pop. 247
Scribner	Dodge county, pop. 950
Shubert	Richardson county, pop. 237
Snyder	pop. 280
Steinauer	Pawnee county, pop. 87
Stromsburg	Polk county, pop. 1,250; fdd. by Swedish Stromburg family in 1910
Tilden	fdd. in 1868; pop. 895
Tobias	Saline county, pop. 127
Weissert	

| Wisner | fdd. in 1850s, platted 1871, pop. 1,200 |
| Wolbach | Greeley county, pop. 280 |

Total	46
"South"	18
"North"	26
descriptive	4
poss.-comm.	37
shift names	2

11. *Places named GERMAN, State of NORTH DAKOTA , in 53 counties, 360 municipalities, ca. 1360 townships*

NB in 1818 the 49th parallel between North Dakota and Canada was agreed upon by the US and Britain

Belden	Mountrail county, pop. 149
Berlin	Lamoure county, pop. 32
Bismarck	named 1873, "Bismarck Tribune" fdd. as well; made state capital 1883; Burleigh county, pop. 55,000; 28 churches; Adventist Academy; Art School; museum; State Archives; colonel George A. custer explored it; Univ. of N. D. 1883; N. D. Farmer alliance; Laura Eisenhuth 1. state super-intendent; national divorce mecca until 1899
Bowman	pop. 1,741
Bremen	Wells county, pop. 108
Burnstad	"a ghost town", 20 residents
Buttzville	Ransom county, pop. ?, named for Buttz in 1896
Danzig	Mcintosh county
Dresden	Cavalier county
Eckman	
Egeland	Towner county, pop. 701
Emrick	
Enderlin	Ransom county, pop. 943; free building lot promised to builders on website
Epping	Williams county, pop. 64
Fryburg	
Gackle	fdd. by Russlanders; "Hutmacker" from Bessarabia on the Black Sea; pop. 221
Garske	
Golden Valley	
Gwinner	Sargent county, pop. 585

Hamar	Eddy county; fdd. by Norwegians and Germans
Hamberg	Wells county, pop. 19
Hannover	Oliver county
Hensel	Pembina county, pop. 121
Hensler	Oliver county
Hesper	Benson county
Hettinger	Benson county, pop. 3,174
Karlsruhe	Mchenry, pop. 143
Kempton	Grand Forks county
Kramer	Bottineau county, pop. 51
Krem	
Kulm	Lamoure county, pop. 514
Lehr	Mcintosh county, pop. 191
Lidgerwood	Richland county, pop. 1,845
Manfred	Wells county
Millarton	
Munich	pop. 310
New Leipzig	pop. 326
Osnabrock	Cavalier county, pop. 214
Raub	McLean county
Reeder	Adams county, pop. 252
Rhame	Bowman county, pop. 186
Roth	
Ross	Mountrail county, pop. 61
Sanger	Oliver county
Steubenville	
Strasburg	fdd. 1902 by Russlanders; Lawrence Welk (1903-1992) hometown; pop. 553; LW TV show starting in 1955
Walhalla	city established in 1845; Pembina county, pop. 1,131
Zahl	Williams county, pop. 94
Zapp	

Total	49
"South"	19
"North"	30
descript.	6
poss.-comm.	41
shift names	1

12. Places named GERMAN, State of SOUTH DAKOTA, in 66 counties

Alpena	pop. 251

Astoria	pop. 155
Baltic	Minnehaha county, pop. 1,839
Bison	Perkins county, pop. 451
Brandt	Deuel county, pop. 123
Enning	Meade county, pop. 275
Erwin	Kingsbury county, pop. 42
Frankfort	Spink county, pop. 192
Frederick	Brown county, pop. 241
Forestburg	Sanborn county
Fruitdale	Butte county, pop. 43
Hereford	Meade county
Herreid	Campbell county, pop. 488
Herrick	Gregory county, pop. 139
Hosmer	Edmunds county, pop. 310
Humboldt	Minnehaha county, pop. 468
Kaylor	Hutchinson county, pop. 223
Kingsburg	Bon homme county
Kranzburg	Codington county, pop. 132
Ladner	Harding county
Langford	Marshall county, pop. 298
Langlake	
Mansfield	Spink county, pop. 92
Mound City	pop. 89
Norbeck	Faulk county
Redig	Harding county
Renner	Minnehaha county, pop. 1,444
Shindler	Lincoln county
Sisseton	Roberts county, pop. 2,181
Strandburg	Grant county, pop. 74
Tripp	Hutchinson county, pop. 664
Vienna	Clark county, pop. 93
Wagner	pop. 1,462
Winfred	Lake county, pop. 54
Witten	Tripp county, pop. 118
Total	35
"South"	13
"North"	22
descript.	7
poss.-comm.	25
shift name	1

B. *Extended South*:

I. KY, TN, MS, AL
II. LA, AR, TX, OK

III EAST SOUTH CENTRAL

13. Places named GERMAN, State of KENTUCKY, in 120 counties

Bethel	Bath county
Bloomfield	establ. 1790, Nelson county, pop. 845; 7 churches
Boaz	Graves county, pop. 1,609, 1 Church of Christ
Brandenburg	est. 1825; Meade county, near Ohio river, pop. 1,831
Briensburg	Marshall county
Crayne	Crittenden county
Crider	Caldwell county
Dycusburg	pop. 47
East Bernstadt	Laurel county, pop. 8,589
Frankfort	fdd. 1786 in Virginia; named after a Mr. Frank? Franklin cty.; state capital; pop. 27,741; Aaron Burr charged with treason there
Gansdale	
Germantown	settld. 1788; fdd. 1794, Bracken and Mason counties; pop. 213
Grahn	Carter county
Gratz	Owen county, pop. 65
Hadensville	Todd county
Happ	
Harlan	fdd. 1819 as coal miners town; Harlan county, pop. 2,686
Heidelberg	Lee county, pop. 605; St. Theresa mission church
Hickman	Fulton county, pop. 2,689
Hindman	fdd. 1884, Knott county, pop. 798
Hyden	pop. 375
Keltner	Adair county
Lawrenceburg	settled in 1780; Anderson county; fdd. as Kaufmann's Station; pop. 5,911
Louisa	Lawrence county, pop. 1,990
Lucas	Barren county, pop. 415
Mayfield	"Chickasaw Purchase Area", Graves county, pop. 9,935; tobacco
Millersburg	Bourbon county, pop. 937; Military Institute of Kentucky
Mitchellsburg	Boyle county
Myers	Nicholas county

Nelse	Pike county
New Hope	Nelson county
Ritner	Wayne county
Sibert	Clay county
Stab	Pulaski county
Stade	
St. Joseph	
Tilden	Webster county

Total	37
"South"	14
"North"	23
descript.	4
poss.-comm.	33
shift names	0

14. Places Named GERMAN, State of TENNESSEE, in 95 counties, 326 municipalities

Alpine	Overton county; pop. 441
Bloomingdale	Sullivan county; pop. 10,953
Brunswick	Shelby county
Castellan	
Clingmans	
Crump	Hardin county; pop. 3,028; Technology Center
Deckerd	
Dresden	Weakley county; pop. 2,488
Ellendale	Shelby county
Englewood	Mcminn county; pop. 1,611
Friendship	pop. 467
Friendsville	fdd. by Quakers in 1790; chartered in 1807; Blount county; pop. 792
Fruitland	
Germantown	Shelby county; pop. 36,396; "beautiful parks"; no tangible intellectual center description
Goreman	
Harms	Lincoln county
Henning	pop. 802
Hickman	Smith county; pop. 836
Hohenwald	Lewis county; pop. 3,760
Holston Valley	Sullivan county
Hornbeak	pop. 445
Humboldt	Gibson county; pop. 9,664

Jasper	pop. 2,80
Keipers Fork	
Kerrville	
Kinzel Springs	
Laager	(Gruetli Laager) pop. 1,10
Linden	pop. 1,99
Lobelville	pop. 830
Maynardville	Union county; pop. 1,98
Mitchellville	pop. 193
Mosheim	(Moosham) Greene county; pop. 1,51
Neubert	
Newbern	Dyer county; pop. 2,15; Technology Center
Rosemark	Shelby county
Samburg	pop. 374
St. Bethlehem	Montgomery county; birthplace of olympic black sprinter Wilma Rudolph
St. Joseph	pop. 789
Shouns (Schanz)	
Saulsbury (Salzburg)	Hardeman county; pop. 106
Wartburg	Morgan county; pop. 932
Wildersville	Henderson county; pop. 2,828
Zach	
Total	43
"South"	18
"North"	25
descript.	7
poss.-comm.	32
shift names	3

15. Places Named GERMAN, State of ALABAMA, in 67 counties

Alpine	Talledega county; pop. 3,062; 7 churches
Altoona	pop. 960
Boaz	settled by Georgians in 1878; incorporated 1897; Marshall county; pop. 7,610
Bolinger	
Bolling	Butler county
Bremen	Cullman county; pop. 3,448; 2 churches
Buhl	Tuscaloosa county; pop. 1,662
Coker	Tuscaloosa county; pop. 5,747
Cullman	fdd. 1873 by the German American colonel John Gottfried

	Cullman, who came from cincinnati, OH in 1866; Benedictine sisters; modern sister city Frankweiler
Fackler	Jackson county; pop. 396
Frankfort	Franklin county
Fruitdale	Washington county; pop. 848
Fruithurst	Cleburne county; pop. 177
Gallion	Hale county; pop. 599
Guntersville	pop. 7.041
Hackleburg	Marion county; pop. 1,161
Hayden	Blount county; pop. 385; named after major H. before the civil War
Heiberger	birthplace of Coretta Scott King (Martin Luther King's wife)
Holt	Tuscaloosa county; pop. 4,125
Ider (Eider?)	pop. 671
Jasper	Walker county; pop. 13,553
Kellerman	Tuscaloosa county
Linden	Manengo county; pop. 2,548
Marburg	
Nectar	fdd. in the early 1800s; Blount county; pop. 238
Newbern	pop. 222
Odenville	pop. 796
Opp	Covington county; pop. 6,985
Pletcher	Toroughbread horse breeding
Ramer	Montgomery county; pop. 1,712
Speigner	
Sprott	Perry county; pop. 1,191
Stroud	Chambers county

Total	33
"South"	14
"North"	19
descript.	5
poss.-comm.	27
shift names	1

16. *Place Named GERMAN, State of MISSISSIPPI, in 82 counties, 280 municipalities, no townships;*
NB the web mentions the names of more than a tousand blackmen who were lynched in Mississippi until 1964

Becker	Monroe county
Belden	Lee county; pop. 4,441
Bethlehem	Civil War Battle in 1862; cemetery

Corinth	Alcorn county; pop. 11,820
Cruger	pop. 548
De Kalb	Kemper county; pop. 1,073
Fruitland Park	
Gattman	Monroe county; pop. 120
Gluckstadt	Madison county
Gross	
Hamburg	Franklin county; the black man William Williams was lynched Oct. 6, 1897
Heidelberg	pop. 981
Helm	
Hermansville	
Keirn	
Lambert	Quitman county; pop. 1,131
Lorman	Jefferson county; pop. 668
Mayersville	Issaquena county; pop. 329
Mize	pop. 312
Oldenburg	
Schlater	named after Schlatter; Le Flore county; pop. 404
Sontag	Lawrence county; pop. 1,953
Stringer	Jasper county; pop. 1,367
Tilden	Itawamba county
Total	24
"South"	6
"North"	18
descript.	1
poss.-comm.	22
shift names	1

IV. WEST SOUTH CENTRAL

17. Places Named GERMAN, State of LOUISIANA, in 64 parishes, 350 municipalities

Alsatia	East Carroll parish
Beekman	Mourehouse parish
Des Allemands	pop. 2,504
Donner	Terrebonne parish
Dubach	Lincoln parish, pop. 843
Effie	Avoyelles p., pop. 447
Epps	
Erwinville	West Baton rouge p., pop. 225
Gallion	
Geismar	pop. 225
Greensberg	
Hahnville	pop. 2,599
Heismer	
Hornbeck	pop. 427
Jena	La Salle p., pop. 2,626
Kaplan	pop. 4,535
Kenner	laid out in 1855; Jefferson county, pop. 72,033; museums
Kinder	2 brothers Kinder owned a store there in the late 1800s; agriculture; pop. 2,246
Klotzville	
Kraemer	
Mansfield	De Soto p.; pop. 5,389
Melder	
Minden	establ. in 1836 by Charles Veeder; Webster county;German Harmonist colony town; Confederate Army Camp; a "Nation's cultural resource"; descendents say: "valuable part of our life today"; pop. 43,000
Oberlin	pop. 1,808
Odenberg	
Ringgold	pop. 1,856
Rosefield	
Roseland	pop. 1,093
St. Joseph	pop. 1,517
Sieper	pop. 474
Singer	pop. 2,374
Sondheimer	East Carroll p.; pop. 887
Swartz	pop. 3,698
Vienna	pop. 404

Waldheim	established by German founders turned Methodist
Zimmermann	

Total	36
"South"	12
"North"	24
descript.	5
poss.-comm.	31
shift names	0

18. Places Named GERMAN, State of ARKANSAS, in 75 counties

Altheimer	fdd. by Louis Altheimer, Jefferson county; pop. 1,192
Beirne	Clark county
Bergman	pop. 324
Bethel Heights	pop. 281
Bigelow	pop. 340
Bismarck	pop. 1,291
Buckner	pop. 325
Corinth	pop. 63
Denning	pop. 216
Dutch Mills	Washington county; skirmish in 1864
Felsenthal	National wildlife Refuge; pop. 95
Friendship	pop. 160
Hamburg	Ashley county; pop. 3,39; 5 churches
Hartman	Johnson county; pop. 846
Hickman	
Huttig	pop. 831
Imboden	Lawrence county, pop. 616
Jasper	Newton county; pop. 332
Keiser	Mississippi county; pop. 805
Lambert	
Lind	skirmish in 1863
Mansfield	Scott county, pop. 2,07
Maynard	Randolph county, pop. 354
Mitchellville	pop. 513
Rohwer	
Roland	Pulaski county, pop. 1,24
Roseland	
Schaal	
Shoffner	
Snyder	

Stuttgart	"The Rice & Duck Capitol of the W."; pop. 10,10; processing center; Agricultural Museum
Trumann	pop. 6,04
Ulm	Prairie county; pop. 193
Waldenburg	pop. 103
Weiner	pop. 655
Wirth	
Wiseman	pop. 26
Witter	Madison county; pop. 179

Total	38
"South"	14
"North"	24
descript.	5
poss.-comm.	30
shift names	2

19. *Places named GERMAN, State of TEXAS, in 254 counties, some 1065 cities & towns* after Pennsylvania; more counties than any other state; after PA more Gn place names left than in any other state; checked against *The Handbook of Texas Online*; accordg. to which 251 of 290 home-rule cities have a population in access of 10,000

Adrian	Oldham county, pop. 220; originated in 1900, named after Adrian Cullen
Arp	fdd. 1868, named after William Arp, popular newspaper editor 1899; 1936: pop. 2,500; 1990: pop. 812
Aspermont	platted 1889, Latin for "rough mountain"; incorp. 1909, pop. 1,214
Ballinger	named for W. P. Ballinger, a Galveston atty., "a ruffian town" in 1888; pop. 1990: 3,975
Barnhart	named for a RR agent; establ. 1910, pop. 135
Bergheim	
Biegel	fdd. 1832 as first German settlement in cty. of Fayette; pop. 50 in 1896; was inundated by the Lower Colorado River Authority
Bloomberg	
Blum	establ. 1881; named for Alsatian-American philanthropist, Leon Blum; pop. 358
Boerne	laid out in 1849 by Low German speaking settlers, named 1852 for Ludwig Boerne, (1786-1837) German poet, freethinker and publicist; incorp. 1909, present pop. 4,274;

101

"Gn cultural tradition has dominated"; Schützenverein; treasure Low German Bible, printed in Lunenburg, Germany, 1614; motto: "to grow gracefully"

Boling	
Booker	
Borger	promoted in 1926; has little to do with German traditions, despite Och's dictum
Brownfield	
Brownville	
Brownwood	chartered in 1910
Buna	established in 1893; pop. in 1990: 2,127
Bushland	named for William H. Bush of Chicago; dedicated in 1908, pop. 130
Byers	estabvlished 1904; pop. 510
Carlsbad	fdd. 1907, pop. 100; 2 businesses
Chappell Hill	laid out in 1849, pop. 310; Ch.H. Historical Society
Chriesman	established 1830; renamed to Chr. in 1885, a local pioneer; pop. 30
Cohn	
Comfort	(Point Comfort?) fdd. in the 1840s; monument "*Treue der Union*" celebrating 35 anti-slavery, anti-Confederacy executed German American farmers
Dalhart	Ballam county; platted 1901; 1rst public library in TX 1921; pop. 6,241
De Kalb	named by Davie Crockett in 1835; pop. 1,976
Eastland	fdd. in 1875; hometown of Janis Virginia Little; pop. 3,690
Elbert	Throckmorton county, pop. 950
Elmendorf	established 1885; named in honor of a mayor of San Antonio; pop. 568
Everman	established 1830; renamed E., a RR man, in 1904; pop. 5,701; near Dallas
Fabens	1665 Spanish-Mexican mission San Felipe; townside sold 1887; pop. 5,599
Fieldton	named in 1924; pop. 126
Forestburg	settled in the 1850s; pop. 200; 8 businesses, 1 post office
Frankel City	renamed 1948; pop. 126
Fredericksburg	Gillespie county; fdd. 1845, by J. O. Meusebach, for the New Braunfels *Adelsverein*; the majority was for the Union during the Civil War; Gillespie County Historical Society Museum; Christkindl Market
Freer	mentioned 1876; *Wochenblatt*, 1877; frontier oil town; pop. 6,934
Friendswood	Quaker settled in the 1880s; suburb of Galveston; pop. 22,814

Groesbeck	settled in 1835; named after an RR director; pop. 3,318
Gruver	"found" 1907; incorporated 1930; pop. 1,172
Hansford	named for physician and frontier judge H. in the 1880s; no more populated today; just a cemetery
Hardeman	now a county; pop. 5,283
Harlingen	-; Army Air Field, pop. 48,700
Hasse	fdd. 1892; pop. 43
Hockley	settled 1829; pop. 300
Hurst	farmers began to settle in the 1840s; named in honor of a Tennessean H.; pop. 33,600; Bell Helicopter workforce, near Houston
Jasper	settled 1824-1830; named in honor of a hero of the American Revolution J.; pop. 7,267
Justiceburg	fdd. by rancher J. D. Justice in 1910, pop. 76
Kaufman	land named for lawyer David Spangler Kaufman in 1848; pop. 5,238; 108 businesses
Kemp	first post office 1851; RR attracted settlers; cattle production; pop. 50
Kellerville	began settlement 1920 as oiltown; first post office 1935; pop. 1,184
Kerens (Krenz)	establ. 1881 by judge Krenz of St. Louis; pop. 1,702
Knipp	
Kountze	2 brothers K. financial backers of RR joining track 1902; lumber; pop. 2,056
Kress	fdd. 1840; incorporated 1953; pop. 729; 42 businesses
Linden	fdd. 1852; named after Linden,TN; lumber boom 1890; pop. 2,439; 38 busin.
Longworth	establ. 1902; RR 1907: "macaroni line"; pop. 65
Louise	renamed L. in 1881 by Italian count Telfener; "cotton joined rice"; pop. 310
Lubbock	named after the family of a Texan governor L. (Lübbecke, Westf.?); home of Texas Tech University 1976; northwest of Dallas; incorpor. 1909; 13 banks; home of Texas Instruments 1980 187,000 inhabitants; 250 (sic) churches 1 saloon; L. Christian University
Lucas	last mentioned 1989; no buildings, no people left: dead place
Lueders	named after Fred. Lueders, a Texan Texas Revolution soldier; pop. 365
Mansfield	fish camp; pop. 731
Merkel	named after first settler S. m. Merkel; incorp. 1906; pop. 2,469
Mertzon	named after banker M. l. Mertz; incorporated 1933; pop. 778

Middle Water	fdd. 1888, pop. 10
Minden	begun to be settled 1849 from M., Louisiana; pop. 350
New Baden	fdd. 1881 by M. Leber, J. G. Meyer and A. B. Langermann; pop. 105
New Berlin	fdd. 1870 by Ed. Tewes 1. store; incorpor. 1980; pop. 188
New Braunfels	fdd. 1845 under the auspices of the *Adelsverein* of Prince Carl of Solms-Braunfels; colonizer Nikolaus Zink; 400 settlers arrived first summer; The *Adelsverein* acquired 3,878,000 acres. N.B. became the fourth largest town in TX for a while; there is a seizable collection in the Beinecke Rare Book Library at Yale University, WA Collection, MSS. S-1291 that would need to be consulted. New Braunfels-Herald Zeitung fdd. in 1852; B. Academy 1858; pop. 27,334
New Bremen	settled 1900 by "slowly scattering German immigrants" up to 1940; now only cemetary left
Olden Switch	RR town; pop. 110
Pflugerville	fdd. by German Henry Pflüger in 1849; boom town 1980s; pop. 4,444
Powderly	originally "Lenoir" settled 1860s; renamed for a labor leader; pop. 185
Reese	settled 1860s; camp 1890; RR 1901; pop. 75
Riesel	settled by German families 1880-90; pop. 839
Royse City	platted 1886 by G. B. Royse; pop. 2,206
Rosenberg	named in honor of Henry R., a Swiss from Galveston, RR. magnate; 234 businesses; pop. 22,577
Rule	RR station 1905; started as a bank in the 1889s; pop. 789
Sachse	named after the Sachse family in 1896; pop. 5,000
Sagerfort	
Samnorwood	established in 1931, pop. 110
Sanger	fdd. in 1886; pop. 3,508
St. Hedwig	first settled in 1852 by a Silesian john Demmer; more Silesian settlers as of 1897 , mainly from Groß-Strehlitz, Upper Silesia; pop. 1,400
Schertz	fdd. as a store in 1875; named after Sebastian Sch. in 1899; pop. 10,555; 86 businesses
Schulenburg	fdd. 1873 by 48er Ernst Baumgarten; cottonseed industry; pop. 2,455
Snyder	fdd. by Mennonite families in 1907, named after their minister; "now dead"
Spearman	platted in 1917; RR 1931; pop. 2,147
Spur	subdivided from the Spur ranch in 1907; pop. 1,300
Summerfield	fdd. during the civil War; later became part of Judson, TX

Tell	fdd. in 1887; pop. 63
Tilden	fdd. in 1858; named after presidential candidate 1876; pop. 500
Ulm	now Neu Ulm; settled in 1841; *Turnverein*; pop. 650
Umberger	
Waelder	surveyed in 1874; named after attorney Jacob Waelder; pop. 745
Weimar	fdd. 1873; incorporated 1875; pop. 2,052
Weinert	fdd. in 1880s; named in honor of a senator; pop. 235
Welch	started in 1924; pop. 110
Wellman	fdd. in 1918; named for an RR official; pop. 239
Wentz	began 1910, named after promoter C. C. Wentz; dead
Westhoff	fdd. 1906 as Bell, then named Bello, finally after pioneer W. 1909; , pop. 410
Windthorst	
Wink	began 1926; originally called winkler, then shortened; oil town; pop. 1,189
Yoakum	built in 1835; RR train stop 1888; named after RR general manager; eventually became "tomato capitol of the South"; pop. 5,611

Total	101
"South"	35
"North"	66
descript.	12
poss.-comm.	87
Shift names	1

Rudolf L. Biesele. *The History of German Settlements in Texas, 1831-1861*. Austin, TX 1930 rp. 1964.

20. *Place named GERMAN, State of OKLAHOMA, in 77 counties, 559 cities and towns (sic)*

Berlin	
Binger	Caddo county, pop. 724
Blocker	
Brinkman	established as RR town in 1910; now ghost town
Frederick	Tillman county, pop. 5,221
Garber	Garfield county, pop. 959
Hartshorne (Herzhorn)	Pittsburg county, pop. 2,120

Healdton	fdd. in 1883 as Mason; renmaned after postmaster Ch. H. Held; oil boom after oil discovery 1913; pop. 2,872
Heavener	La Flore county, pop. 2,601
Hess	
Hoffman	Ockmulgee county, pop. 175
Kiefer	pop. 962
Krebs	pop. 1,955
Lambert	fdd. by Ezra Lambert, pop. 11
Luther	Oklahoma county, pop. 1,560
Mayfield	Buckham county
Overbrook	pop. 283
Ringold	pop. 97
Roff	Pontotoc county, pop. 717
Rosston	
Schulter	
Snyder	Kiowa county, pop. 1,619
Springer	pop. 485
Stigler	Haskell county, pop. 2,574
Stroud	Lincoln county, pop. 2,666
Vinita (Vineta?)	Craig county, pop. 5,804
Wagoner	started in 1872; 1st postmaster 1887; town platted 1893; pop. 7,310
Wann	pop. 126
Wirt	

Total	29
"South"	7
"North"	20
descript.	3
poss.-comm.	5
shift names	1

C. *Extended Atlantic*:

I. PA, NY, NJ, DE
II. VA, WV, MD, NC, SC, GA, FL
III. MA, CT RI, ME, NH, VT

V MIDDLE ATLANTIC

21. *Places Named GERMAN, State of PENNSYLVANIA, in 67 counties and about*
    50 cities and 125 colleges and universities

Adrian	Armstrong county, pop. 726
Altoona	Blair county; pop. 51,81; 9 churches
Arendtsville	Adams county, pop. 693
Arnold	started by Arnold McCrea in 1781; incorp. 1896; pop. 6,13
Aultman	
Baden	pop. 5,74
Berlin	Somerset county; pop. 2,64
Berwyn	fdd. 1877; one of five different names; Chester cty; pop. 9,82; 7 churches
Bethel	Berks county, pop. 3,23
Bethlehem	fdd. by Moravian brethren (count Zinzendorf) in 1741; incorp. 1845; pop. 71,000; The Moravian Museum of Bethlehem
Bigler	
Blandburg	
Bloomsburg	Ludwig Eyer laid it out in 1802; Columbia county;incorpor. by Samuel Bloom in 1870; pop. 12,439
Bloomsville	
Blossburg	settled by Aaron Bloss in 1792; Tioga county; pop. 571; coal festival
Boalsburg	Centre county, pop. 2,206; military museum; birthplace of Memorial Day
Claysburg	Blair county, pop. 1,399
Clearfield	pop. 6,633
Clymer	Indiana county, pop. 1,499
Conestoga	Lancaster county, pop. 4,493; Conestoga, originally called *Dutch,* wagon originated here in 1725; up to 16 ft. in length, broad rim wheels, could carry up to 8 tons, carried by 6-8 sturdy horses, covered 20-25 miles a day; used until 1850, "camel of the prairies" / "p. schooner" manufactd. by the thousands

107

East Berlin	Adams county, pop. 1,287
Ebensburg	Cambria county, pop. 3,872
Effort	Monroe county, pop. 3,817
Ehrenfeld	pop. 307
Emmaus	Lehigh county; pop. 11,157; 11 churches
Frankfort Springs	pop. 134
Fredericksburg	pop. 2,338
Fredericktown	
Freeburg	Snyder county, pop. 640
Freemansburg	pop. 1,946
Friendship Hill	
Fryburg	
Gallitzin	Cambria county, pop. 2,003
Geistown	Cambria county, pop. 2,749
Germantown	see New Germantown below
Gettysburg	the son of the early settler Samuel Götz, James Gettys, laid out Gettysburg in 1786, Adams county; they lived from carriage making; pop. 7,025 (1990); the battle of G. had 23,000 casualties on the N. side , 31,000 casualties on the S. side; Nov. 19, 1863: Lincoln's "Gettysburg Address"; L. "dedicated a position of that field" [now Evergreen Cemetery Gatehome] to the "proposition that all men are created equal" and wanted us that "we take increased devotion to that cause"
Grassflat	pop. 2,208
Hamburg	Berks county, pop. 3,987
Hanover	York county; battleground 1863; pop. 14,399
Harmony/Harmonsburg	fdd. by George Rapp 1805; The Harmony Museum
Heidelberg	York county, pop. 1,238
Heilwood	
Hereford	fdd. by Mennonites
Hindman	
Houtzdale	pop. 1,204
Iselin	
Jennerstown	pop. 635
Karthaus	pop. 932
Kayler	
Kempton	Berks county; pop. 2,387; 3 churches
Kist	
Koppel	pop. 1,024
Kresgeville	Monroe county; pop. 1,125
Kunkletown	Monroe county; pop. 4,924
Kulpsville	pop. 5,183

Kutztown	Pennsylvania German Cultural Heritage Center; Kutztown University
Lampeter	Lancaster county
Lander	
Lanse	pop. 814
Lehman	established 1829; pop. 507
Lenhartstown	
Lititz	Moravian settlement
Lottsville	
Loysburg	pop. 656
Luthersburg	pop. 2,249
Mainesburg	pop. 1,140
Manheim	fdd. in 1762 by iron- and glassmaker H. W. "Baron" Stiegel and the Stedman brothers; Lancaster county; Shearer's Covered Bridge; pop. 5,011
Mansfield	laid out in 1824; Tioga county; pop. 3.538; M. University
Markletown	
Markleysburg	Fayette county; pop. 320
Martinsburg	pop. 2,119
Marienville	pop. 1,374
Marietta	Lancaster county; pop. 2,778
Mayburg	
Mechanicsburg	pop. 9,452
Mertztown	Berks county; pop. 4,058
Meyersdale	Somerset county; pop. 2,518
Mohntown	
Mohrsville	Berks county; pop. 3,473
Myerstown	pop. 3,236
Nazareth	fdd. 1741; Northampton county; pop. 5,713; 12 churches
New Berlin	Union county; pop. 892
Newburg	pop. 312
New Eagle	Washington county; pop. 2,222
New Germantown	bought for the original 13 Krefelder (Düsseldorf diet) in 1681; motto: "America was the perfect solution to ... religious persecution" ; arrived, led by lawyer Francis Daniel Pastorius, on the *Concord* in Philadelphia in 1683; Gt. fdd. in the same year; first (German and English) written protest against slavery in 1688; first paper mill in America 1690; school directed by Pastorius, 1701-1718, first primer in America; first German Bible printed in America by Christopher Saur 1743; most famous native son, astronomer David Rittenhouse (1732-1796); battle against British troops 1777 ; pop. 455 (1990) nowadays

	part of Philadelphia
Nuremburg	
Oswigsburg	
Osterburg	pop. 174
Pennsburg	Schwenkfelder Library and Heritage Center
Petersburg	Huntingdon county; pop. 469
Philipsburg	pop. 3,048
Rainsburg	pop. 175
Reamstown	pop. 2,649
Rebersburg	pop. 816
Reedsville	Mifflin county; pop. 1,030
Rimersburg	Clarion county; pop. 1,053
Rohrersburg	(Rohrer family is Palatine)
Roseville	established 1801 by William Rose; Tioga county; pop. 230
Rossiter	Indiana county; pop. 1,858
Rouzerville	pop. 1,188
Rummersfield	
Saegertstown	
Saltsburg	fdd. in 1813 for abundance of salt; Indiana county; pop. 990
Schaefferstown	Lebanon county
Schellsburg	Bedford county; pop. 245
Schnecksville	(Schoenecksville) Lehigh county; pop. 1,780
Schwenksville	Montgomery county; pop. 1,376
Shillington	Berks county; pop. 5,062; birthplace of John Updike
Shinglehouse	pop. 1,243
Shippensburg	pop. 5,467; Sh. University
Shoemakersville	Berks county; pop. 1,443
Shunk	Sullivan county; pop. 300
Sigel	Jefferson county; pop. 1,103
Sinhamahoning	
Smidsburg	
Snydertown	Northumberland county; pop. 416
Spangler	Cambria county; pop. 2,068
Strasburg	Lancaster county; Amish village
Strausstown	Berks county; pop. 353
Stroudsburg	fdd. in 1778 by colonel J. Stroud for survivors of the Wyoming Massacre; Monroe county; pop. 5,312
Upper Strassburg	
Wellersburg	
Wernersville	Berks county; based on St. Isaac Jogues novitiate Jesuit School fdd. in 1930; pop. 5,056
Windber	Somerset county; coal mining town established before the turn of the 19th to the 20th century; pop. 11,421

Winterdale	
Womelsdorf	Berks county; Bethany Children's Home; pop. 4.034; Conrad Weiser Homestead
Yeagertown	Mifflin county; pop. 2,197
Zelionople	fdd. by "Baron" Dettmar Basse in 1802

Total	127
"South"	43
"North"	82
descript.	16
poss.-comm.	106
shift names	1

22. *Places Named GERMAN, State of NEW YORK, in 62 counties, 62 cities, 931 towns, 556 villages* [NB.: *New Yorker Staatszeitung* is one of the 59 dailies in the US]

Altona	Clinton county, pop. 1,003
Bergen	pop. 1.103; Bergen Museum
Berne	Albany county, pop. 2,293
Bloomington	Ulster county, pop. 845
Brant	Erie county
Brinckerhoff	pop. 2,756
[Brooklyn	comes from Hollandic *Breuckelen]*
Buffalo	held by the Holland Land Company; fdd. by J. Ellicot in 1801; Army Camp in the War of 1812, container drums marked US= "Uncle Sam" used by German American soldiers; launchg. of the steamer *Vandalia* 1841, went to Chicago, hence known in IL; city of 1832 with 10,000 residents; University of B. fdd. as college in 1846; Canisius College; breweries; mayors Wells, Fargo 1862-67; of the 50 m.s only 5 had German names from 1898-1937; modern subway; e-motto: "Bringing up the past into the future"; downplaying of the masses of German immigrants from 1830 to end of 19th cent.
Corinth	Saratoga county, pop. 2,474
De Kalb	St. Lawrence county
Dresden	Yates county, pop. 339
Ellenberg Center	
Fleischmans	
Frankfort	Herkimer county, pop. 2,693
Frewsburg	Chautauqua county, pop. 1,817

Friendship	Alleganny county, pop. 1,423
Germantown	established 1710 by Palatines; pop. ? [see text PART TWO chapter 4]
Hamburg	fdd. in 1812; Erie county (south of Buffalo); first German settlers (farmers) arrived in 1830; pop. 53,735
Herkimer	pop. 7,945
Knapp Creek	Cataraugus county
Mechanicsville	
Mecklenburg	Schuyler county
Mendon	Monroe county, pop. 864
New Bern	www. mix-up with P. Lang Verlag New York and Bern
New Berlin	
New Bremen	Lewis county
Newfane	Niagara county, pop. 3,001
New Paltz	fdd. 1678 by Abraham Hasbrouck on behalf of Huguenots; Ulster cty; pop. ? State University Campus
[New Amsterdam/ New York]	fdd. by non-Germans in early 1620s; ca 13% of her inhabitants were German Americans around 1900; there were "Little Germanies" in her 10th, 17th, and 19th wards until end of 19th century
Oppenheim	
Otto	
Pawling	
Potsdam	fdd. by D. Clarkson & G. Van Horne as Unionville in 1802; St. Lawrence county; pop. 10,251
Rhinebeck	fdd. by Palatines in 1710; Dutchess (*sic*) county, pop. 2,725
Rhinecliff	
Roseboom	Otsego county; pop. 8
Sandusky	
Shenevus	settled as Jacksonboro in 1793; Otsego county; renamed *Schoenevos {ursp. wohl auf Plattdeutsch " schöner Fuchs" bedeutend}* in 1843; pop. 513
Wayland	pop. 1,976
Wurtsboro	fdd. called Rome by N. Y. Yankees end of 18th century; Sullivan county; renamed W. by German settlers in 1812

Total	37
"South"	12
"North"	25
descript.	7
poss.-comm.	29
shift name	1

23.   *Paces Named GERMAN, State of NEW JERSEY, in 21 counties, 53 cities, 234 townships*

Alpine	Burgess county; pop. 1.716
Bergenfield	Bergen county; incorporated 1894; pop. 24.458; Museum
Berlin	fdd. 1867 Camden county; pop. 5,672
Brunaw	
Brunswick	17th century beginning; Middlesex county; Sephardic Jews came from the Ottoman empire 20th cent.; Rutgers university; pop. 49,000
Buttzville	
Carlstadt	
Clementown	
Closter	
Colonia	
East Brunswick	Middlesex county; fdd. by John Longfield, 17th cent.; pop. 43,548
East Hanover	Morris county; pop. 9,926
Englewood	settled 1674; Bergen county; regist. 1859; named after Engle family; incorporated 1896
Guttenberg	Hudson county; pop. 8,268
Hainesburg	Warren county
Hamburg	Sussex county; "Old Monroe Stone School House"; pop. 2,566
Hornerstown	Monmouth county
Johnsonsburg	originally Johannesburg
Linden	Union county; pop. 36,701
Lyndhurst	Bergen county; pop. 18,262
New Brunswick	Middlesex county; pop. 41,711
North Brunswick	Middlesex county; same as East Brunswick until 1860; Old Bridge Turnpike
Riegelville	
Roseland	Essex county; pop. 4,847
Rosenhayn	pop. 1,053
Sicklerville	Camden county; pop. 29,949
South Brunswick	see Brunswick
Vienna	
Whitesbog	

Total	29
"South"	12
"North"	17
descript.	5

poss.-comm.   23
shift name   1

24. *Places Named GERMAN, State of DELAWARE, in 3 counties and 60 cities and towns*

Bethel	Sussex county; pop. 178
Ellendale	Sussex county; pop. 313
Elmhurst	
Frankford	Sussex county; pop. 591
Hickman	
Leipsic	1 of 2 towns, pop. 236
Nassau	Sussex county
Winterthur	Museum

Total	8 [in 13% of total of place names]
"South"	4
"North"	4 [only State where these two numbers are equal]
descriptive	1
poss.-comm.	7
Shift names	0

VI SOUTH ATLANTIC

25. Place Named GERMAN, State of VIRGINIA, in 95 counties, 41 cities, 189 towns

Bastian	Bland county; pop. 1,656; 2 churches
Bergton	Rockingham county; pop. 341
Birchlear	
Brownsburg	
Critz	Patrick county; pop. 260
Christiansburg	Montgomery county; pop. 15,004
Esserville	Wise county
Ettrick	fdd. mid-1700s by Buchanan from Ettrick, Scotland; Chesterfield county; pop. 5,290
Franconia	Fairfax county; pop. 19,882
Fredericksburg	Spotsylvania county; pop. 19,027; no independent city; 30 dead in World War II
Fredericks Hall	schools for young women oprated 1858-1880
Fries	Grayson county; pop. 690
Goldenvein	
Hanover	pop. 3,796
Hartfield	Middlesex county; pop. 797
Haysi	pop. 222
Herman-Maxie	
Holston	
Honaker	pop. 950
Horntown	Accomack county; pop. 132
Keeling	Pittsylvania county; pop. 2,651
Keezletown	Rockingham county; pop. 1,204
Lennig	
Linden	Warren county; pop. 352
Lunenburg	pop. 156
Maurertown	Shenandoah county; pop. 1,483
Mechanicsburg	Bland county
Mechanicsville	Hanover county; pop. 22,027
Riner	Montgomery county; pop. 2,947; Blue Ridge Mountains
Roseland	Nelson county; pop. 2,333
Rustburg	Campbell county; pop. 4,723
Snell	Spotsylvania county
Strasburg	
Sutherlin	Pittsylvania county; pop. 1,018
Thornburg	Spotsylvania county
Trammel	Dickenson county; pop. 51

Vienna	Fairfax county; pop. 14,852
Waidsboro	Franklin county
Weber City	Scott county; pop. 1,377
Wirtz	Western community College; 1 church
Zepp (Zipp)	Shenandoah county

Total	42
"South"	17
"North"	25
descript.	4
poss.-comm.	36
shift names	2

26. *Places Named GERMAN, State of WEST VIRGINIA, in 55 counties, 230 municipalities*

Adolph	
Albright	Preston county; pop. 195
Alpena	Randolph county
Arnoldsburg	Calhoun county; pop. 1,683
Berwind	McDowell county
Bethlehem	pop. 2,694
Bismarck	Grant county
Boaz	Parkersburg county; pop. 1,137
Brandywine	Pendleton county; pop. 941
Crum	Wayne county; pop. 763
Eckman	McDowell county
Elbert	McDowell county
Ellenboro (Ellenburg)	pop. 453
Erbacon	Webster county; pop. 318
Friendly	pop. 146
Frankford	Greenbrier county; pop. 814
Gormania (not Germania)	settled by Jacob Schaeffer, originally named after him; renamed after Senator A. P. Gorman from MD in 1839; pop. 823; 1 church left
Hanover	Wyoming county; pop. 1,523
Harmony	religious colony; Lewis county
Harper's Ferry	confluence of Shenandoah and Potomac rivers; John Brown's (born 1800 in CT, hanged Charleston, SC 1859) rebellion, had originally wanted to found a fugitive slave state in the mountains; Sept. 15, 1862, largest Union

	troops' capture, 12,400, during the Civil War; National Historical Park; college
Iaeger	
Kasson	Barbour county
Kessel	Hardy county
Keyser	fdd. around 1866; Mineral county; pop. 9,579
Kieffer	Greenbriar county; pop. 2 (*sic*)
Kistler	Logan county
Kline	Pendleton county
Kopperston	Wyoming county
Lahmansville	Grant county; pop. 32
Linden	Roane county; pop. 270
Lorentz	Upshur county
Lubeck	pop. 1,579
Manheim	Lee county
Martinsburg	fdd. in the 18th century; Berkeley county; RR junction 1850; pop. 4,073
Mathias	fd.. 1797; Robert E. Lee family cabin
Mayers	
Maysel	fdd. before 1858; Clay county; pop. 223
Metz	Marion county; pop. 924
Minden	Fayette county
Moser	
Mostville	
Newburg	Preston county; pop. 378
New Martinsville	Wetzel county; pop. 6,461 (1998)
Ruddle	Pendleton county
Seebert	Pocahontas county
Shepherdstown	Jefferson county; pop. 1,287; college in town
Steubenville	
Vienna	Wood county; pop. 10,862
Welch	McDowell county; pop. 3,028; "the longest running Veterans' Day Parade" (82 years)
Wendel	
Wymer	Lewis county
Wormelsdorf	
Total	52
"South"	23
"North"	29
descript.	6
poss.-comm.	46
shift names	0

27. Places Named GERMAN, State of MARYLAND. in 23 ccounties

Aspen Hill

Baden   fdd. by people from Baden, Germany; Montgomery county; pop. 45.494

[Baltimore]   fdd. by non-Germans; but high % age of German immigrants until the end of the 19th century; f. i. Justus E. Kuhn, portrait painter arrived in 1706; Otto Mergenthaler (1854-1899) in 1872; he invented the *linotype* there; German residents peaked at 42,000 (of 365,000) then

Berlin   (not contracted from Burleigh Inn) fdd. 1790; incorpr. 1868; pop. 2,686

Boring   Baltimore county

Bozman   Talbot county; pp. 847

Brandywine   Prince George's county; pop. 7,627 (1990)

Clements   Sainte Mary's county; pop. 303

Colmar Manor   pop. 1,249

Creagerstown

Crysfield

Eldenburg

Ellerslie   Allegany county

Ellerton   A. Buttman(n), Huguenot Palatine; one of first 18th century settlers

Emmitsburg   laid out 1785; named after Irishman Sam Emmit; German settlers arrived end of 18th century; pop. 1,688

Ferndale   pop. 16,355

Finsburg

Forestville   pop. 6,731

Frederick   town laid out in 1745 by D. Delaney for German settlers; Reformed Lutheran Congregation 1747 by M. Schlatter; newspaper 1786; 50,000 residents; Hood College

Frizellburg

Friendship   Anne Arundel county; pop. 853 [requires comment!]

Friendsville   Garrett county; likely Quaker settlement; pop. 577

Frostburg   Allegany county; State University; pop. 8,075

Fruitland   Wicomico county; pop. 3,511

Funkstown   pop. 1,136

Gaithersburg   fdd. as logtown 1765; 1850 named Forest Oak; 1878 incorporated as G'burg; Montgomery county [Fair]; pop. 50,000; noticeably high children ratio; motto "G'burg has it all"

Germantown   fdd. 1790 by Waters brothers; renamed Germantown because of residents' heavy accent (*sic*); during Civil War many gn residents were against slavery, and "had their sons fight for the Union"; freed slaves worked in a section of town called "Browntown" (*sic*)

Grouna (Gronau?)	
Hagerstown	originally called Elizabeth town; incorpor. in 1813; Washington county; held ransom by Confederate troops; biggest city in Western MD; ca. 36,000 residents
Hanover	Anne Arundel county
Hereford	Baltimore county
Kempton	Garrett county
Kemptown	Frederick county (this county was founded in 1748)
Keymar	Carroll county; pop. 1,691
Kitzmiller	pop. 275
Leitersburg	Washington county
Lenz	
Lutherville	Baltimore county
Marbury	pop. 1,244
Mayberry	Carroll county
Marydel (Marienthal)	pop. 143
Mechanicsville	in St. Mary's county, fdd. in 1637; Ste. Mary's College; pop. 17,326
Millersville	pop. 16,436
Myersville	Frederick county fdd. in 1748; pop. 464
New Bremen	Frederick county, settled by J. F. Adelung, born in Reitlingen, who established glassworks here in 1784; the premier American glassmaker of the late 18th century
Oldenton	
Prince Frederick	Calvert county; pop. 1,885
Reisterstown	pop. 19,314
Ringgold	Washington county
Rohrersville	Washington county; pop. 200
Rosedale	Baltimore county; pop. 18,703
Ruthsburg	Queen Anne's county
Shaft	
Steyer	Garrett county
Sudlerville	
Trappe	started as a small hamlet in 1760 in Talbot county; incorporated town 1856; pop. 794
Vienna	Dorchester county; pop. 264
Waldorf	named after South German farmers from Würtemberg; Charles county; pop. 15,058; Afro-American Heritage Museum

Total	57
"South"	24
"North"	33
descript.	7
poss.-comm.	47
shift names	2

28. *Places Named GERMAN, State of NORTH CAROLINA, in 100 counties, 470 municipalities*

Bethel	Pitt county; pop. 1,842
Boomer	Wilkes county; pop. 2,146
Brunswick	pop. 302
Crumpler	Ashe county; pop. 2,32
Drexel	Burke county; pop. 1,46
Dunderrach	
Effland	
Enfield	fdd. 1740 as oldest town in Halifax county; a riot against "the British tyranny" in 1759; tobacco planting
Engelhard	Hyde county; pop. 1,822
Erwin	Harnett county; pop. 4,061
Hildebran	pop. 790
Hoffman	Richmond county; pop. 348
Hubert	Onslow county; pop. 8,527
Kernersville	Forsyth county; pop. 10,836
Louisberg	
Mecklenburg	
Misenheimer	Stanly county; teacher education college called "Pfeiffer University"
Momeyer	
Neuse	Wake county
New Hanover	
Otto	Macon county; pop. 2,297
Rennert	Robeson county; pop. 217
Riegelwood	Columbus county; pop. 2,038
Rominger	Watauga county
Rosman	Transylvania county; pop. 385
Spies	Moore county
Stedman	Cumberland county; pop. 577
Troutman	pop. 1,441
Turnerburg	
Wagoner	Ashe county

Wallburg	Davidson county

Total	31
"South"	10
"North"	21
descript.	4
poss.-comm.	27
shift name	0

29. Places Named GERMAN, State of SOUTH CAROLINA, in 46 counties

Bamberg	Bamberg county; pop. 3,843
Bowman	Orangeburg county; pop. 1,063
Ehrhardt	Bamberg county; pop. 442
Filbert	York county
Givhans	Berkeley county
Huger	named after Daniel Huger, senator 1842-46; pop. 1,964
Kline	pop. 285
Neeses	Orangeburg county; pop. 410
Orangeburg	pop. 13,739; S. C. State University; 5 churches
Pelzer	Anderson county; pop. 81
Plum Branch	McCormick county; pop. 101
Ritter	5 churches
Saxon	pop. 4,002
Shulerville	9 churches
Snelling	pop. 125
Spartenburg	
Steedman	fdd. by one of the Steedman brothers
Tillman	Jasper county; pop. 1,679
Ulmer	Allendale county; pop. 90; 5 churches
Wagener	pop. 950
Walhalla	Oconee county; pop. 3,755; Oktoberfest

Total	21
"South"	8
"North"	13
descript.	2
poss.-comm.	19
shift names	0

30. Places Named GERMAN, State of GEORGIA, in 159 counties

Adel	Cook county; pop. 5,093
Adrian	pop. 615
Berlin	pop. 480
Bloomingdale	Chatham county; pop. 2,171
Bremen	Haralson county; pop. 4,356 [Robinson Crusoe's birthplace]
Brunswick	town grid laid out by general James Oglesby in 1771; one of the five original ports of the colonies; Glynne county; incorpor. 1836; Ritz theater; pop. 16,443
Corinth	pop. 136
Dasher	Lowndes county
De Kalb	
Ebenezer	Walton county; Salzburg protestants moved here in 1736; grid plan by Matt. Seuffert; reverend J. Bolzius; Fort E. erected in 1757
Elberta	Houston county
Hinesville	Liberty county; pop. 21,603
Jasper	pop. 1,772
Ludovici	
Luthersville	Meriwether county; pop. 741
Mansfield	pop. 341
Mechanicsville	Gwinnett county
Metter	pop. 3,707
Mitchell	Glascock county; pop. 181
Nuberg	Hart county
Offerman	Pierce county; pop. 4 churches
Phillipsburg	pop. 1,044
Rentz	Laurens county; pop. 364
Rhine (Rheine)	Dodge county; pop. 466
Ringgold	Catoosa county; pop. 1,920 (1998)
Santa Claus	pop. 154
Sauter	
Schley	pop. 3,588 (1990)
Tell	Fulton county
Thalman	
Troutman	Stewart county
Vienna	Dooly county; pop. 2,708
Total	32
"South"	11
"North"	21
descript.	2

poss.-comm.	29
shift name	1

31. Places Named GERMAN, State of FLORIDA, in 67 counties

Altoona	Lake county; pop. 1,743; 5 churches
Barth	Escambia county
Basinger	Okechobee county; settled in the 1880s
Casselberry	Seminole county; pop. 24,961 (*FL Almanac:* 18,911)
Clearwater	originally Clear Water; pop. ca. 100,000
Elfers	pop. 12,356
Englewood	[guide with music!] pop. 15,025 (no such place in the *FL Almanac!*)
Felda	Hendry county
Fellsmere	Indian River county; pop. 2,179
Fort Myers	Lee county; still *Deutschenhochburg*, pop. 45,206; university
Frink	Calhoun county
Fruitville	pop. 9,808 (part of Fruitland Park; Lake county?)
Haines City	Polk county; pop. 11,683
Holder	Citrus county
Jasper	Hamilton county; pop. 2,099
Jensen Beach	Ste. Lucie county; pop. 9,884
Lutz	Hillsborough county; pop. 31,081 (not in the *FL Almanac*)
Newberry	Alachua county; pop. 1,644
Overstreth	
Sebring	fdd. by George Sebring in 1911; pop. 8,900
Seffner	post office opened 1884; Hillsborough county; pop. 37,000 (not in the *FL Almanac*)
Sparr	Marion county
Winter Garden	Orange county; pop. 9,745

Total	23
"South"	7
"North"	16
descript.	3
poss.-comm.	20
shift names	0

VII NEW ENGLAND

32. *Places Named GERMAN, State of MASSACHUSETTS, in 14 counties and 39 chartered cities, and 312 incorporated towns*

The Commonwealth of Massachusetts website "is part of an ongoing initiative"

Berlin	Worcester county; pop. 2,293
Hanover	first settled in 1649; incorporated 1727; Plymouth county; pop. 11,912; some 19th century shipbuilding; "a friendly blend of culture and country"
Lunenburg	incorporated in 1728; Worcester county; pop. approx. 10,000
Mansfield	township in 1775; had practically no German resident in 1790; pop. 16,676
Saxonville	Middlesex county

Total	5
"South"	0
"North"	5
descript.	0
Poss.-comm.	5
Shift names	0

33. *Places Named GERMAN, State of CONNECTICUT, in 8 counties, 169 towns and 22 cities*

Baltic	New London county; pop. 3,188
(East)Berlin	Hartford county; pop. 1,021
Bethel	named in 1759, township 1855; Fairfield county; pop. 17.939; firefighter museum
Hamburg	New London county
Hanover	New London county
Mansfield	18th century settlement; Hartford county; became part of Storrs Mansfield; pop. 16,117
Mechanicsville	Hartford county

Total	7
"South"	2
"North"	5
descriptive	1
poss.-comm.	6
Shift names	0

*34. Places Named GERMAN, State of RHODE ISLAND, in 5 counties, 8 cities, 31
      towns*

there are none

Total	0
"South"	0
"North"	0

*35. Places Named GERMAN, State of MAINE, in 16 counties, 22 cities, and 475
      towns*

Bethel	fdd. in 1774; Oxford county; museum
Brunswick	incorporated in 1739; Bowdoin College; Maine's largest town; was French-Canadian by 54% in 1904; boat building; pop. 14,683
Dresden	settled in 1752; incorporated1794; German settled together with French Huguenots; pop. 1,500
Frankfort	Waldo county; pop. 1,141
Fryeburg	Oxford county, pop. 1,580
Hanover	Oxford county; pop. 272
Haynesville	
Hermon	Penebscot county
Lubec	fdd. in 1811; Washington county; easternmost point of the US; gateway to Campobello island, President F. D. Roosevelt's summer hide-out Pop. 2,349
Newburgh	
Sangerville	Piscatauguis county; pop. 984
Steuben	Washington county; pop. 773
Vienna	Kennebec county
Waldoboro	fdd. 1740; pop. 1,420

Total	14
"South"	4
"North"	9
poss.-comm.	14

36. Places Named GERMAN, State of NEW HAMPSHIRE, in 10 counties, 221 towns

Berlin	settled in 1825; incorporated 1829; Coots county, "Berlinite"; pop. 11,824
Epping	Rockingham county; pop. 1,384
Hanover	settlers arrived from connecticut; town chartered 1769; Dartmouth College established 1769; world-famous private college; town pop. 9,530
Henniker	Merrimack county; pop. 1,693

Total	4
"South"	1
"North"	3
poss.-comm.	4

37. Places Named GERMAN, State of VERMONT, in 14 counties, 9 cities and 237 organized towns

Bethel	Windsor county; pop. 2,725
Hinesburg	Chittenden county; pop. 3,187
Lunenburg	Essex county; pop. 854

Total	3
"South"	1
"North"	2
poss.-comm.	3

D. *The West*:

CO, WY, MT, ID, UT, NV, NM, AZ

VIII MOUNTAIN

38. *Places Named GERMAN, State of COLORADO, in 63 counties and 261 municipalities*

Anton	Washington county; pop. 240
Black Forest	Pondarosa pines reminded German immigrants of their "Black forest"; pop. 8,143
Byers	Arapahoe county; pop. 1,065
Deckers	Douglas county
Eckley	Yuma county; pop. 211
Egnar	
Elbert	pop. 1,808
Englewood	fdd. in 1800s; settled first by Irishman Th. Skerritt in 1860; originally called Orchard Place; pop. 31,750
Flagler	Kid Carson county; pop. 564
Frederick	pop. 988
Hartman	Prowers county; pop. 108
Hayden	
Hereford	Weld county
Hoehne	Las Animas county
Jansen	Las Animas county
Keenesburg	pop. 570
Kremmling	Grand county; pop. 1,166
Lindon	
Lucerne	Weld county
New Ragmer	
Peetz	Logan county; pop. 179
Roggen	Weld county; pop. 150
Seibert	Kid Carson county; pop. 181
Snyder	Morgan county; pop. 134
Strasburg	Adams county; pop. 1,197
Swink	pop. 584
Walsenburg	Huerfano county; settled originally by Spanish farmers as Plaza de los leones middle 1800s; renamed by the mine owner Fred Walsen in 1870; pop. 3,300
Yoder	El Paso county; pop. 511

Total	28
"South"	10
"North"	18
descript.	2
poss.-comm.	26
shift names	0

39. Places Named GERMAN, State of WYOMING, in 23 counties

Alpine	pop. 200
Bosler	Albanany county; pop. 22; calls itself "ghost town"
Casper	settled near the Platte river in 1888; Natrona county; second largest city of WY; pop. 49,000; rodeos
Egbert	Laramie county
Emblem	Big Horn county; 11 churches
Kemmerer	Lincoln county; pop. 3,020; "Fossil Fish Capitol of the World"
Leiter	Sheridan county
Lingle	Goshen county; pop. 473
Nelber	
Otto	Big Horn county; pop. 120
Ulm	Sheridan county
Wolf	Sheridan county; pop. 32
Worland	fdd. 1906; named after station master "Dad" Wurland"; Washakie county; on the Old Bridger Trail;pop. 6,000
Yoder	Goshen county; pop. 136

Total	14
"South"	5
"North"	9
descript.	1
poss.-comm.	12
shift names	1

40. Places Named GERMAN, state of MONTANA, in 56 counties, ca. 125 municipalities

Bozeman	almost 30,000 inhabitants; Montana State University
Butte	Silver Bow county; was started as a silver mining place in 1864; township fdd. 1893; Gallatin county; Museum of Mining; pop. 33,941

128

Fromberg	Carbon county; pop. 370
Geyser	Judith Basin county [second such named after a woman]; pop. 289
Haugan	Mineral county
Hogeland	Blaine county; pop. 143
Lambert	Richland county; pop. 655
Loring	Phillips county; pop. 243
Luther	
Opheim	Valley county; pop. 145
Rad(k)ersberg	
St. Ignatius	pop. 778
Silesia	Carbon county
Telgen	pop. 481
Wagner	Seminole county
Zurich	Blaine county
Total	17
"South"	7
"North"	10
descript.	2
poss.-comm.	15
shift names	0

41. Places Named GERMAN, State of IDAHO, in 44 counties

Bern	Bear Lake county; pop. 261
Buhl	fdd. 1908 due to irrigation projects; pop. 3,516; "Rainbow Trout Capital of the World"
Burgdorf	ghost town
Cobalt	Lemhi county
Dietrich	fdd. 1909 due to irrigation projects; Lincoln county; pop. 127
Dingle	Bear Lake county
Ferdinand	pop. 135
Fruitvale	Adams county
Hagerman	Gooding county; pop. 600
Hamer	Jefferson county; pop. 79
Hansen	Twin Falls county; pop. 848
Hauser	pop. 380
Heise	Caribou National Forest
Huetter	pop. 82
Keuterville	

Lowman	Boise county; pop. 63
Nordman	Bonner county; pop. 446
Rupert	Minidoka county; pop. 5,455
Weippe	Clearwater county; pop. 532
Weiser	named after Peter Weiser who travelled with Lewis and Clark; Washington county; pop. 4,571
Wendell	pop. 1,963

Total	21
"South"	8
"North"	13
descript.	2
poss.-comm.	18
shift name	1

42. *Places Named GERMAN, State of UTAH, in 29 counties and 40 incorporated areas with 5000 or more inhabitants*

Altonah	Duchesne county; pop. 10
Alpine	settled in 1849; pop. 5,200
Dutch John	fdd. in the 1950s as Daggett city by the federal Bureau of Reclamation; pop. 174
Elberta	Utah county
Fruitland	Duchesne county
Lindon	Utah county; pop. 7,000
Maeser	named after principal of [the forerunner of] Brigham young University in Provo, UT; Uintah county; pop. 2,598
Yost	Box Elder county

Total	8
"South"	2
"North"	6
descript.	3
Poss.-comm.	5
shift names	0

43. *Places Named GERMAN, State of NEVADA, in 16 counties*

Gerlach	Washal county; pop. 469
Humboldt	
Luning	Mineral county; pop. 501; "ghost town"

Minden	Douglas county; pop. 1,441
Overton	Clark county; pop. 8,191; Lost City Museum
Schurz	Mineral county; pop. 617
Yerington	Lyon county; pop. 2,763

Total	7
"South"	3
"North"	4
descript.	0
Poss.-comm.	7
shift names	0

44. Places Named GERMAN, State of NEW MEXICO, in 33 counties

Carlsbad	near the Pesos river; pop. 24,952
Deming	Luna county; pop. 10,970
Engle	
Fruitland	San Juan county; pop. 819
Grier	"ghost town"
Hagerman	pop. 961
Hanover	Grant county; pop. 271
Hayden	
Springer	Colfax county; pop. 1,262

Total	9
"South"	3
"North"	6
descript.	1
poss.-comm.	8
Shift names	0

45. Places Named GERMAN, State of ARIZONA, in 14 counties

Alpine	Apache county; pop. 243
Christmas	claims started 1878; mines discovered Christmas 1881; Gila county; name change 1902; first post office 1905; homesteading began in the early 1800s; first known and settled by Eagar brothers as "Union" in 1888; renamed 1892; Apache county; White Mountains; incorporated 1948; pop. 4,840
Ehrenberg	La Paz county; pop. 1,226

131

Elfrida	Cochise county; pop. 1,655
Hayden	Gila county; pop. 909
Hereford	Cochise county; pop. 1,762
Houck	Apache county
Humboldt	(=Dewey-Humboldt) Yawapai county; pop. 3,640
Leupp	Cownino county; pop. 857
Linden	Navajo county
Mayer	Yawapai county
Olberg	Yawapai county; pop. 3,248
Seligman	Yawapai county; pop. 693
Springerville	established as a trading post by Henry Springer in 1878; incorporated as town in 1948; Apache county; pop. 2,085
Wenden	La Paz county
Wickenberg	
Winkelman	Gila county; pop. 676; mining and agricultural area
Wintersburg	Maricopa county
Wittmann	Maricopa county; pop. 789

Total	20
"South"	7
"North"	13
descript.	1
poss.-comm.	18
shift names	1

E. *Pacific Coast*:

CA, OR, WA
AK, HI

IX PACIFIC

46. Places Named GERMAN, State of CALIFORNIA, in 58 counties

Anaheim
: begun as a colony of German farmers and vintners founded by George Hansen in 1857; incorporated in 1876 in Orange county; orange growing center 1880 until 1960; 23 notable growers' firms; Disneyland [Disney is ironically a Würtemberg town name] 1955, Micky Mouse the most famous celebrity; 10th largest city of CA; pop. 301,176 (1998); principal street names from Adele to Wilhelmine named after Gn-Am pioneer women

Alpine
: fdd. by Benjamin Arnold because of asthma, "best climate in US; pop. 9,695

Belden
: Plumas county; pop. 52

Bieber
: Casson county

Bowman
: Craighead county

Carlsbad
: coastal city near San Diego; incorp. 1952; "Alt Carlsbad Hanse House Museum," mineral well; pop. 78,247

Caspar
: Mendocino county; pop. 349, "ghost town"

Coloma Site
: Sutter's Mill and the Goldrush to California 1848, replica of Saw Mill

Gerber
: Tehama county; pop. 3,337

Gorman

Healdsburg
: Sonoma county; pop. 9,469

Hornbrook
: Siskiyou county; pop. 905

Johannesburg
: Kern county; pop. 306

Kingsburg
: pop. 7,205

Korbel
: Brown-Korbel Champagne firm fdd. 1882, Humboldt county; pop. 187

Lucerne
: Lake county; pop. 2,011

Nicolaus
: Sutter county; pop. 802

Randsburg
: ex mineral ghost town, Kern county; Mojave desert; pop. 200

Rohnerville
: Humboldt county

Sanger
: began as saw mill in the late 1800s; incorp. 1911, Fresno cty; pop. 19,050

Shafter
: Kern county; pop. 8,409

| Sutter | named after Johann Augustus Sutter (1803-1880) "founder of California"; see entry Coloma; on whose farm gold was found |
| Wendel | Lasson county |

Total	22
"South"	8
"North"	14
descript.	1
Poss.-comm.	20
shift names	1

47. Places Named GERMAN, State of OREGON, in 36 counties

Adel	Lake county; pop. 190
Adrian	Malheur county; renamed after a town in Illinois; RR received right of way in 1911; pop. 140
Alpine	Benton county
Astoria	explored in 1792, and by Lewis and Clark, in 1802; Clatsop county; pop. 34,300
Birkenfield	
Breitenbush	
Coburg	Lane county; pop. 763
Elsie	
Gearhart	By the Sea; pop. 1,027
Gunter	
Haines	Baker county; pop. 405
Harlan	
Hauser	Coos county
Heppner	named for storekeeper Henry Heppner in 1887; Morrow county; pop. 2,127
Hereford	Baker county; pop. 287
Hildebrand	Klamath county
Imbler	"The grass seed capital of the world"; Union county; pop. 450
Jasper	Lane county
Keizer	Marion county; pop. pop. 21,884
Kernville	
Metzger	pop. 3,149
Mitchell	first post office in 1873; Wheeler county; pop. 163
Newberg	Oregon's first Quaker hamlet; Yamhill county; pop. 16,962
Paulina	Crrok county; pop. 98

Ritter	Grant county; pop. 71
Roseburg	Douglas county
St. Benedict	
Sutherlin	Douglas county; pop. 5,020

Total	28
"South"	11
"North"	17
descript.	2
poss.-comm.	26
shift names	0

48. Places Named GERMAN, State of WASHINGTON, in 39 counties

Benge	Adams county; pop. 2 (lowest figure given in whole US)
Bingen	(on Gorge river); pop. 645; Gorge Heritage Museum
Bremerton	fdd. by William Bremer from Germany on Puget sound as a port town in 1891; Kitsap county; pop. 38,142
Dishman	pop. 9,671
Elbe	Pierce county; pop. 103
Elberton	Whitman county
Ellensburg	pop. 12,361; Central Washington State University; rodeos
Fruitland	Stevens county; pop. 515
Geiger Heights	
Hansville	Kitsap county; pop. 1,256
Heisson	Clark county
Husum	Klickitat county
Keller	Ferry county; pop. 255
Lucerne	Maple Valley
Lynden	settled in the 1860s; Whatcom county; pop. 12,896
Mansfield	pop. 31
Marlin (Krupp)	Grant county; pop. 856
Mohler	Lincoln county
Nordland	Jefferson; pop. 738
Prosser	pop. 4,476
Rosburg	Washkiakum county; pop. 279
Seabold	
Shoultes	
Waitsburg	Walla Walla county; pop. 990

Total	24
"South"	7

"North"	14
descript.	4
poss.-comm.	20
shift names	0

49. *Places Named GERMAN, State of ALASKA, no counties, but 8 boroughs and 128 municipalities*

Bethel
Deering
Dutch Harbor
Fritz Creek
Hyder
Meyers Chuck

Total	6
"South"	2
"North"	4
descript.	1
poss.-comm.	5

50. *HAWAII No Places Named GERMAN*

Total	0

Comparative Results:

Total US	1,664	100%	1990	
"North"	1,056	63%	1990	
"South"	588	36%	1990	
Non-German	20	1%	1913-1990	
Loss of Names	388	~ 23%	1913-1990	
Gain of Names	524	~ 47%	1913-1990	[partially overlapping with the above]
Net Surplus	166	~ 24%	1913-1990	[partially the same names]
Total CANADA	318	100%	1996	
"North"	176	55%	1996	
"South"	135	43%	1996	
Non-German	32	10%	1996	
Net Loss	88	~ 32%	1867-1996[11]	

No over-all pattern in the types of places founded (except the adaptation to the American "grid" system) is discernible. The whole gamut of hamlets, villages, communities, neighborhoods, home towns, district (or larger) towns, and cities, is represented. Obviously, "Little Germanies", on the other hand, do not exist in the Old Country.

Further research in settlement patterns needs to be carried out on a state-by-state and a provincial basis.

---

[11]Cohortive German groups stay intact geographically longer in the US than their brethren in CANADA; Germanness is made still cohesive in Saskatchewan and Manitoba by the continuous use of *Plattdeutsch/Plautdietsch* making for cultural differences.

Chapter 4
Comparative results and hindsight perspectives on the
co-founding processes

During a seventy years time span, 1820-1890, the twelve WEST NORTH
CENTRAL "states" were founded, integrated and admitted to statehood. On an
administrative level they consist of roughly more than a thousand counties. I
compared Dr. Joseph Och's figures of co-founded "German" places (1913,
reflecting the 1910 census) with *Funk &Wagnall's Hammond World Atlas*
(1980) entries which had stayed extant and were included. I checked the names
against the internet website entries of these places as to the year of their co-
founding, if known, and their present population (reflecting 1990 or 2000), as
well as their history, if listed there. Usually the so-called "City Resource Guide"
became my source. It was not always listed in first place, but occurred
sometimes as late as page 20 on their material to be scrolled from *Google.de,*
downloading *America. Digital-Neighbors* or *City Resource Guides*. The
Canadian statcan.ca is easier to handle, since it indicates the name's continuation
of a township even to the level of a subdivision.

A. US

In this WEST NORTH CENTRAL census area there are retrospectively roughly
630 German named places left shortly before the end of the 20th century, in size
anywhere between 20 (rarely only 7) and 50,000 inhabitants. Of the places
referred to as villages, municipalities, towns or cities [with varying numbers of
divisions among them], roughly 400, or 64%, belong to the Northwestern
German naming sphere. These name givers left the Old Country not necessarily
from exactly the namesake area or town, but as a rule, not too far from there. I
am not arguing that the founders of all Hanovers originated from Hannover.
Often the dynasty was meant to be honored. But those giving the names felt at
least an attraction for the name that, in their mind, possessed certain qualities
and made them reminisce e.g. of the dukedom or the dynastic line of King
George IV, who has a statue honoring him in front of the great hall of the
Landesuniversität Göttingen, where many English and American students liked
to study until 1900, if not longer. The remaining percents are not exactly 36%
Southern German on the dot, but roughly so. At least they belong to that
different sphere of influence close to that percentage, with the exception of a few
non German name co-foundations, f. i. Grand Island, Quincy, and a few others.

There might have been an attraction by American mountains and
mountainous states on High German speaking South Germans. It is characteristic
of the Mountain states that they sometimes look "alpine" to Germans, as the
flatlands normally should have been attractive to the "Low German" speaking

138

Plattdeutsche. But we found no simple correlation of that sort in our deliberations. Far Western states are not densely populated by German immigrants as is the Middle West to begin with. The percentages, 63% of the places, somewhere named in the Northwestern German fashion, vs. 36% the Southern German kind elsewhere are every bit as real as the same percentage-wise distribution of cities in the Old Country's German urban history.[12] If immigration history happens on a sufficiently large scale, the laws of big numbers seem to hold true on a different continent, settled by such people also. This is different in Canada, where many German immigrants, whose primary loyalty concerned the language use, and not their origination from the *Reich*, started their emigration in Russia, where they had been invited to by the Czarina Catherine the Great.

The possessive-commemorative naming category in the sense of Adrian Room shows at least 481 names, and some 100 descriptive, and 35 shift names, in the NORTH WEST CENTRAL census area of the twelve states, which happen to have the highest percentage of "German" immigration during the 19th century. There are roughly 25 names, two on average per state within the EAST and WEST NORTH CENTRAL areas that were co-founded by "German" settlers commemorating an American personality. The reader is requested to compare the figures in the end tables with the ones of areas or area groups, named here for convenience, A to E.

Of the nine large cities none has a recognizable "German sounding" name. They may have a larger or smaller percentage of German heritage Americans left, but these would be more difficult to ascertain nowadays than, shall we say, a hundred years ago. The self-identification with the "German sounding" co-founding past is easier to fathom in smaller rural surroundings, where people have known each other sometimes for generations.

This book does not enter into speculation about whether particular towns admit, betray, or fancy an larger than average ethnic heritage, unless such places, large or small, make such a point of self-identification on their website with official sanction. To my knowledge there are on average no more than two to four such places left per state with a critical mass to maintain identification with or just be sentimental about the Old Country from the perspective of past local history. Sometimes this heritage is a true part of local resources, and is then interesting and differentiated enough to be mentioned as part of a common history. Ironically there come to mind two or three non-German sounding city names, Washington, MO, and the old capital of Illinois, named Vandalia, IL,

---

[12]Keyser-Stoob, *Städtebücher*, elaborated throughout their 5 volumes that this very cofounding statistical distribution, 64% of all historical German cities *(Gründerstädte)* in the Old Germany area were Northern or Northwestern placed, 36% Southern and Southeastern placed, off the Benrath line. Our statistics bore out that similarity between the two countries' settlement areas. It follows that the Mason-Dixon line *cannot* be compared to the Benrath line.

which district young congressman Abraham Lincoln once represented in the House of Representatives, as well as perhaps Sheboygan, WI. Another irony might be seen in the name of the hometown of Lawrence Welk, Strasburg, ND, founded by Germans from Russia, among them his parents, one year before his birth. Ironically the *kitschige* Lawrence Welk Show, ("A one, a two...") begun on television in 1955, a critical time, may have done more for re-evaluating solid, but pleasurable things German than anything in the format of talk shows or parades could have.

Obviously some of these solid and protective heritage traditions, for instance in Missouri, are five generations strong by now, some are more recent. How did they meet or conglomerate? We don't know in detail, and therefore cannot construct a model. But the most important component and factor may well be the inter-ethnic marriage pattern.

The intermarriage cohort pattern, practised in 17th and 18th century New York may have been continued only partially here. "Cohortiveness" here (and subsequently) may refer only to a vague reputation, or to shared reminiscences, rather than the residue of genuine ethnic loyalty. Was there wide-spread primary and secondary loyalty in the first generation toward "Germany", followed by the feeling for the U.S., and, in the second generation, first toward the home country, the US, and a subordinated loyalty toward the Old Country, as formerly represented by one's parents or grandparents? The longevity of one`s secondary loyalty cultivation does not depend on the size of the home community, except that the use of the German language during the Lutheran Sunday sermon could survive longer in such small towns, as Altenburg, MO, or New Melle, MO. This attachment, according to Kamphoefner, may have had quite a bit to do with Westfalian stubbornness. But there is more to it.

In the *Plattdeutsch* speaking household the most important cohort is the farmer's wife, and her control of the farm home, which combined most farm functions, including stalls.. The Lower Saxon combined farm house had one or two posts (*Ständer*), and was never "clapt up" like a Massachusetts farm house without cellar. The purpose of this Dutch farm house was maximum space with a high ceiling, which could be cleared by a hay wagon returning home. The hearth really formed the center of a housewife's and mother's activity. From that vantage point she was able to see and control pretty much every activity without frenetically moving about, at one and the same glance seeing the fire, smelling the dish, seeing the children and the cattle, and for that matter, the people coming and going, and the traffic to and from the farm. The people had to come to her, as it were, and receive orders from her as if she minded a commando bridge. The 18th century Osnabrück cultural critic , the so-called *Anwalt des Vaterlandes* (comparable to attorney general) Justus Möser,(1720-1794), who was governed by a British royal bishop,[13] was full of praise for this farmhouse

[13]Frederick, Duke of York, King George III's son; see the entry for Osnabruck, Ontario.

140

construction. He stated that even Vitruvius could not devise a better plan.[14] These types of practical farm houses were brought over to Pennsylvania and Missouri, and must be considered part of the home's success story. Nothing supports a house better and protects all dwellers than one secured by posts carrying the roof overall providing security and comfort to all members.

Our observations verify that rural areas seem to preserve traditions longer and ultimately also see them wither away or phase out and die. This is literally true: cemeteries survive even ghost towns. This process is due to a lack of a critical mass of inhabitants. Big cities may more openly preserve traditions and reminiscences and collect them as well as invite research of the heritage's ultimate origin as a research endeavour at the university or museum level. Apart from adjustments and frequent American intermarriages, the pattern registered betrays interior mobility within a census area or across the length of the US, or a move from the city to the suburbs, e.g.. from Cleveland, OH, to the surrounding Cuyahoga county, where four times as many inhabitants with a large "German American background" live presently than used to live in Cleveland. Such a flight from the inner city may reflect and sometimes reconstitute a heritage in a secondary way. It is likely that some Americans of the heritage in question feel only "fully" like German Americans during festivals, such as Octoberfest, Bremenfest in New Bremen, OH, or during a Steuben Parade, but not consistently during the working part of an entire calendar year.

It would be very difficult to come up with a model in regard to the inclusion of rural-suburban villages a couple of miles up or down the river that preserve markers of their former significance in "German American" profiled cities such as Cincinnati or Cleveland[15]. The different former and subsequent population percentages cannot simply be subtracted or added, except by comparing other rising or sinking heritage percentages. In other migration research this is conveniently represented by circular diagrams in the shape of a pie. But even those lose significance and become less representative as time wears on.

Whichever major and minor groups participated in the making of North America, their descendants do not necessarily remember their adequate share quantitatively, and may not have been reckoned with and counted in every modern census.[16] Also it must be admitted that descendents who no longer

---

[14]"Die Häuser des Landmannes im Osnabrückischen sind in ihrem Plan die besten," *Osnabrücker Intelligenzblätter* v. 7. 3. 1767, rp. vol. III, chapter XXXVI, p. 143, ed. by his daughter J. W. J. v. Voigts, geb. Möser. Möser had been in England and was thus familiar with other farm houses.

[15]Neither named after the Rhenish name nor after President Grover Cleveland, but after the Connceticut surveyor Moses Cleaveland, measuring Connecticut's Western Reserve.

[16]Fredericksburg, TX, according to the *Handbook of Texas Cities. Online*, was omitted from the census before 1930. One may duly wonder how widespread such incidences may have been, and for what reasons other than negligence these lapses occurred.

understand, let alone speak or read German understandably may relate differently to *Olle Kamellen* (old family lore and anecdotes).

I find remarkable how a smaller town such as Little Oldenburg, NE, can organize annual *Plattdeutsche Konferenzen*, to actively keep the local knowledge of Low(er) German alive. On the other hand it is almost equally impressive how a medium-sized city such as Jasper, IN, as a living entity "reflects the predominantly German heritage." Most impressive I find the electronic self-representation of Milwaukee, WI, "as an intellectual capital of the State" in terms of its multi-slide website design offering the multi-cultural facets in images of energy and drive toward making use of the heritage as resource. A prospective visitor or someone on the move to Milwaukee can take heed of the residual resource value without the community belaboring its worth. For example. the old "German-style" downtown facades, restored to new sheen, offer services and protection to all Milwaukeeans alike. That can make the restored Flemish Renaissance style of the old City Hall appealing to every citizen (or visitor), whatever his or her background. This city seems to have found a method of splicing together the majority and the minority taste, the old, but well-worn, and the expectant new. Both features seem to share a technical focus and *Gemütlichkeit* as well for enjoying and for working, but really for enjoying working. It does not even expressly mention the German American heritage. There is just a lingering suggestion of it that makes you care. On the other hand, to my mind, with all due respect, the city of Cincinnati may slightly overstate the role of her "deep German heritage." This may be due to long-term neglect and deprecation. But it may only sound like an overstatement to an outsider, and may be mellifluous to many a Cuyahogan ear? The sigh of relief can be understood and appreciated that "the lingering stigma of things German" has finally been overcome. Besides it is a good sign of growing urban tolerance of the majority and of self-assurance of the strengthened minority. However a more unequivocal welcoming of the new downtown black tenants might have cushioned the blow of having to admit to "abandoning subway transit tunnels". This urban neglect leading to decay is officially stated with an obvious bad conscience.

Concerning the smaller towns: without heritage libraries or museums it would have been that much harder to preserve and integrate the heritage worth preserving. Concerning the larger cities: colleges and universities may preserve the surrounding (sometimes sponsoring) collective heritage as intellectual part resource or by sheer exuberance in digging up roots in different media.

In the 21st century, where images will play such substantial roles, the website self-representation of a place makes a big difference. Nothing is more self damaging than having to state in the www. city guides under statistics and facts: "N/A," that is, "non-applicable." This clearly is an admission, we don't want you to know how low the number of residents has sunken. Some guides laconically supply the information: seven residents in one case. You can take pride in such a small number of people as well. In these cases founders would like to maintain: some of these good people are still around. We are not yet a ghost town!

If we now see the EAST NORTH CENTRAL census area as a unit with the strongest rural and city representation of German Americana, well above the national average, and compare the WEST NORTH CENTRAL area as a unit, we can state these differences to the next settled group unit, in the SOUTH CENTRAL area, fewer but still better than average representation took root on the countryside, and developed through a century and a half of constantly replenished, though ebbing, cultivation by "Germans". Contrary to the North no big city with above average German influx developed into an above average German American peopled city. That is so even in Texas, where the influx was strong and lasting, e.g. into the San Antonio and the early Galveston areas. Three medium seized cities of above 10,000 residents come to mind, New Braunfels with 27.334 residents, Rosenberg with 22,577, and Schertz with 10,555 residents in Texas. We find one city, planned as a German Harmonist colony town of nowadays 43,000 residents.

Obviously the strength of this great rural influx lay in the agricultural achievement, methodical and stubborn improvement by crop rotation and the right amount of fertilization with the result of a larger than average yield per acre, sometimes due to better farm equipment and community practices and use.
The Louisiana Sale and Purchase provided the US with the greatest granary reservoir the nation has. The joining of Texas with the largest longhorn cattle breeding provided the territorial size and the grazing ground. The German American farmers in both the NORTH CENTRAL census areas provided outstanding and recognized craftsmanship in respect to husbandry. They worked as cohorts, that is successfully together. Generally substantial wealth was gained for these farmers themselves and for the good of the country.

If one now compares WEST and EAST NORTH CENTRAL states as a double unit group to WEST and EAST SOUTH CENTRAL, also as a double unit group, that is in a "quadrupled" way, we clearly have an antagonism between the US "North" and "South", both before and after the Civil War. There are no big German American style metropolitan cities in the whole "South", not even in Texas that were planned as German foundations or co-foundations. There are several strongly residual medium seized cities in Texas. But these cannot be compared with the metropolitan areas around the Upper Lakes or in the Mississippi-Missouri Valley. In fact, the German North[western]erners, broadly speaking, founded their places mostly among the American North[west]erners. In the four census areas attracting the most Germans to America, the Northern leaning states WI, IA, [ND], NE, MN, IN, OH, and the border state MO stand first, followed by PA. TX stands out as the Southern state with a strong 19th century German American component. Florida is moving up in the last decade. The "rest", as huge as it is, with the exception perhaps of Kansas,

143

ebbs off in this respect. The pivotal border states of the Civil War, MO/KY/WV, produced enough regiments, among them prominent German companies, to tip the scales in favor of the North.

The fourfold block areas, *Extended North* and *Extended South*, with 3,500,000 km², feature mainly agriculture as their main means of production. This is not only heartland USA, but also the nucleus of the German American heritage territory as well. It is different in the *West* with its eight mountain states of together 2,237,000 km², which are mainly breeding and feeding cattle areas. It is a much less densely populated area, and hence has fewer Americans with this particular ethnic background than the *Extended North/South* areas. According to the standard work of German geography[17] the majority of "Germans" historically migrated to the rural areas of North America, in the 17th century to New York; in the 18th century to Pennsylvania, Virginia and Georgia, in the 19th century to Missouri, Wisconsin, and Texas until roughly 1870.

Their knowledge of Low(er) German or *Plattdeutsch*, coupled with their protestant denomination, "alleviated this assimilation [process]".[18] The later 19thh century push went into the bigger towns, harbor towns, and cities generally. Preference was given to Milwaukee, Chicago, and Baltimore (see end table 8). Milwaukee, WI, is generally considered the most German looking city in the USA, but Wisconsin as a state is not necessarily the number one state in this regard. It is probably surpassed by Missouri and Indiana as to the number of German ancestry concentration. The two states have readers for their *Abendpost und Milwaukee deutsche Zeitung*, which absorbed the *Detroit Zeitung* in 1991, and is also read in Chicago. Sheboygan, WI, has an active city twinning program with Esslingen, Würtemberg, Germany. Another higher concentration of German heritage elements or roots is found in Indiana, the "Hoosier" state. Although not listed as a viable explanation among American nicknames, I would like to define *Hoosier* as a German word *"Hausier"* (instead of *Hausierer*, as it is used today), a "circuit riding small businessman or *"Kurzwaren[wander]händler,"*(haberdasher[19]) with a meaning very similar to "yankee". Indiana is a state of great diversity, has fertile plains in the North as well as industrial steel production, mineral resources such as bituminous coal, petroleum and natural gas. Indiana, slightly before Illinois, but equally as strong as Wisconsin, has a strong German heritage, and all three had the largest residual population of German Americans with their diversified heritage.[20] Individually, by the sheer

[17]*Harms Erdkunde Band VI Amerika.* 1970.

[18]*Harms*, p. 20.

[19]Although the dictionaries mark a Middle French origin, it would be challenging to prove that it originated from an old German imperative, *"habe das hier"* (buy this one!) with a meaning of "measuring dealer", along the lines of *habenichts, haberecht*.

[20]See the old figures of 1890 represented by a "pie structure" in *Deutsche in Amerika.* TU Dresden 1994.

force of numbers, as well as thanks to their ancestors' founding activities in these states from the beginning until roughly 1900 they retain German heritage. According to *Hammond Atlas of the United States History* (1989) the cities Pittsburgh, Cleveland, Detroit, Cincinnati, Milwaukee, St. Louis, Kansas City, and Denver are surrounded by "a predominantly German [American] population".[21] This includes the cities themselves, which would be in continuation of the data collected by Rossnagel[22] in the late twenties of the last century, perhaps slightly stretching the point. Thus there would be a belt encompassing a huge across-the-board East-West stretching area from Pennsylvania to Northern and Central Ohio, Indiana, including the entire WEST NORTH CENTRAL area with its seven states, Montana, and northern Idaho.

Although my studies basically concur, I arrived at my findings in a different way and by collecting different data. If one would allow for two groups of very large cities, in which a certain amount of German immigrant influence was constitutive and still visible, the most pronounced would be Milwaukee, St. Louis, and Chicago, in that order, followed in group II by Philadelphia and, with some reservations, Baltimore. In the separate category of State capitals, only Bismarck, N. D. and Madison, WI should be listed. In the category of states, my comparative observations lead me to this ranking of measurable German American resource stamina: Texas, Missouri, Indiana, Iowa, the Dakotas and Pennsylvania, Wisconsin and Ohio, in that order. Possible corrections and qualifications to the massive ethnic distribution pattern were gleaned from my state tables, First to Fiftieth State. Lacunae – e.g. no German place name found in the State of Rhode Island – and their "losses" are expressed by blanks in the US, and by a hyphen in Canada."Losses," in my opinion, express or camouflage adverse economic conditions, natural disasters, or sheer remoteness, and the dwindling of the populations, rather than an oddity of a foreign sounding German place name and culture. Although an equally noticeable belt is found north of the border to Canada, Saskatchewan and Manitoba have strong minority ethnic territories and area pockets themselves.

The German immigration to the *West* came too late, and stayed comparatively too individual, island-like, non-chain-settling to make a sizeable dent in the majority "ethnic pie". Although there remain sizeable pockets of "German" settlements in Colorado, Oregon and Northern Washington, our point of view focuses on urban comparisons, founding by area. It has proven the practice of a very solid cohort settling technique with roots, immigrant presence, and on-going projection into the future.

[21]Page U-54.

[22]Paul Rossnagel, *Die Stadtbevölkerung der Vereinigten Staaten*. Tübingen 1928; see also my Table 7.

B. Canada

Nobody today views Canada from an old-fashioned Eurocentric point of view. That is to say, Canada should not be eyed through a map manufactured in Europe (or the US, for that matter) centuries ago. The vast available space for settlementshould not be defined as a Northern annex to the modern US dominated continent.

The perspectives on group history of the German Canadians were dominated by American, rather than Canadian scholars, well into the 20th century. *Deutsch-Kanadische Landesgeschichte* as a discipline is rather colorless to read.[23] Actually the scientific inquiry into this geographical history branch was started by exhaustive field work of a young professor-to-be Heinz Lehmann (1907-1985). He published his trailblazing work in two volumes.[24] After a time lapse of almost fifty years a noted German Canadian modern historian, Gerhard P. Bassler, translated, edited and introduced the two parts in one well-integrated volume as Heinz Lehmann. *The German Canadians 1750–1937: Immigration, Settlement and Culture*. Jesperson Press St. John's, Newfoundland 1986. Realizing that Lehman and himself had achieved groundbreaking spade work, professor Bassler followed up by striking out with a handier volume, which he intended to become a standard historical reference book. It is true that this reference book is written from a federal perspective and published in both languages. It follows the method, then en vogue, of proceeding backwards from the 20th to the 19th, 18th and finally the 17th century. It also adheres to the filiopietal approach. I did not have the chance to compare the original English version of 1991/92 with the German edition, which I have, of 1993.[25] He compares Canadian main history with German Canadian contributory history, whereas I compare German American settlement history with German Canadian settlement history with respect to the founding of places in either country.

Independent of the point of view of the place where settlements took place, immigration history has to come to grips with the fact that eventually the push into which ever remote area has to thin out and thus lose steam. Different from the Western settlement by some Germans in the US, the Canadians who brought the use of the German language to Western Canada often did not hail from Germany, but were Mennonite[26] "Russlanders" speaking a version of *Platt-deutsch,* called *Plautdietsch* by them. They migrated from an array of other non-

[23]Karl Lenz, Wissenschaftliche Länderkunde Band 30. *Kanada. Eine geographische Landes-kunde.* Wissenschaftliche Buchgesellschaft Darmstadt 1988.

[24]*Das Deutschtum in Ostkanada* (Stuttgart 1931) and *Das Deutschtum in Westkanada* (Berlin 1939).

[25]Gerhard P. Bassler, *Das Deutschkanadische Mosaik Heute und Gestern.* No copyright. Deutschkanadischer Kongreß Ottawa 1991, recte 1993 (?).

[26]See *Journal of Mennonite Studies*, ed. by Harry Loewen, 16 vol.s issued so far; *Mennonite Historian*, ed. by Lawrence Kleppenstein, 25 vol.s so far.

German countries, which do not exist in the same borders any more today. Changing a treeless prairie into wheat country such as in Sasketchewan is not the same as changing woods into beef grazing country in Wyoming. It may not only call for a different background, but perhaps also for a different mentality.

Professor Hartmut Froeschle from the University of Toronto in his research report[27] stresses that a new, modern discipline, which he refers to as "Canadistics" (*Kanadistik*) had arisen as a sub-discipline of history, which was to be freed from US American (political) value judgments.[28]

The problems involved in this *desideratum* are not as easily handled and overcome, as one might assume. To begin with, after the 1850s, the German Canadian immigration caused congestion in southwestern Ontario, so that Lutheran protestants prevailed as competitors over Catholic settlers in Canada too, as they had in the US from the very beginning, except for Maryland. Most researchers erroneously assume that the Catholic German immigrant was the more frequent emigrant, ,an unfounded opinion. In Eastern Canada a German Canadian middle class could form in medium seized to bigger seized townships. In Western Canada a predominantly agricultural populace formed settlement islands. Since chances for a survival and then growth of a minority enclave rise in proportion to their level of cultural attainment, this achievement switched its primary loyalty to English and its implied guiding function. The faster the upward mobility, the lesser the bond to the old-ways culture. It follows that the original ethnic bond weakens as the center of one's ethnic identity. This is not a matter of absorption alone, but of inevitable growth of adaptation, and voluntary commitment to citizenship.

One of the key questions to tackle now is: do Canadians of German descent occasionally transit back to grandmother's seemingly outworn values, or have they abandoned reminiscences of that sort altogether? Will, for example, some readers who know or suspect that they have such a background, look up one of the lists, to find the place where his or her grandparents landed, Or will the collective feeling for things and people in the present prevent majority Canadians from reopening the past? What, furthermore, is the experience of Canadian viewers of Museums, say in Lunenburg, [29] Nova Scotia, or a memorial hall for Sir Adam Beck (1857-1925), the founder and "king" of the Ontario Hydro Power company. It is he who was knighted for his services to Canada by King George V in 1914. For Sir Beck from Germany was, in Heinz Lehmann's words, "the only German in Canada, who has made history."[30]

---

[27]"Deutschkanadische Studien: Entwicklung, Stand und Problematik", *Zeitschrift für Kanada-Studien.* 15. Jahrgang/ Nr. 2, vol. 28 /Augsburg 1995), pp. 131-140.

[28]This caveat was first advanced by Don H. Tolzmann, Cincinnati, in 1988.

[29]This is the way *Lüneburg* was spelled in the 18th century.

[30]*The German Canadians 1750-1937*, p. 73.

It is the two Canadian railroads that were left over from the conglomeration fight, the CNR and the CPR, that established a rail net which transformed the continent,[31] the Queen's Highways (the Canadian equivalent to the US Interstate), the electric and telephone companies, and now the internet connections, which made the twentieth century kind to Canada. Canada was pulled beyond her protective international boundary and her differentiated cultures. This continentalism sooner or later had to be challenged by some of the more favored provinces such as British Columbia.

But British North America managed not only to settle its own West north of the 49th parallelwhich had been fixed in 1818 and guaranteed in 1846. The Act of reuniting the "Upper" [Ontario] and Lower [Quebec] Canadas of 1841 helped as much as the fusion of the Hudson Bay and the Northwest companies had twenty years before. Bytown-Ottawa was chosen capital of Canada. And their own Canadian goldrush (not yet *ho for Clondike!*) helped in the founding of British Columbia by attracting "worthies" to the West.

The Free Trade Reciprocity Treaty concluded with the U. S. in 1854 stabilized commerce on either side of the new border. While the Canadian founding representatives where busy negotiating the British North America Act of Confederation, Washington instead of Ottawa snatched away the last big prize of the Northwest: Alaska.

While the German speaking wheat farmers produced the food for the people of the rapidly expanding Canadian West, peace in the land was kept by the Royal Northwest Mounted Police, much respected and nicknamed the "Canadian Mounties", who still control the order of the day on horseback like in the good old days, as if patrolling Piccadilly Circus.

As we have seen, the change and loss of names is a rather common phenomenon in North America. It is not so much a matter of the changing of the guard in colonial power structures and control from abroad. Rather the residents themselves wish to change their identity. This may be triggered by the wind of political change, new immigration waves, different notions of looking at the past and so on. Also the appreciation of foreign names abroad must stay pegged to the general estimation of the minority culture, which may sink lower than anticipated by the time of the name giving. Since Canada suffered higher per capita military losses during World War Two than the US, the percentage of German place name loss is higher. First the name losses in Canada (1.) , then the ones in the United States (2.) will be introduced.

---

[31] James E. Vance, JR (1925-1999), *The North American Railroad: Instrument of National Development*. The Johns Hopkins University Press 1995.

C. A Comparison of name losses in Canada and the US

1. Lost German Place Names in Canada by the 1996 Census

Albergthal
Alt-Altona
Beisecker
Berfeld
Bernhart
Berlin
Bismarck
Blumenfeld
Blumenhof
Blumenhorst
Blumenstein
Blumenthal
Didsburg
Edenthal
Eichenfeld
Eisner Cove
Engelfeld
Frankburg
Frankfort
Freiburg
Friedenthal (twice)
Friedrichsburg
Gaetz Cove
Gleichen
Gnadenfeld
Gnadenthal
Goerlitz
Gorlik

Gotha Point
Grossweide
Grunwald
Herbert
Hiebert
Hoffnungsfeld
Hoffnungsthal
Jacobsberg
Josephsberg (twice)
Josephsburg
Karmelheim
Katharinenthal
Koch's Point
Kronberg
Krothal
Kronsthal
Krugersdorf
Landau
Landestreu
Landsheet
Landshut
Lorembec
Lutherhort
Lutz
Mariahilf
Neuanlage
Neu-Elsass
Neuendorf

Neu-Kronsthal
Oldenburg
Olgafeld
Osterwick
Osterwieck
Rastatt
Rheinfeld
Rheinfeldt
Rheinland
Rhineland
Rosenbach
Rosenthal (twice)
Rudolf Point
Sanstaedt
Schanzenfeld
Schefferville
Schoendorf
Schoenfeld
Schorle
Seltz
Siemens
Staufer
Strassburg (twice)
Vogler Cove
Vollmer
Waldheim (twice)
Wien

Total	88
"North"	39
"South"	48
descript.	9
poss.-comm.	74
shift names	5

2. Lost German Place Names in the US since 1913

Abert
Ableman
Ackerman(ville)
Ackerville
Adam
Adelwolf
Allard
Alplaus
Anhalt
Arnt
Audenried

Brachmanville
Banner
Barthold
Bechler
Bechtelsville
Bergholt
Berholtz
Bittner
Blocksburg
Boardman
Boleman
Bonner
Brandsville
Brenner
Buckman
Burbank
Burgen
Burgetstown
Buschberg

Cleversberg
Coesfield
Constance
Cushing
Cushman

Dahlgren
Denman

Diller
Dolberg
Drehersville
Dresbach

Dryburg
Durst

Ebensburg
Eberle
Eckmansville
Emaus
Eno
Enoch
Erasmus

Farnum
Felden
Fetterman
Feuersville
Friedberg
Friedens
Friedensau
Friedensburg
Friedheim

Gano
Gans
Gail
Gnadenhütten
Godefroy
Goethe
Goetz
Goldner
Goodhart
Gorner
Gosper
Graffschap
Grönup
Greiner

Grimms
Groesbeck
Grundy
Gutman

Haasville
Hagamann
Hagansport
Haglerville
Halleck
Hardman
Hardtner

Hartmonsville
Hartranft
Harz (Harts)
Hausertown
Haverstraw
Hecktown
Heidenheimer
Heidlersburg
Heidtville
Heilmansdale
Heilsberg
Heim
Heineman
Heinrichtown
Heislerville
Heller
Hellertown
Helmer
Hemple
Heun
Hilgard
Hillmann
Hinkle
Hinze
Hitterdal
Hiteman
Hites

Hochheim
Holder
Holderbaum
Homan
Hostetter
Houcktown
Hubbard (Hubert)
Huff (Hoff)
Huffman
Hultman
Hurt
Hutton (Hutten)
Hyman
Hyndman

Immermere
Interwald

Jansenville
Janssen

Kalmer
Kantner
Kantz
Kehler
Ketterman
Kidder
Kieferville
Kiel
Kieler
Klaus
Kleburg
Klecknersville
Klinger
Klink
Knittel
Knoll
Knopf
Koehler
Kohn
Koelztown
Koepenick

Korn
Kramer
Krams
Kreamer
Kreidersville
Kreischerville

Lamborn
Landeck
Landenburg
Landgraff
Landisburg, -ville
Lang
Langedahl
Lebeck
Leber
Leisenring
Lenzburg
Lester (Leister)
Levering
Lick
Lindermans

Macksburg
Mecksville
Mariastein

Martin (ville)
Mehlville
Melber
Meltzer
Meppen
Mertens
Mott
Mühlenberg
Munch

Nagle
Naumburg
Neffs
Neihart
Nix

Nordhoff
Nussman
Nyman

Oberon
Oerman
Olden
Osterhout
Overbeck
Overpeck
Oversteg

Paderborn
Palatine
Pender (grass)
Plumer
Plaummer
Pommerania
Primus

Quitman

Raber
Raft
Ram
Rang
Ranger
Ranken
Rappsburg
Raubsville
Rauchtown
Rauschs

Rieder
Reck
Reckford
Reichert
Rein
Reinholds
Reisor
Rembert
Rempel

151

Rex/Rix -burg
Rexford
Rexville
Rhinehard
Rittman
Rober
Rock
Roding
Rodman
Rohrsburg
Rosser
Roten
Rothville
Rucker
Rucksville
Ruckman

Sanders
Saxony
Schalks
Schaapman
Schaumberg
Schell
Schenevus (Schönfuß)
Schiller
Schleicher
Schleisingerville
Schlesser
Scholls
Scholten
Schulenburg
Schwartsburg
Schwanville
Seigler
Seigling (sville)
Seiling
Selden
Selig

Setser
Sett
Schiffer

Schaver
Scheller
Schellman
Shiner
Shoup (Schupp)
Shubert
Shuff
Shumansville
Sigel
Siglerville
Sigman
Siler (Seiler)
Simonsville
Sittler
Spangler
Spann
Speight (Specht)
Speelman
Sperbeck
Spilmann(s)
Staatsburg
Stahlstown
Steger
Steinman
Steinmetz
Steinsville
Steintal
Stine (sville)
Stites (Steitz)
Stover (Stober)
Strang
Straubville
Straus(s)
Strickersville
Strickland
Strickler
Strobel
Strother
Stroups (Strupps)
Studebaker (Stutenbäcker)
Stuebner
Stultz

Sunderlin (Sonderling)
Swart

Tannehill
Tanner
Teck
Thielman
Thiensville
Tice (Thciss)
Timmermann
Trout- (Traut-)
Tuckerman

Ulen
Uhland
Uhler
Ulman

Wacker
Waggaman
Wagram
Waikel
Waitman
Waller (Pilger)
Walther
Waltz
Wareneck
Warne
Warnecke
Waymansville
Weber
Weida
Weigand
Weikert
Weil
Wein
Weisburg
Weisenburg
Welker
Wetsel
Wetzel
Wever

Weyerts	Wiltsee	Zanesville
Waidman	Wishart	Zeigler (-ville)
Wiehle	Witmer	Zittau
Wier	Worner	Zollarsville
Wightman	Wuerttemberg	Zornville
Wilber	Wurtsboro	Zucker
Wilholt	Wy(c)koff	Zumwalt
Wilmer	Wyman	Zwanzig
Wilmerding		

Total	380
"North"	200
"South"	180
descript.	9
poss.-comm.	366
shift names	2

3. Comparison of the name losses

In comparing the disappeared or disused GERMAN names of CANADA to the ones given up in the US it can be stated that they do not correlate. Not a single same place name other than one or two of world renown is found on either list that overlaps. Although the two active names lists correlate slightly, particularly by making use of the same commemorative material, there are a few "losses" on the Canadian list which stayed in use as place names in the US. The leading German place name losers are:

Pennsylvania with 31 losses or 20%, Indiana with 22, 3%. Michigan with 19%, 4 a/b Kansas and Illinois at 16% each, 5. Minnesota with 13, 6% a/ b Maryland and Tennessee with 11% each, and 7 a/ b/ c Missouri, North Dakota and Louisiana with 10% each. By comparison Texas gave up on 8% of her German derived place names, just as much as Ontario did. Whether this has something to do with the fact that the first German settlers arrived during the time when Texas was an independent republic with reverberations of some special kind, needs not to be decided here. Texas is non-pareil as a "Lone Star" and as such defies comparisons. Ontario again took in the most of German hyphenate Canadians of all provinces after World War II.

The loss of percentages are much higher in CANADA. Alberta experienced a loss rate of GERMAN named places of 40%, Nova Scotia of 35%, Manitoba 31%, Saskatchewan 30%, and Ontario 8%. Traditionally the colony of Upper Canada and the successive Province of Ontario with the highest German immigration rate in all of CANADA explains the much lower loss rate.

Since the majority of the names in disuse are possessive-commemorative (84% on the Canadian, 96% on the American list), the name loss is not tied to far-fetched descriptions or to name shifts. I venture to guess that people memorialized were perhaps not famous enough, or were forgotten officials whose reputation did not surpass the confines of their county area. Most likely the loss of economic success of a place tended to help make the memory of a particular man fade.

And man it was since women are almost never honored by German names in the United States or Canada, and probably not by Anglo-Saxon names either. I recall only two female county names in two thousand four hundred US counties. The loss list does not contain women's names that are recognizably feminine.

It is a sad testimonial to the pioneer women sice they had a equal share of the burden to shoulder. One gathers the same neglect and unfairness on 18th US graveyards – I recall a horticulturally beautiful one in Rhode Island – only married women are marked in the first place. Unmarried ones are forgotten. Otherwise it goes: so and so gave birth to x number of children, perhaps one or two stillborn ones, and she passed in loving memory. We learn the years and months and the exact number of days. What she did, suffered, and may have achieved has gone from memory.

The "going Dutch" regularly lasted only until death did the couple part. The bill of life has been paid in full by woman alone. Place names are paternalistic, not receptacles of love. Their loss does not call for an enduring bereavement.

Chapter 5
The differences

Urban life would give every citizen enough leisure to make it possible, perhaps desirable, to give the German Canadians their due for the part they played with committed citizenship in Canada's deelopment. Surely they played s o m e part in the majority history. Without counting their impact on it, one might have a bilingual, English-French dominated fractious history. Only that is not the way it was. The Francophone Canadians may be condemned to playing the unthankful role of the runner-up of the Canadian dichotomy civilization in all provinces but Quebec. So this is not a grand invitation to open up a shaft to the past rural and urban history in the Dominion and the Commonwealth of Canada. If this hidden strength might have any resource power left, it is likely to concern urban more than rural life.

A city asks its citizens all for sharing efforts to promote the sum total of their ethnic existence. Minorities do not have to move on from older to ever newer (suburban) areas, but stay, pause or unwind from the continuous upward mobility. Cities and their urban quarters do not have to decay, but could be infused with more ethnic life, as is very visible in the metropolitan area of Toronto. People, by admitting foreign-born forebears, deconstruct an assumed Anglo-Saxon monocultural family style, and an hermetic zoning system.

Has Canada, in other words, denied especially German Empire Loyalist history or settlement history which took place long before the *Kaiserreich* (1871–1918), as well as the Weimar Republic (1919–1933)? And did it perhaps ignore its role and veneer legitimacy as a genuine and laudable effort to enrich Canada? This was perhaps harder to do in the rural areas, where the agricultural prowess in husbandry, cattle grazing and vegetable planting was obvious to all buyers of food and staples. Does Canada follow the pattern of throwing away pockets and parcels of settlement history?

In Canada no deference to monolithic Anglo corporative power is asked of integrated minorities with their coherent planning and participatory power any longer. In the ethnic family account a minimum amount of ethnic social security may safely be deposited and provide for socially accepted identification on the outside.

Roots in US America are affected by more militancy in clamoring for fiscal support. To quote a Trudeauism, "Canada is more of a welfare than of a warfare state." If applied to the greening of ethnic roots, it supplies part of the answer. Germans are usually not mentioned, when there was simple merit involved, straight achievement called for. It is taken for granted. But, on the other hand, they were rarely violently excluded in Canada, which knows of civil unrest, even rebellion in its labor movement, but had no civil warfare.[32]

[32]Gregory S. Kealy, *Workers and Canadian History.* McGill-Queens University Press 1995;

Since World War II a large amount of German immigrants were welcomed to Canada once again. Whereas the impact of recent German immigrants to larger US cities may be negligible, the impact on urban living styles in the largest Canadian metropolitan cities is considerable. In Canada you have Bloorstrasse in Toronto or Robsonstrasse in Vancouver, B. C. Finally, there is compatibility which you look for in vain in America, concerning minority culture. In Gainesville, FL, the *"Wienachtstolly"* (German Christmas cake) had to be ordered in advance to be imported from Dresden in time. My point is: despite the US richer and more diversified ethnic cultural background, *ethno-urbania* is a myth in the frequently decaying US metropolis, except, as we have seen, in Milwaukee, or, as in the Twin Cities, Minnesota. In many other places ethnic people cannot live without fear. This contrast in the perception of the city, and its blurred image, the fearless walk (*"der aufrechte Gang"*) is still to be walked in all major Canadian cities, including the inner city blocks. Since this is true for both minorities as well as majorities, most likely men and women, there are some general far-reaching consequences to be drawn:

1. the concept of the *one* "North American City" type is a myth;
2. the seemingly invisible international boundary between Canada and the US represents clearly differentiable histories and cultures;
3. the greatest myth is that their majority in both countries sprang from the same source, Britain. While this is culturally true of British Canada, it needs to be qualified for the whole US.
4. a fundamental founding difference is the vast mass of Germans pouring into the US, and more per capita than Canada could have absorbed by herself
5. this differentiation should throw light on the judgment as to how deeply "anglicised" German Americans really are compared to German Canadians outside the province of Quebec
6. the respective assimilation, as "mirrored" in the city images in Canada, seem to run deeper, and gave them a freer and constantly adjustable reign, and a public image, justifying the drop of the hyphen between German and Canadian.

Culturally German Canadians may surface freely today, whereas in the US cities, these features of adjustment would long be internalized, despite the fact, that nobody seems to be concerned about it. These features are forgotten except on ritualized days as Steuben Parade, or the essentially hollowed-out German American Day (October 15?). This is not meant to belittle the deep rural roots of German Americana south of the border. All I am saying, the perceptual geography is changing in both countries. The economic ranking of cities where

Richard J. Van Loon and Michael S. Whittington, *The Canadian Political System Environment, Structure and Process*. Fourth edition McGraw-Hill Ryerson Ltd. Toronto etc 1987.

German settlers helped in the co-founding phase, is higher than where they only sporadically penetrated.[33]

Another contrast effecting the integration of minorities in Canada and the US is found in the habitation of the central cities. A substantial part of Canada's middle class remain in the cities by choice, and within this trend, generations of German Canadians as well. But in the States the white middle class feels forced to retreat to suburban areas, or even to the countryside. This staying on in Canadian cities makes for a different role of inner city public parks, European style, in Canadian Centre Cities, and with it less crime, more public subsidy by the confederate government in Ottawa for the poor, handicapped and elderly. Concerning education in Canada the provinces pay a major share of the costs of primary and secondary schools. In the US more than fifty percent of the costs is paid by the municipalities, the local school boards. Thus the enrichment programs of the underprivileged become the dilution of the privileged. Neither are the causes of poverty related to the choice of the locality where one is living (or forced to live), nor are localities principally preferred or deprecated as such by ethnic minorities. Welfare payments are higher or lower depending on the area and its price of living index, which is pegged to the standard of living, and not the substandard of the living area.

The impact of immigrants on urban life styles in the US is smaller than in Canada's inner cities. Professionalism may not only be correlated to the immigrants' educational standards and achievements, but also to the immigrants' general preference for urban rather than suburban or even rural living. The mystique of constantly reinforced frontier individualism, fancied by Americans, runs counter to notions of social responsibilities.[34] The social responsibility is ethnically non-correlated and perhaps encompassingly human. One must not belong to an ethnic group to do good, but one must belong to s o m e ethnic group to be "patched into the mosaic "[35] at all. Thus one can have a germanophile private family view coupled with a public Anglophone perspective. That would suggest that Canadian cities tolerate and evolve within the cultural framework of the societies within which they are l o c a t e d [36] This phenomenon, according to Goldberg and Mercer, ultimately leads to a differentiated behaviour in Canadian cities (including, as we may add, "Little German" blocks or remnants of them), a behaviour which is coupled with respect for authority and self-

[33]Michael A. Goldberg and John Mercer, *The Myth of the North American City: Continentalism Challenged.* Press Vancouver 1986. I like to thank Michael Sharpe of Memorial University of Newfoundland for copying some Urban Studies on Canada for me and for taking time out for a long fruitful discussion.

[34]Edward Higbee, "Centre Cities in Canada and the United States," chapter 11, T. Watson & T. O'Riordan, ed.s, *The American Environment and Perception and Policies*, 1976. p. 145-160.

[35]Michael A. Goldberg and John Mercer, *The Myth of the North American City: Continentalism Challenged.* Vancouver 1986, p. 27.

[36]Ibidem, XVII, 5-6.

restraint. This, in turn, leads to orderly government. In American cities, on the other hand, assertive behaviour (an aggressive one in N. Y. C.) is coupled with distrust of authority and leads to self-indulgence and experimental pursuit of individual happiness.[37] These value differences[38] would push ethnicity[39] aside as a debatable trait as rarely useful resource in this line of enquiry. In the US, areas where the revolutionary/early immigrants landed and started out, outstanding landmarks have become shrines, in Canada the Loyalists' generated settlements in Ontario and New Brunswick have become leading cities. This has indirectly and intuitively anglicised German Canadians from the root. It has also prevented the German Canadians from sticking out and choosing to become allies of the economically neglected Francophones. This ultimately, it seems to me, is the reason why German Canadians, often without realizing it, silently belong to the dominant group. Accordingly, they are a non-vociferous group in terms of sharing political power, even closer to the political center than German Americans who identify with the correct political majority in the US. There is no suspicion attached to an assimilative stance among Anglo-Canadians and German Canadians, at least not a deep-seated discriminatory one.

Anglo-Americans would be puzzled over the retention of old ways. Immigrants to the US ritually have to undergo a remaking in a remade country. In Canada they are allowed to grow differently at their own pace. One cannot conceive of separate German language schools (different from Benjamin Franklin's surrounding) in modern Pennsylvania or a separate Spanish language school in Phoenix, AR, but there are separate English-language public schools in Quebec, and separate Catholic French teaching public schools in Ontario. An immigrant becomes homogenized in America (*love it or leave it*) almost as if he/she were a retailed personality. To perform this assimilation was much easier for Germans, who have an ethnic trait other than Anglo, but more or less look alike, and are, in any case, of the same race. Koreans settling in Los Angeles might be ethnically obvious for two to three generations; the son of the North German immigrant to Bozeman, MT, might easily become a ranger, perhaps already following his dad's footsteps, for he had studied forestry in Germany and was qualified for the job during the zero generation level.

It may be bold to summarize: immigration stays a federal matter in the US and hence the steps leading to citizenship in federal bureaucratic hands. Provincial government enters into the assimilation process and therefore may help on the way, rather than threaten as in Big Brother Land.

---

[37]Ibidem, p. 14-15.

[38]Lienhard Lötscher, *Lebensqualität kanadischer Städte*: Ein Beitrag zur Diskussion von methodischer und empirischer Erfassung lebensräumlicher Qualität. *Basler Beiträge zur Geographie*. vol. 33. Basel Wepf 1985.

[39]Ed. Alfred Pletsch, *Ethnicity in Canada. International Examples and Perspectives. Marburger Geographische Schriften*. vol. 96. Geographisches Institut Marburg 1985.

These differentiations may not have much to do with the perception of metropolitan centers (or centres). However, the American urban adage, "if you have seen one, you have seen them all" could not fairly be uttered while describing bigger Canadian cities. As far as I have seen them they are different and distinctive, in fact, they are distinctively different when expressing and allowing citizens to express residual ethnic values as resources. Seen in this light, the Canadian city is an unfragmented projection of Canadian society and of its accompanying spectrum ideology (from English to French to German to Italian to Jewish, and so on) onto s p a c e .

The traditional city dominated areas [from Baltimore to St. Louis] are no longer the pace-setters in the US, but this perceptual geography has been transformed and pushed contemporary settlement into the *Sunbelt,* where the Germans traditionally settled less to begin with. As a result, the new sunbelters become rather mobile, possibly "rootless" twice over, at least more so than the former inhabitants of the Old South are. New Canadian city living must continue to dominate in a formerly void territory, in a *Snowbelt* within 250 miles of the frontier, the 49th parallel Latitude North. So the movement toward new dominance stays flush with the former immigration direction: due West. Whatever roots may have been allowed to dominate by nature, are sown in the soil and grow. The Canadian mobility to the West with new dominance patterns does not economically hollow out the old dominant provinces Manitoba and Saskatchewan, carved out of the Hudson Bay's Old Rupert Land Grant only in 1905; on the contrary, it strengthens them. The Canadian East is neither effete, nor is the West Marlboro Man country. Both newly dominant areas plus Alberta, and above all British Columbia, as well as the added census areas SOUTH ATLANTIC, EAST SOUTH CENTRAL, WEST SOUTH CENTRAL, NM and AR are wide h o r i z o n country, the four Canadian provinces very cold in the winter, moderate to not so cold the six American states. The four enumerated provinces will, for historical reasons, fortify the German Canadian residual power in the West, where it was and is strongest or deepest, The latter six US states, also for historical reasons, will tend to lessen the German American remnants, which were never too deep there in the first place.

Hence the Canadian West will stay harnessed to their traditional social liberation philosophy, the American sunbelt to traditional political conservatism. Canadian s p a c e , city as well as country, expands west in an evolutionary logical direction: West. The American s p a c e , new economy and all, conquers the South for a second time, this time without civil war, but still in ol' yankee style. There is no rebellion at hand, but a revolutionary expansion in s p a c e it is.[40] No

---

[40]James E. Vance, "Revolution in American Space since 1945, and a Canadian Contrast," R. D. Mitchell and P. A. Groves, eds., *North America – The Historical Geography of a Changing Continent,* pp. 439-459. It remains clear that Quebec's immobility in this connection will prevent its people from spreading Canada-wide, and will set the Francophonie even further apart.

part is recreated, there almost was none (see Gertrude Stein's motto of this book). Rather Teddy Roosevelt's prediction is fulfilled, "to make the desert bloom." (*"eine blühende Landschaft..."*) A new present is created before our eyes. An arid void is greened and filled with people.

PART FOUR

ASSIMILATION AND ACCULTURATION PROBLEMS:

Language as deconstructing resource[1]

Chapter 1
From 1st generation primary German speaking to 2nd generation English speaking

In the context of this chapter acculturation is understood as a consequence of professional activity, success, and advancement in the new surrounding. Assimilation takes place while the acculturation is going on. As the immigrant accepts the role models of conducting himself or herself in English, he/she disengages from public conduct and communication in German. The end of an initial self-ghettoization is reached when a look-alike speaker such as a German immigrant can more fully converse in English and "get things done" in that language. The more the speaker copes with the required conduct rules, including speaking idiomatically, the sooner he/she assimilates. A social and economic recognition follows the successful acculturation phase. Here we have a fundamental difference to internal European migration, say from Warsaw to Vienna or from Minsk to Berlin. Within this immigration's context you have to learn German first and then depending on the accultured adjustment may rise in the esteem of your fellow Germans. If the acculturation is achieved by the cohort group, say in Missouri a "Little Germany" is well on its way to assimilate to the outside and then individually and collectively become "reborn" as a "Little America". The main source of help for accelerating the assimilative process is to make sure that the immigrant and his/her group wants to stay. The assimilative acceleration is greatly enhanced by successful economic integration. The key to it all is the assimilative use of the English language, while the German usage steps into the background. This requires a linguistic as well as psychic adjustment.

The process can be demonstrated by using an every day example, the use of a car. An immigrant like any native driver occasionally needs spare parts.[2] The use of a car is governed by a shared experience of a collective daily life cycle. The

---

[1]Allan C. Hutchinson, "From Cultural Construction to Historical Deconstruction," Book Review of *When Words Lose their Meaning: Constitutions and Reconstructions of Language, Character and Community*. By James Boyd White. U of Chzicago Press 1984.Yale Law Journal, vol. 94 (1984/5), p. 209-238.

[2]Most immigrants will remember the moment when their car's *"Vergaser"* changed into a *"carburator"*, because it became part of a vehicular artifact language, which was so named for identification purposes by the repair shop or the gas station.

161

confidence that the *"Vergaser"* is doing its job is reinforced by using a carburator functionally like everybody else who might be talking about it in the neighborhood. The comparability of parts pertains to the idea of human equality, and a temporary equilibrium between the immigrant's communication skill in the imported language (even if he speaks with a heavy accent) vs. the primary language, in our context, German. The clerk can only find the spare part number if he knows what the spare part is referred to in English. Sooner or later the identification of parts, comparable to the "labelling" of grammar rules, becomes subordinated to the growing familiarity. Once a certain degree of facility is reaching or surpassing the level of the old language, a new usage superimposes itself. An adherence and loyalty to the new language is built up and completed. Such a new model of communication is formed and is usually almost totally in place in the second generation. The former linguistic loyalty is more often evaded, first in public, then in the family, then in one's mind, and finally in one's dreams.

The son who speaks English to his (or her) old-fashioned father acts like a deconstructionist demolishing beyond hope of repair the construction of a mother tongue spoken abroad. The reason for that happening is not oedipal, but the loss of confidence (to stay in our example) of getting the vehicle repaired, or of getting the communication between him and his father, his former teacher, "going", renewed or perpetually enlivened. Deconstruction into English by an immigrant in North America seeks to demonstrate that words, utterances, or texts lead to an alloy of thought, the entry to which, once it is opened, will never be closed again. It did not primarily open to find new meaning, rather is crossed into for the sake of added knowledge. Labels such as *Auspuff, Vergaser, Zündkerze*, etc., now identified as muffler, carburator, spark plug, etc. deconstructed the formerly constructed German labelled spare parts. Not that *Zündkerze* regains hegemony-in-naming over one's mind more than temporarily. Spark plug by itself is no more operative than *Zündkerze*. The English equivalent, however, has become an automatic response in North America for the deconstructionist as speaker, listener, purchaser, or tax payer, etc. In this way the preponderance in the primary response achieves acceptance of the speaker's perception and guarantees adequacy of the result-oriented response, and becomes an exchange of business along expected lines. The son notices that he gains power by speaking in the jargon of primary loyalty.

It follows that in the colonies of the Low German speaking Mennonites, where automobiles were taboo, this deconstruction was slowed down or stalled. Now, until about 1740 the German immigrants to North America were using farm tools, equipment, or Conestoga wagons with the special tarpaulin, technologically at least on a par basis, if not at times of slightly better quality. After 1815 ff., with the exception of the Grey Forty-Eighters, who were considered "Latin" farmers, immigrants with a dwindling surplus knowledge of the latest technology and the corresponding know-how arrived, so that Senger speaks of a deficit across the board, a *Modernitätsdefizit*.[3] He ties this lack of know-how to the prevailing miserable state of the German economy and the lack of constitutional freedom. It was from these conditions the very immigrants wished to escape en masse. Hence they learned English with a special fervor so that they would not have a linguistic replacement problem with a spare part, as described above.

Another sixty years later, the Premier of Ontario, J. P. Whitney, welcomed to Berlin, the seat of Waterloo county, as many Germans as he could get, "in order to get them instructed in enterprise and progress".[4] Can the claim be made that the "modernity lag" (*Modernitätsdefizit*) entails taking second place in direct competition with such technical labelling in English? It is not the word material as such, but the deconstructed usage of segments as repair parts that decides.[5] Secondly, the increase in exposure to a modern economy and a technology made them participate in free enterprise, coupled to the deconstructionist switch (rather than mere code switch)[6] from Low German to English which was easier to achieve for these speakers. The signposts of modern technology were less clearly marked, before they came, than in High German speaking territories. The Low(er) German speaker could be deconstructed from a native minority language place surrounding them in the Old Country before, superimposed by "modern" High German. Parallel to this situation, the newly achieved linguistic loyalty to English in North America required less linking effort.

The primary issue, which the first native born generation faced, lay not so much in the correct usage, but in the sharing of the generally accepted subsistence level, and finally in reaching the first rungs on the ladder to self-governing power with newly won freedom. Thus the new language used as deconstructed resource relegates the old language brought from the homeland as less apt in the new surroundings to the shelves. Often this linguistic adjustment must have been a painful process. It needed not to have been utterly transparent to the successfully adjusted immigrant. He was being treated with respect if he succeeded in this perceptual effort in an ultimately social enterprise. His status rose, and the primary loyalty to English reinforced his settling new identity.

---

[3] Stefan v. Senger und Etterlin, *Neu-Deutschland in Nordamerika*. 1991, p. 3.

[4] Gottfried Leibbrandt, *Little Paradise. Aus Geschichte und Leben der Deutschkanadier in der County Waterloo, Ontario, 1800–1975*. Kitchener 1977, p. 95.

[5] According to Günter Moltmann, in *Festschrift für Fritz Fischer*. 1978, Germans immigrating to the US during the 19th century were likely seen as "security *valve*" [sic!] by their German governments for letting off the steam of social unrest or upheaval.

[6] Which does not equal a "degeneration of the [Low] German language", as H. Lehmann, *The German Canadians*. 1986, p. 287, assumes.

Chapter 2
German Bibles as pillars of resistance in North America

Until the Age of Goethe or in some cases even until the end of the 19th century the High German Bible was the most widely read, esteemed and the most often quoted book of the entire land. High German by becoming the vessel of the Holy Spirit which helped Martin Luther to translate from the traditional Church versions of the Hebrew , Greek and Latin Testaments to German had elevated German on to a higher plain. Luther's sound and adroit judgment in giving his translation of the whole Bible (1522–1534) the rhythm and the right deconstructionist frame – copied later on by Catholic re-translations – in turn placed protestant German theology to the forefront in Europe. Still in the perspective taken by the church hierarchies it did not raise German to the rank of *lingua sacra*, reserved for Hebrew, Greek and Latin. So the various Bibles had to make it clear to immigrants that there was more than one way to approach religion.

Luther's Bible immediately took German Christian religious seekers by storm and settled it in people's hearts, buttressing ordinary man's belief in God and a possible redemption. Luther's Bible version was retranslated into Low German several times. It must therefore be assumed that German family bibles, taken over as precious belongings to the US or Canada, could have been Low or High German Bibles. Yet even among Low German speakers, after the breakdown of the Hanse, which was described in PART ONE, their written language was not considered a totally adequate vessel of faith for holding down the heavenly messages written down in the Bible. And this had little to do with a lack of expressive power (*Sprachfähigkeit*) or aptness as a vehicle for transporting belief, but rather with traditions of church history and local practices.

The Low German church language was deconstructed into the High German of commerce, law and most newspapers, before the settlers came over. The Northwestern Germans were getting used to such constructionist pressures. My point is: the immigrants who came over from north of the Benrath Line to America often still understood Low German, and may have spoken it frequently on their farms, but they had been overwhelmed before by a linguistic spread, which had proved irresistible, and they had adjusted to the printed media, which followed the requirements of the High German print market. Why would they not "triumph" again? The pace setting city making the deconstructionist switch first was none other than Berlin in Brandenburg. There High German replaced most of Low German as early as 1504, before Luther had started his work on the translation of the Bible into High German. But the Low German biblical tradition is as old, and has a venerable tradition of its own, spread and carried on until today.

The five principal Low German speaking tribes of landsmen, the Westphalians, Oldenburgers, Hanoverians, Schleswig-Holsteiners, and Pomeranians streamed into the new territories in the following order: Ohio, Indiana, Missouri, Iowa, and Wisconsin, and founded Low German=speaking churches--*Plattdeutsche Kirchen.* Their settlements witnessed a small but vigorous linguistic counter-current today. Their talking Low German still makes disagreements disappear: (*Mit Platt Düütsch fallt de muurn.*")

The Low German New Testament by itself is still used in Schleswig-Holstein and Mecklenburg-Vorpommern in re-issued form, but also in new translations manufactured in Manitoba and Kansas.[7] The television stations of the Norddeutscher Rundfunk Hamburg and the two studios CFAM in Altona, and CHSM in Steinbach, Manitoba, send programs in Low German periodically. Low German became a recognized regional language in Germany (*Gesetzblatt Jg.* 98II 25) on July 16, 1998. Almost 10% of the German population can understand it nowadays.

[7]*Dat Niee Testament Plattdüütsch* vun Rudolf Muuß. Breklumer Verlag 1975. *Dat Niehe Tastament Plautdietsch* fonn J. J. Neufeld äwasat, Winnipeg, Manitoba – Hillsboro, Kansas 1987; Herrmann Rempel, *Kjenn jie noch Plautdietsch? A Mennonite Low German Dictionary.* Winnipeg 1984, re-ed. Rosenort, MB 1995; Jack Thiessen, *Mennonite Low German Dictionary.* Marburg 1977; Reuben Epp, *The Story of Low German and Plautdietsch.* Hillsboro Kansas 1993; Victor Peters, *Plautdietsche Jeschichten.* Marburg 1990. The Mennonite Heritage Centre in Winnipeg, Manitoba, issues *Mennonitische Rundschau* and *Journal of Mennonite Studies.* Whereas Lehmann-Bassler estimated some 160,0000 Mennonite Low-German Canadian speakers living in Western Canada after WW II, Reppmann believes that there are now 200,000 Mennonite Low German speakers in Saskatchewan and Manitoba alone (by 1994). So the number of *"Plautdietsch"* speakers seems to be on the rise. The same phenomenon holds true for *"Plattdüütsch"* in the New Bundesland Mecklenburg-Vorpommern, where the constitution appeared in Low German beside High German also, as well as in Lower Saxony, Schleswig-Holstein, Hamburg, and Bremen.. Almost 10% of the German population or 8 million speakers at least passively understand Low German nowadays again.

There are numerous Mennonites in Mexico, Paraguay, Brazil, and Bolivia, according to *Mennonite Encyclopedia*, vol. V (1990) 121-124. Whether they still converse in Low German is not known to this writer.

Chapter 3
Pennsylvania Dutch, a German American Dialect

In order to make sure that a modern hindsight perspective on Pennsylvania Dutch is broached to the reader I am quoting from the website of the Wellesley Icon Township, Pennsylvania:

"Vass Is Deitsch"?

"Deitsch (pronounced diech) or *Deitsh* (Ohio spelling) is a German dialect still spoken in parts of Alsace, in France, and in some German states, as well as Pennsylvania, Ohio. Indiana, Ontario and other states and provinces in North America. While it is the mother tongue of many conservative groups of Amish and Mennonites, (the "Plain" *Deitsche*), many others still know and use it. In fact, in Pennsylvania, the "Fancy" *Deitsche*, (Lutherans, Reformed and others of non-Mennonite persuasion) maintain an interest in the language through research at universities, ets., and *Grundsow* (Groundhog) Lodges, in which the language is used in meetings. Members are fined if they use English when a *Deitsch* word is known.

In the USA, it is called Pennsylvania Dutch, and in Ontario, it is called PA Dutch by some. It is also referred to as low German by some who regard it as an inferior kind of German, but it is a distinct language, and real students of the language resent the term "low". However, there is a Low German language, spoken by a group, often referred to as Russian Mennonites whose language originated in the northern Lowlands of Germany [editor's comment: actually in West Prussia]. It is not a low or inferior language either, but *Deitsch* is not Low German [editor's comment: true enough, for the *Pfalz* (Palatinate) is a High German territory on the French border].

Deitsche (pronounced die-chee) is the name given to those who speak *Deitsch.* Often referred to as the Pennsylvania Dutch, they trace their roots back to settlers who came to the USA and Canada from Europe. In Ontario, the majority of Mennonites trace their ancestry directly back to Pennsylvania, while the Amish, Catholics and Lutherans who still know the language, trace their ancestry directly back to Europe, especially Alsace-Lorraine. In Ontario, only the most conservative groups continue to use it in their homes so many young people are not taught the language any more.

Two great historical events, that caused *Deutsch* (pronounced doych) to overshadow *Deitsch*, occurred in Europe years ago. When Luther translated the Bible into German, he used *Deutsch* as the language of choice. The unification of the many states and duchies into modern day Germany was led by those who spoke *Deutsch*. There are still areas in France and Germany where *Deitsch* is ... spoken and many visitors from Waterloo county have easily converted with the *Deitsche* there. Until the late 1800's, the language was unwritten, but many

166

efforts to refine spelling, pronunciation, syntax and grammar are being made. In the 1960's, an orthography was developed. In 1993, in Ohio, a committee consisting of both Old and New Order Amish worked under the auspices of the Wycliffe Bible Translators and completed and printed the New Testament in *Deitsch*. It is estimated that over 200,000 speak *Deitsch,* which many claiming it as their first language. Until now, the New Testament was available to them only in Standard German or English.

There is dialect variation among the many groups in the States and Ontario. Even in Wellesley Township there are variations. In spite of the differences, however, the various "tongues" are mutually understandable."

Although I consider some parts of the above statement a bit "adventurous," I still find it instructive as an example of website self-presentation.

The above excerpt is seconded by another more circumspect self-presentation, which is quoted from *The Columbia Encyclopedia*, Sixth Edition. 2001:

Entry "Pennsylvania Dutch":
"[Ger. *Deutsch*=German], people of E. Pennsylvania of German descent who migrated to the area in the 18th cent., particularly those in Northampton, Berks, Lancaster, Lehigh, Lebanon, York, and adjacent counties. The colony of Pennsylvania, established by William Penn as a refuge for Quakers, offered other groups the prospect of religious freedom. In 1683 the village of Germantown was established by a group of Mennonites led by Francis Daniel Pastorius, and in succeeding years other groups, such as the Dunkards and the Moravians, settled in Pennsylvania. However, the bulk of immigration occurred after 1710, when the Germans from the Palatinate first arrived. [editor's comment: what is meant is, for a second time]. Many of these people had sought economic and religious freedom in England; from there a number were sent to the Hudson valley to engage in the production of naval stores, [see PART ONE chapter 5] but with the failure of that project many Palatines moved to Pennsylvania. Enthusiastic reports brought other settlers from Germany, until by the time of the American Revolution the population of Pennsylvania, according to Benjamin Franklin, was one-third German.

At first the large influx of German settlers antagonized the English, but those were gradually accepted, and during the Revolution they provided valuable assistance. Most of the settlers engaged in farming, at which they were extremely successful. For the most part they maintained their own language and customs; the family became the principal economic and social unit, and the church was next in importance.

The aim of the various religious sects was to establish a Christian, democratic society; for many years they opposed public schooling, preferring to retain their own standards and manners, and they strongly resisted signs of progress and worldly living. Several of the sects are completely pacifist, such as the Amish and the Mennonites. The Amish are particularly strict in the matter of dress, maintaining a simple but distinctive garb, and also have a strong aversion to automobiles, electric lights, and telephones. The Amish have continued to oppose public schooling, and the U. S. Supreme Court ruled in 1972 that the Amish were exempt from state compulsory education laws. The Church of the Brethren, incorrectly but popularly known as the Dunkards or *Dunkers* from their manner of baptism, and the *Schwenkfelders* are two other sects.

The Pennsylvania Dutch, or Pennsylvania German, language is a blend of several dialects, essentially Palatinate, with some admixture of standard German and English. A substantial Pennsylvania German literature, art, and architecture exists. Many written records were adorned with illuminated writing, and such articles as pottery, furniture, needlework, and barns made use of decorative motifs, often of a highly artistic nature. Their buildings are usually of heavy stone and timber construction, with steep roofs and small, irregular windows. Pennsylvania Germans have contributed much to the culture of Pennsylvania. The Pennsylvania-German Society, organized in 1891, has published much material relative to the history and folklore of the Pennsylvania Dutch."

Editor's additional comment: Lancaster county, PA is the heart of Pennsylvania Dutch country.

For convenience's sake the reader is provided with a Pennsylvania Dutch Bibliography:

J. F. Sachse, *The German Sectarians of Pennsylvania, 1708–1800* (2 vol., 1889; rp. 1971); W. Beidelman, *The Story of the Pennsylvania Germans* (1898, rp. 1969), L. O. Kuhns, *The German and Swiss Settlements of Colonial Pennsylvania* (1901, repr. 1971); A. Long, *The Pennsylvania German Family Farm* (1972); J. J. Stoudt, *Pennsylvania German Folk Art* (rev. ed. 1966) and Sunbonnets and Shoofly Pies, *Pennsylvania Dutch Cultural History* (1973); Earl C. Haag, *A Pennsylvania German Anthology* (1988); E. C. Haag, *A Pennsylvania Reader and Grammar*. Keystone Books. Penn State Press 1982.

For a visit to the Pennsylvania German Heritage the following clip from <slidea.gif> may be helpful:
"The Pennsylvania German Cultural Heritage Center at Kutztown University is a place, a museum, and a year-round program. The Center represents the commitment of Kutztown University to the preservation of Pennsylvania German ("Pennsylvania Dutch") history, lore, and traditions. It is part of the University's educational and cultural program.

168

The place is a 60-acre 19th century farmstead with a stone farm house, barns, and smaller buildings which are being authentically restored, a one-room school house, circa 1870, and a visitors' center.

The museum is a collection of more than 10,000 artefacts representing Pennsylvania German rural life in 19th and early 20th centuries, and extensive genealogical records of several thousand Pennsylvania German families dating to the mid-1700's.

The program is a year-round series of events celebrating Pennsylvania German culture and traditions - music, children's programs, classes in the Pennsylvania Dutch dialect, talks and demonstrations on topics such as home life, foods, and crafts. The one-room school experience is re-enacted in the 125-year old Freyberger School.

"*Heemet Fescht*" (home festival) is our autumn weekend celebration of Pennsylvania German life as it was in the late 19th and early 20th centuries. The dates for Heemet Fescht in 2000 are September 16-17.

Of special interest is the Kutztown Pennsylvania German Festival , a nine-day celebration of Pennsylvania Dutch life and lore. The festival, held annually in the time period around the Fourth of July, features taste-tempting foods, pageantry, crafts, quilting, folklore seminars and children's activities. The dates for the 2000 Festival are July 1 through July 9.

Send for a free descriptive brochure about the Pennsylvania German Cultural Heritage Center. Our E-mail address is: henry@kutztown.edu and our telephone number is 610-683-1330. Our mailing addresss is Pennsylvania German Cultural Heritage Center, Weisenberger Alumni Center, Kutztown University, Kutztown, PA 19530.

Kutztown PA German Heritage Center Library

Sing, Schpiel,Unn Danz. Join in our German Heritage Adventure - May 24–June 7, 2000."

Hau di thu? Sank you wary much.

The Pennsylvanian German dialect is still used in religious services, including Sunday school, in theater performances, and by writers of primary literature, above all in contemporary plays today. See Don Yoder, "Die Pennsylvania-Deutschen. Eine dreihundertjährige Identitätskrise ," *Amerika und die Deutschen*, ed. Frank Trommler. 1986, p. 65-88.

Chapter 4
The "Dutch uncle" humor or Galgenhumor and its critics

The characteristic feature of American humour is its distinctiveness and a peculiarity in taking one's point of view. On the one hand, there is a willingness to see things as they are unrobed of the traditional European reverence. Thus Mark Twain, in his *Innocents Abroad* (1869) humorously draws a funny picture of Europe as seen from the top of the Rocky Mountains. His "innocent" pilgrims are equipped with mock superiority. The narrator makes them arrive in the Old World with only a "yarn spinner shrewdness" to compensate for an abundance of ignorance.

The most devastating rebuke of German humor came to me, when I heard the quip somewhere in New England that "German humor is no laughing matter". According to that cliché a migration would import an unfunny cultural background, a German *Landschafts-Humor* from the Old Country, before it could release its preserved energy in the New Country. This could not possibly be true. It may be quite hard to rival in the basic expressions of the major culture humorously, when one`s vocabulary and sense of arrested expression is not yet assimilated enough to voice the impulses of your heart and raise them verbally to the level of your funny bone. The pronouncements risked might be mistaken for "double Dutch"(*Kauderwelsch)*, and not be laughed at, or laughed at for the wrong reasons. The comic effect of German American jokes told in English garb in the US before a single native or a group is unfortunately often of the involuntary kind. Here a historical sample from Leland's "Hans Breitmann" Ballads, the rage of the Musical Season in Buffalo of 1878, may illustrate voluntary (ironic) humor with mispronouncing words phonetically (with the "clipped" accent). In this fashion the humour would show a mixture of good-natured to intentionally nasty comical lines:

> "Hans Breitmann shoined de Turners:
> Mein Gott! How dey drinked and shwore,
> Der vas Swabians und Tyrolers
> And Bavarians by de score ...
> Hans Breitmann shoined de Turners:
> Mit a Limburg cheese he coom.
> When he open de box it shmell so loudt,
> It knock de musick doomb ..."[8]

Behind these mock amusing lines lay a serious struggle of German lips and throats for coming to terms with mastering the language tools to equip oneself with an immigrant's identity. The music may have softened the tension surrounding this black humor a bit.

[8]Charles G. Leland issued such continuation stories serially even in London.

One could perhaps separate humour growing out of typical and repetitive situations calling for comic relief from stock yard jokes, army jokes, or feeble bank clerk jokes and arrive at self parody. Even the strongly sarcastic gallow's humour requires ironic distance from one's maladjustment, or occasional hopelessness. Humour, well sprinkled in conversation, or interspersed in newspaper clippings, requires observation and character. But character again is a cultural construct described and modelled by writers such as Mark Twain in the US or Stephen Leacock in Canada, or Justus Möser and Theodor Fontane in the Old Country.

Humor, even the stern "Dutch uncle" humor (sometimes deliberately hurled at a hapless victim of one's vilification) needs to diffuse tension rather than merely oversimplify of stereotypic funny situations. The German immigrant listener is involved in first understanding and then in facing the funny intention on the one side and the mock rejection by a native group on the other. In such a typical situation we would likely find a confrontation occurring between fellow Americans (or Canadians) and community-isolated German Americans or German Canadians learning to banter verbally.

It must have been clear to many of these German immigrants, as it was to the over-critical majority that only a strong and recognized identity could lead to lasting recognition, no longer based on one's ethnic background. In that sense this unabashed addressing of their peculiarities may have cleared the way in the process of overcoming some of these oddities which were perfectly normal back home in privacy.

Ethnic sayings about matters "Deutsch", rarely come across in Canada, are abundant already in colonial North American time. While the writer is not a sociologist, it makes sense to group my collection into four categories: 1. useful things, tools; 2. negativel criticisms; 3. slurs containing reprimands; 4. nasty anti-German insults. These sayings contain, accompany or illustrate shifting considerations. They did not occur in the order presented, but with the help of the press usually originated in the East. This ethnically almost overwhelmingly strong and capable minority received closed scrutiny in the public view of their times.

Expressions of the first category, in my opinion, originated around 1750-1780; the second category has to do with the culturally different ways people looked at resting during Sundays, and the inactivity that should accompany it in Anglican eyes. These expressions originated after 1800 some time during the first half of the 19th century, because of noted German American osten-tatiousness making merry in beer halls on Sundays. The third category expressions presuppose the modern American "Deutsch" (Dutch) to be out of tune with their epoch and point toward surfacing during the latter part of the 19th century. The fourth category containing slurs may have originated within the Labor Movement or in response to alleged Prussian atrocities during the Franco-

171

Prussian War of 1870/71 on the part of the American public or the newspaper reader. It is noteworthy that the learned or bookish term "German" did not substitute the continuously popular term "Dutch", for "Deutsch" kept on attracting mischievous comments.[9]

DEUTSCH AND ANTI-*DEUTSCH* CLICHÉS

1. different but useful things or tools

Dutch Wagon	Conestoga wagon
Dutch 200	a perfect bowling score
Dutchman's breeches	a plant *dicentra*; a striped blue sky after a storm
Dutch door	a two-sectional wind breaking door
Dutch oven	originally *Kochkiste* [in Conestoga wagons]; later heavy kettle
Dutch lap	overlapping shingles on a roof
double Dutch	two jumping ropes; *Kauderwelsch*

2. negatively filled criticisms

Dutch treat	both pay their own way
Dutch reasoning	an endless (pointless) debate
Dutch uncle	administering a stern lecture
Dutch medley	everyone plays a different tune
Dutch feast	a party where the host gets drunk first
Dutchman's drink	the last sip in a bottle
Dutch courage	false courage gleaned from one drink too much
have Dutch courage	you have your alcohol level tested
Dutch bargain	a deal concluded while intoxicated
Dutchman's headache	a hangover
Dutch comfort	misery which could be worse
Dutch auction	a dropping price auction
put your Dutch up	put your "dander" up

3. slurs containing reprimands

dutchy	funny looking
are you in Dutch?	are you in trouble?

---

[9]These stereotypes are a far cry from "huns" and other nasty modern 20th century propaganda terms reserved for "ugly Germans", Günter Trautmann, ed., *Die häßlichen Deutschen. Ausblicke, Essays und Analysen zur Geschichte und Politik*. Wissenschaftliche Buchgesellschaft Darmstadt 1991.

I'd be a Dutchman if I do   I'll be a liar if I do
Dutch praise   a thorough condemnation
to get one's Dutch up   to get angry at somebody
to get into Dutch   to get into trouble
I would rather be a Dutchman than do what you ask me

4. anti-German insults

a Dutch nightingale   a frog
Dutch gold   simple brass
Dutch reckoning   pure guesswork and no skill
"Dutchman"   a plug indicating bad carpentry or stone cutting
Dutch bellied   highly pregnant or very fat
Dutch widow   a prostitute
Dutch defense   a surrender
Dutch infidel   hell as place for unbelievers
Dutch route   suicide

With the possible exception of the *dicentra* plant name, all sayings are directed at the Germans, not the Hollanders or Netherlanders.[10] Surprisingly, these sayings have little if anything to do with language loyalty or with hating another language, the only exception being "to speak double Dutch", i. e. talk incomprehensibly. The resentment zeros in on behavioural habits. Hence most of these expressions from group 1 to 3 must have originated on the streets and the newspapers likely before 1916. We understand from this, perhaps not totally complete list that German behavior in the US became an issue surrounded by discomfort and tension. The way this tension could be addressed and hopefully defused, was to make fun of it. *Deutsch* humor did not automatically become a laughing matter in a free ride of shared laughter. Toughness invites rigorous scrutiny and can best be attacked vicariously by auxiliary weapons of a particular arsenal.

On the other hand this American ethnic humor entails expressions of reprimand, based on an unwillingness for deeper understanding. It does not unmask German American humorlessness, rather it betrays a "walled" thinking. The laughter at the expense of these German Americans who used to stand together as a cohort group and were now isolated is not funny by itself, but stern. Ultimately this overdrawn criticism of German American humorlessness is no joke. It points at the limits of tolerance. It does not create comic relief, hence does not help soften the worry and anger on the part of the majority. Neither

[10]Only the term "Dutch elm disease" is directed toward the Hollanders not preventing the export of their bark beetles to the US, which committed heavy damage.

does this kind of pointed anti-ethnic humour survive for a long time, but requires constant adjustments. If German Americans had accepted this kind of humor voiced at their expense as authentic cliché, it had to amount to an imposed burden of "gallow's" humor or *"Galgenhumor,"* to which German Americans were largely resistant.

We do not know how many cliché challenges lie hidden in the mass of unpublished German American literature, written in German in response to these slurs, or in the thousands of *Jahrgänge*, decades of newspaper numbers, deposited in libraries, and all sorts of papers down to last wills in German. Recently the public has been made aware of how many German books were printed and published in the US until 1861-1865.[11] The Civil War must have been the great linguistic leveller. A continuation of this line of inquiry for the later 19th and the 20th century will be eagerly awaited. In as much as German has largely disappeared from use in the US melting-pot, critics are usually not willing to show more than antiquarian interest in this untapped comparative field of early American Literature that might have been or was written by American writers in response to German American assimilation problems. In which genre should American writers interested in acculturation problems have penned them? Surprisingly the contributors to the volume on Conflict and Cooperation between Two Cultures 1800-2000,[12] do not look into this matter.

But we know about some prominent North American writers in this context. And their criticism carries a great deal of weight. Three influential trails of theirs have left permanent traces and cliché labels on the way in which Anglo Americans or Canadians have looked upon German Americans and German-Canadians. And almost equally important – how did these folks look upon themselves? Did these feelings get on paper as well?

Nineteenth century writers taught their readers what they wanted to hear: that only the dominant white American history was constitutive for understanding North America and its complexities, but that their continental European background sprang only from the realm of myth, and not from relevant written sources like all the fledgling American written material on good taste. Secondly, books written about these backgrounds were supposed to be humorous shortened fables, produced for mass consumption, rather than enlightening treatises. They were, thirdly, to be written so well as if Englishmen rather than Americans or Canadians had penned them. Hence the professional taste of the premier English

---

[11] Robert E. Cazden, *A Social History of the German Book Trade in America to the Civil War*. Camden House, S. C. 1984. Consult the most comprehensive collection *European Americans*: A Chronological Guide to Works Printed in Europe Relating to the Americas, 1493-1750. Six volumes until 1992. Readex Canaan, CT. It has 32,000 entries, at least a third of which (if not more) relate to German, which was widely used by printers in 17th and 18th century Scandinavia also.

[12] Ed. Frank Trommler and Elliott Shore, *The German-American Encounter*. Berghahn Books New York Oxford 2001.

174

writers in England decided on their esteem in England, while their popularity in North America was of secondary importance.

[Sir] Walter Scott (1771-1832) was the most influential literary potentate of his time, poet, sheriff of the court of session, novel writer, grave clerk of the court, publisher and critic. He, like two of the American writers, shone as a humorist and taste setting satirist. He came from the reservoir of the British commonwealth humor, traditionally replenished by borderland Scots, from Edinburgh.

We must not be surprised that their "humorous systems" were set up to please English tastes, to participate in what the English public wanted to read, what had to be "the rage" to be read at all in London, in New York and even in Albany, N. Y. Scott's and his American admirers' and emulators' stories were really serialized comic stories, contrived at the traveller's desk, heavily influenced by all sorts of questionable "sources". Quite a proportion of these two American writers' stories were written in England. Luckily for the writers, English critics felt that these Americans "scotched" the old prejudice held against literature of so fine and funny a fabric, *could* have been produced in America at all.

A. Washington Irving (1783-1859)

Washington Irving was born in New York City the youngest of eleven children –a sibling and pecking order position of great help for social and anti-social satire – , of a Scottish father and an English mother. As a young man he received but a checkered education. It is not known how he, given his unsuitedness for his family's hardware business, could escape going to college. He was allowed to go on trips to both Montreal and Quebec City early in his life. Furthermore, his brother liked him well enough to send him on an "educational tour", during which he visited France, Italy, Switzerland, Belgium, The Netherlands, and last but not least Britain.

Through a long literary career this much admired "first American man of letters" turned into and "remained an arbiter of American taste, and an example of the literary attainments of the young republic."[13] Since he set out on a tour in search of health, pleasure, and education, and to emulate literary models, he managed to establish contacts with Madame de Staël who had praised Germany and German manners in her main literary work, published first in 1810, in a gesture directed against Napoleon's arrogance.[14] But not only did she admire Germany's beginning resurrection in her life-and death struggle against the French yoke, in 1806 ff., Walter Scott did also.

Irving upon returning from the continental tour began to read law in different law offices. Betraying a genius for self-education he passed the bar examination.

[13]Stanley T. Williams of Yale University, *Encyclopedia Britannica*, vol. 12 (1959) col. 696.

[14]*De L'Allemagne*, par Mme la Baronne de Staël. Nouvelle edition revue et corrigée. A Paris chez Treuttel et Würtz, Libraires, 1835.

But as with other *Dichterjuristen* [poetic lawyers and/or lawyering poets] such as Theodor Storm (1817-1888), the author of our second motto, the territory Irving had known since his childhood, left an indelible stamp and thorough impression on him. Seemingly out of nowhere, knowing the Catskill Mountains since his childhood and equipped with a thorough familiarity of the Hudson Valley, Irving as a young man about town wrote and published a burlesque on the ancient "Dutch Valley History".[15] He whimsically but carefully grafted splinters of the real on the far-fetched fictionalized "history" of his boyhood holiday homeland. He manufactured a semi-accurate, humorous tall-tale about it.

He prepared the public for expecting and accepting this story in ads placed in the New York Evening Post, to the effect that " a very curious kind of written book had been found by the innkeeper of a Columbian Hotel, left by a disappeared elderly gentleman by the name of *Dietrich Knickerbocker.* This was going to be the pseudonym under which the twenty-six year old Washington Irving hid his identity.

Walter Scott like Irving a *Dichterjurist* [a lawyering poet] par excellence, praised this "jocose history of New York." It contained welcome elements of narrative skills, a concoction of Cervantes' Don Quichotterie, a dash of Rabelais and a grain of Fielding. whereas the descendants of the portrayed "Dutch" settlers, if they chanced to become readers, were left with smiles in a sweet-sour fashion, the general Anglo readers recognized the humorous flair. But even the writer of social satire, otherwise unsurpassed in the English language, Charles Dickens (1812-1870), who had visited New York, could say of himself in believable fashion: "Dietrich Knickerbocker I have worn to death in my pocket."

In his Knickerbocker Irving pokes fun on a threesome of Hollandic governors of the former New Amsterdam, called Walter the Doubter, William the Testy, and Peter the Headstrong. Even Thomas Jefferson is more or less openly satirized as William or Wilhelmus Kieft. But generally Irwing's targets for satire are pedantic [German-Dutch !] history, and their representative, the irksome governor Pieter Stuyvesant. The exaggerations are part of the satire. For example,. Yankees are summoned by decree to leave the district of New Amsterdam, so that there would not be too much intercourse between the "Dutch" and the "English". The funny thing is that Irving's humor "... seldom becomes wit, for wit is the product of analytic insight",[16] but performs a pendulum swing between sense and nonsense. Ever since that good-natured

---

[15]*Diedrich Knickerbocker's A History of New York from the Beginning of the World to the End of the Dutch Dynasty.* (Christmas 1809; with alterations 1812). A line could be drawn from here to Th. Storm's *Husumerei,* a local patriotic feeling hovering about his small native harbor town of Husum on the North Sea.

[16]Henry A. Pochmann, *Washington Irving, Representative Selections.* American Book Company. w. y., p. LXXI. He started his scholarly career with a 1924 M. A. Thesis from the University of Texas on Mark Twain's Mind.

176

treatment of matters "Dutch", i. e. Netherlandic as an admixture of *Deitsch,* this whole complex has become one of ambiguity, of something treated light-heartedly and is not allowed to be taken too seriously, so that it would become threatening.

While the War of 1812 between the US and Britain, represented by Lower Canada and "Hessian" auxiliary troops, was going on, and as its secondary result, Manitoba was won for Canada, Irving went to Washington as member of a Committee of Merchants, and became an editor there as well. In 1814 he was appointed assistant to governor Tumpkins, with the rank of colonel. In 1815 he set out to England again – only this time to stay for seventeen years. Irving's visit to Scott was followed by a frantic effort to learn German and that amidst social triumphs in London, in which he most likely did not brag about his private foreign language study.

The first fruit of the German "influence" can be seen in the large literary borrowings for his tales "Rip van Winkle", "The Legend of Sleepy Hollow," and the "Spectre Bridegroom". [17] Under the title of a Sketch-Book these legendary stories established his lasting fame and became a literary pioneer work which deconstructed the threatening elements and constructed a bridge between the English speaking majority on the American continent and England so shortly after the War of 1812, which evaporated by 1814. The Sketch-Book contributed to a better understanding of America and Europe,[18] but it also poked fun on native German Americans.

From a coma-like enchanted sleep in the Catskill Mountains Rip van Winkle awakens after twenty years of absence. His rifle has rusted, his dog become wolf-like not recognizing him any more as he snarls at his former master. Rip's house has become forlorn and empty, and looks abandoned like a ghost house. Even the village inn has gone. The story suggests that during Rip's sleep the Netherlandic colony has turned republic. Irving facetiously states that Rip still feels "a loyal subject of the King, God bless him!" The startled bystanders mistake him for a "tory", a spy, or worse, a *refugee.* Rip feels harangued by talks about "the heroes of seventy-six" and of " *liberty*." Apart from Irving poking fun on the state, the reader is also reminded of Benjamin Franklin's letter of 1753, in which he expressed his fear to Peter Collinson that the new post-1710 arrivals from the Palatinate in the Hudson valley were not used to freedom, revising his prior positive assessment of the early Pennsylvania Germans.[19] At least indirectly Irving concurs with Franklin and many other critics of German mass

---

[17]H. A. Pochmann, op. cit., Introduction, LXVI. These stories are contained in *The Sketch-Book of Geoffrey Crayon, Gent. A Posthumous Writing of Diedrich Knickerbocker*. Two vol.s. 1822; published serially first from 1819-20 to America and England.

[18]Karl-Heinz Wirzberger, *Washington Irving The Sketch-Book*. NEB Deutscher Verlag der wissenschaften Ostberlin 1954, p. 17.

[19]*The Papers of Benjamin Franklin*, vol. 4, p. 483f.; see PART TWO, f. n. 8 above.

immigrants to America that they could not always exercise freedom of choice on the promise of American liberty.

At this instant of impending *anagnorisis* Rip recognizes his antiquated self as a *Doppelgänger* (double) with a separate identity of his'. At this very moment "a fresh comely woman" can help lift the veil spread over the old man's identity by being recognized as his daughter, while he learned from her mouth, that her mother, the former Dame Van Winkle, had died, while she "broke a bloodvessel in a fir of passion at a New England ped(d)ler."[20] "Rip now resumed his old walks and habits;" "he was now a free citizen of the United States." "Rip, in fact, was no politician; the changes of states and empires made but little impression on him; but there was one species of despotism ... " ; "petticoat government ..."; "he had got his neck out of the yoke of matrimony." Firmly he had embraced his newly found daughter precisely upon the moment when he came to realize her true filial identity. Here you have it: philiopiety can be folly too.

The author Irving fully realizing that he had obtained this fairy-tale-like legend from the Northern German *Kyffhäuser* stories of the Harz Mountains took the sting out of foreseeable criticism by pinning a Note at the end of the main story:

"The foregoing Tale, one would suspect, had been suggested to Mr. Knickerbocker by a German superstition about the Emperor Frederick *der Rothbart*, and the Kyphaeuser [*sic[21]*] mountain..." " ... Indeed, I have heard many stranger stories than this, in the villages along the Hudson; all of which were too well authenticated to admit of a doubt. I have even talked with Rip Van Winkle myself, who, when I last saw him, was a very venerable old man, and so perfectly rational and consistent on every other point, that I think no conscientious person could refuse to take this into the bargain; nay, I have seen a certificate on the subject taken before a country justice and signed with a cross..."[22]

It may be a bit of an understatement to say that underneath Irving's desire to entertain lies a serious streak (according to the old *prodesse et delectare*); we learn of a stereotypical Harz goat herdsman turned German Hudson-Valley odd settler, with a suspended identity; he has no political skill, but just enough good-natured neighborliness to win acceptance again. Rip finds his identity and

---

[20]Irving's mock diatribe against the yankees is obvious and quite funny occurring at the very moment of self-recognition. I use the *Sketch-Book* edition of Wirzberger, op. cit., p. 87 ff.

[21]To kip means to sleep.

[22]Irving learned this "Peter Klaus *Sage*" from an American translation of Otmar, *Volks-Sagen* (Bremen 1800), as Henry A. Pochmann, "Irving's German Sources in the 'Sketch-Book'", *Studies in Philology*, vol. 27 (1930), Johnson rp., established, and improved it both by adorning it with a different context, and by giving it an American cloak of funniness. See also Walter A. Reichart, *Washington Irving and Germany*. The University of Michigan Press. Ann Arbor w. y.

assimilation capacity back with the help of his daughter, that is, on the next generation level. This forms the link to our main topic of this chapter.

Later on Irving spends eight months in Dresden, Saxony in 1822–23. But he looked for confirmation as well as new inspiration in vain. Maybe he did not know enough German, maybe the freshness of his former approach had out-serialized itself. Still later in his career when he could write what ever he wanted, he allowed himself to be appointed a member of the American Legation in 1826. Henry Hudson and his *Half Moon* are exchanged for Christoforo Columbus and his *Santa Maria.* During the last five years of his life he undertook the labor of patriotism by writing a five-volume biography of George Washington. These serious writings could, however, never erase the grim satire at the expense of the clumsier compatriots from the Hudson Valley, whom he vicariously equipped with a new deconstructed identity. He even fortified his strange image in the equally famous two other legends of his Sketch-Book, "The Legend of Sleepy Hollow", and "The Bridegroom Spectre", both heavy superstition stories from Germany, not the Netherlands. Still, Irving is laughing at his borrowed characters who stay boorish, threatening, but in the end ghoulish and "gothic." Now the region is enchanted by " ... the apparition of a figure on horseback without a head. It is said by some to be the ghost of a Hessian trooper, whose head had been carried away by a cannon-ball, in some nameless battle during the Revolutionary War, ..." [23] The headless horseman a funny apparition with a German background? Which humor is no laughing matter now ? "The Spectre Bridegroom," borrowed from Gottfried August Bürger's [born 1747 in the Harz Mountains] *Wildem Jäger*, has to do with death, not with copulation. If thousands of young Americans read these stories, their original response might have been that of fright in the face of such "Germans". The humour used by Irving is feigned and not really romantic rather it is scary and did not help to heighten the standing of Dutch/German American citizens in the eyes of the majority readers.

B. Thomas Chandler Haliburton (1796-1859)

Thirty years before the arrival of the Empire loyalists 1453 Germans left Halifax (Chebucto), Nova Scotia, and under great hardships moved north to Merliguesh (Malegash) Bay, beginning June 7, 1753. They had founded *Lunenburg* (spelled in Germany thusly) first. They had been promised 50 acres of land for each family around the Halifax area by their shipper who operated out of Rotterdam, The Netherlands, Mr. John Dick, and who had collected a guinea per head for this purpose in advance.[24] They had waited without getting any land of their own

---

[23] Wirzberger's ed. of *The Sketch-Book*, p. 394.

[24] Th. Ch. Haliburton, *An Historical and Statistical Account of Nova Scotia.* Two vol.s Halifax, N. S. 1829; Rp Mika Publications 1973. These data and facts are fully borne out by Andreas Brinck, *Die deutsche Auswanderungswelle in die britischen Kolonien.* Stuttgart 1993.

after arrival since 1750, or almost for three years,[25] while working hard as indentured servants to repay their passage. They were, according to the governor's report "almost incredibly industrious" on their main lot and garden lot. The departure did not occur without a prior rebellion. Since they were clearly defrauded, they planned a forceful exodus by boats. Shortly before their leaving, American privateers had looted some wards of Lunenburg, and had demanded ransom money. It was hard to be defrauded on the one hand by New Scots and be assessed for a share of that ransom extracted by the Yankees.

It is in this political atmosphere that the Constitution Act partitioning "Ontario" from "Quebec" passed in 1791. Shortly after that time, while Lunenburg had grown to 2,213 inhabitants, according to Haliburton's report, it was looted again by American freebooters. It is understandable that the Lunenburg area did not feel friendly toward the southern neighbour. The Atlantic Region was heading to Confederation, and not toward American statehood.

On the other hand, a considerable number of rural, but educated dwellers of New York, New Jersey, Pennsylvania, and Massachusetts could not recover their personal losses incurred during the American War of Independence. Nor did they think highly of their future prospects in these states. As "losers" a sizeable part of the whole population, they figured and decided it was better to stay "loyal to the English crown", and their second-generation King George II. Like their king (he of course, in absentia), some of these "Empire loyalists" had undertaken to transfer themselves from Hanoverians, Waldeckians or Hessians into Britishers by doing service, including military service, in North America. This loyalist decision implied a new trek up North, and a new rooting in the Atlantic Region, above all in New Brunswick and Nova Scotia. These usually Tory-inclined loyalists after their arrival were promoted to the prouder rank of "United Empire Loyalists". They encompassed English, Scottish, and German settlers, and quite a few freedom-seeking Blacks.

A sizeable part of these United Empire Loyalists trekked to and settled in Eastern Ontario first, among them a few clockmakers and sellers from Pennsylvania beginning in 1783-84. Not all of the newcomers were civilians. Many German auxiliaries who had belonged to the First Battalion of Sir John Johnson's so-called "Royal Green" New York regiment, came to settle also. All of these were to function as bulwark against the young, independent U. S., and to counter-balance the Catholic French inhabitants of Lower Canada (Quebec). Captain Michael Grass of German extraction disbanded his former men, shipped them the northern route via the Great Lakes, and let them help to populate and settle Kingston, Upper Canada (Ontario).

Should these many "loyalists" be considered exiles or resettlers in the sense that they became co-founding members of Canada? Of the almost 50,000

[25]Haliburton, op. cit., vol. Two, p. 132f.

estimated United Empire Loyalists, 30,000 arrived in what was to be split off as New New Brunswick in 1784 looking mostly for farmland. Many loyalists were literate, highly skilled, often bilingual (German being their other language).[26] We will see further down what kind of English language they really *spoke*.

Among the loyalists coming to Nova Scotia from New York was a young woman by the name of Lucy Chandler Grant, the daughter of a loyalist major, one of General Wolfe's officers at the Battle of the Plains of Abraham, making Canada British rather than French. Another was a kinsman of the famous novelist, we came across in the last sub-chapter, Sir Walter Scott.[27] Thus arrived among the loyalists from Massachusetts William Haliburton. His son, who had married Lucy Grant, became the Honourable William Hersey Otis Haliburton, Chief Justice of the Court of Common Pleas in Nova Scotia.[28] The scion son of these two distinguished families, Thomas Chandler Haliburton, was born in Nova Scotia in 1796. He went to King's College at Windsor, N. S., modelled after King's College (now Columbia University) in New York. While being educated there his Tory spirit was formed. Next to the influence of his family, the War of 1812 planted the seed in Thomas for comparing his compatriot New Scots with the Yankees. As many a Nova Scotian he feared annexation by the United States, a fear which intensified his attachment to and love for Scotland and England. Haliburton set out for England, wooed and married a distinguished English woman, returned to Nova Scotia, and was called to the bar at Annapolis Royal, a fortress town at the entry to the Bay of Fundy. Both his cousin Walter Scott and Haliburton managed to publish a highly praised historical work each.[29] Haliburton in describing the surrounding settlement expressed the same opinion as Washington Irving had, namely, that the history of every country *in Europe* commenced in the realm of *fable*. Only the beginning *history* of his *new country* was to be accurately describable, and lifted, as it were, on a higher, almost scientific plane. He also became a distinguished and famous *Dichterjurist,* a poetically inclined lawyer. For the big question continued to fascinate him. While he listened to cases and speaking to many as a *Lunenburg* circuit riding

[26] J. M. Bumsted, *Understanding the Loyalists*. Sackville 1986; ed.s Phillip A. Buckner and John G. Reid, *The Atlantic Region to Confederation: A History*. U of Toronto Press/ Acadiensis Press Frederickton, N. B. 1994, and particularly Ann Gorman Condon's Chapter 9; see also the same author's earlier book, *The Loyalist Dream for New Brunswick*. Frederickton, N. B. 1984. Lehmann-Bassler, *The German Canadians 1750-1937*, pp. 52ff., 375, 387; and Gerhard P. Bassler, *Das Deutschkanadische Mosaik*. Ottawa 1991, Chapter XXV.

[27] Scott's tomb is situated in the Haliburton family grave at Dryburgh Abbey in Scotland.

[28] Lorne Pierce, *Thomas Chandler Haliburton*. The Ryerson Canadian history Readers. Toronto 1926.

[29] Walter Scot, *History of Scotland*. Two vol.s 1829; Thomas Chandler Haliburton, *An Historical and Statistical Account of Nova Scotia*. Halifax 1829. This book won Haliburton a high cash reward from the N. S. legislature. Amazingly it was read by Henry Wadsworth Longfellow and perused in his epic *Evangeline*.

judge, he wondered what kind of English did the Empire Loyalists really speak. The religious preference, he noted, often seemed inclined towards various pietistic sects. This is a veiled way of understanding their German background. Did they help that American speech patterns (and cultural values) would survive in his Atlantic Region? The modern historian Bumsted noted furthermore, that these loyalists as an elite helped to preserve a status quo "beyond its usefulness."[30]

In keeping with Haliburton's ultimate rejection of one of his two loyalisms, if not loyalty, by permanently leaving Nova Scotia for England, where he even became a MP for Launceston for six years, before he died in 1859, he developed his mock serious, but still very systematically described theory of *soft sawder*. Its background is formed by the Pennsylvania-Dutch tinged way of *Salbadern*. To be quite clear about the intent: on the one hand the pure and hard High English is defended, the soft sawder, lumped together with deprecated 'yankee speak,' is caricatured. The contrast is couched in humorous terms, f. i.:

"Says you, minister, here's a work that will open your eyes a bit ... It gives the Yankees a considerable of a hacklin, and that ought to please you; it shampoos the English, and that ought to please the Yankees; ..."[31]

Haliburton, MP in the House of Assembly in Halifax, a city more important than Bytown (=Ottawa) at that time, as vigorously as he practised the law, even on the high level of chief justice of the common pleas, continued his literary career. As *Dichterjurist* he believed in Walter Scott's adage: "Literature should be a staff and not a crutch." Haliburton found a friend, the publisher of the Novascotian newspaper who printed a series of humorous albeit *unsigned* articles on a quick-witted yankee clock peddler, Sam Slick of Slickville.

The plan underlying The Clockmaker is a simple one. An English traveller on horseback, called the Squire, lets himself be overtaken by an itinerant Yankee clock seller, also in the saddle. The Tory-inclined Squire feigns liking to hear his new companion's "soft sawder" so much, that he decides to accompany him, first within Nova Scotia, secondly, as far as Connecticut.[32] The Squire is a John Bull-like persona of judge Haliburton, rotund and a little obese, port bibbing, disillusioned, but establishmentarian, otherwise quite reserved. Sam Slick, taller and wirier, represents the Yankee type, a dynamic "bird of prey," sly, vain, talkative, garrulous, irreverently exploiting native Nova Scotian "bluenosers".

[30]In Buckler-Reid, *Atlantic Region*, p. 183.

[31]Quoted from *The Clockmaker; or the Sayings and Doings of Samuel Slick Slick of Slickville*, vol. II, fourth ed. by R. Bentley. London 1839, p. 319. I make use of prior research published in my *Northwest Germany in Northeast America*. Lit Verlag 1997, pp. 40-46.

[32]And much later, in a serialized continuation, all the way to England. See Ray Palmer Baker, *Sam Slick by Thomas Chandler Haliburton*. Doran New York w. y. (ca. 1923).

The educated Squire is mock-attracted by the seemingly rough peddler's educational philosophy: "Books only weaken your understandin' as water does brandy." Slick studied no foreign or classical languages like the judge, "but the language of human natur' ", and as a salesman, uses his soft sawder to great advantage. What matters to him is how to sell $ 6.50 clocks for $ 40. So *The Clockmaker* indulges in talk, small talk, sales talk, contrasting provincial toryism with a peculiar Yankee idiom. Thus I do not think that Haliburton deliberatedly "butchers" the English language. Rather his intent is to transcribe dialogue written in a satirical contrast to standard English.

In his original edition Haliburton wanted to demonstrate indeed how not to speak in Nova Scotia, so that its residents would not be made Nova-Yankees by linguistic default. Haliburton wants to expose the mixed parentage of both his hero, as son of a colonel Slick, hero of Bunker Hill, and grandson of General Van Shleek, who came over to England with King William the "Dutchman", and emigrated to America, "where our name gettin' altered into Slick." For Sam and his family "larfs at everythin' that ain't Yankee." Although women purchase the clocks, their husbands are legally responsible for payment, the purchasing women are relegated to the background. The narrative focus stays predominantly male oriented. The narrator wants to caricature the way New Englanders speak at home and "abroad" in Nova Scotia.[33] He was not sure of the linguistic origin.[34] We have here rather a differentiation between oral speech patterns in language, as it was really spoken, and formal written English; conservatives understand and use both ways, they talk down formally to underlings, but they do not necessarily talk formally among themselves all the time. Haliburton intended to expose the imported Empire Loyalist way of speaking, as the Yankees had brought it up to the Atlantic Seaboard. To transpose this spoken speech into accurate print was no mean feat and proceeded in stages in his subsequent 1843 revision. Within six years the spelling had been changed phonetically.

First Series 1837 ed.	1843 edition
Second Ser. 1838 ed.	1843 edition
[Amerikin]	[Amerikin] (see Fontane's motto)
certain	sartain
chest	chist
fertile [2nd]	fartile
follow	foller
general	gineral

[33] *The Attaché; or Sam Slick in England, Second Series.* London 1844, p. 208f.; Third Series, pp. 142, 148, 152.

[34] I disagree with Elna Bengtsson, "The Language and Vocabulary of Sam Slick I." *Upsala Canadian Studies*, w. y., pp. 1-50, that such was the idiom of "uncultured people".

join	jine
knew	knowed
learn	larn
petikilar [2nd]	pitikilar
politie	perlite
pumpkins	punkins
regular	regilar
soldiers	sodgers
speculation	spekilation
value	valy
window	winder
you were	you was

In our opinion Haliburton tried to put the 'yankee speak' into print. What does it really consist of? There is "corrupted" English, Cohort Low German and Hollandic influences resulting in a genuine American spoken idiom as it was beginning to constitute itself in New Amsterdam and in New York. It must have spread to Long Island and Connecticut and up the Hudson valley during a long incubation period of 1664 to 1792. It brushed off the influence of High English on the Yorker idiom, and formed an anti-Yorker or Yankee idiom, oriented toward speaking, hustling, trading, and selling. It probably spread as an army jargon. It became a linguistic possibility with a practical phonetic system and a grammar of its own.[35] It filled a void left by ex-New Netherlands, which was rapidly peopled by lower class Non-Englishmen as well as by average to higher class Englishmen. It must have been spoken by the man of the street (or rather path in those days). It was an un-English English dialect, a bridging idiom for orally concluded business. The Yankee speech developed into a *lingua franca* (see Bengtsson's dialect system) of the colonial period of the 18th century. Had the War of 1812 not stopped dreams of a North American unification, it might have lasted longer. But the migratory United Empire Loyalists spoke it to death in the Atlantic Region of Canada in formation. The literature to make its speakers sound crass was at hand. The deviations from standard English, in the long run, were not only displeasing to the "Bluenosers", it was considered a slightly uncouth way of sawdering, and did not please fine-tuned educated New Yorker or Halifax ears. And above all, it had been taken up en masse and and promoted by Yankees of the German-Dutch ilk. It was the Rip Van Winkle's and the Sam Slick's sub-standard way of speaking. It was exposed to humor, sarcasm and satire of the finest kind. Example: "Do you seem them are swallers*", said

---

[35]Carefully researched by Elna Bengtsson, showing which vowels and consonants disappeared, when th becomes t (similar to Old High German), how pronouns are used and abused, and forms like "I aren't," and "you be" became standard, and many other characteristic features.

the Clockmaker.[36] Ironically the same Yankee pedlars carried the spelling-book around, without consulting it.

In hindsight it seems rather a shame that this dialect humor was only taken up on a grand humorous scale one more time, and discontinued as a linguistic "gun." Haliburton's primer stayed "one of the excessively rare items in...Canadian Literature."[37] Contemporary readers would recognize in Sam the prototype of Uncle Sam, or, if he was really "older", a caricature of that uncle, which is a stern figure. It is derived from the initials U S and was popularized on supply containers during the War of 1812. Not by coincidence is the first (unauthorized) edition of the novel, Innocents Abroad's cover graced by an image of Uncle Sam. One boy in Hannibal, Missouri, is said to have owned a copy of The Clockmaker, and even read it in church, and later on as a journalist.[38]

C. Mark Twain (1835-1910)[39]

It is difficult to fathom how many sides there were to Samuel Langhorne Clemens's identity and character. In 1850 he started out a typesetter apprentice. At age 27 he renamed himself 'Mark Twain', assuming a nom de plume by which he is better known. This name is owed to the fact that he had been a registered Mississippi river boat pilot beginning in 1859. As a Westerner he served in the Confederate Army in 1861; Twain became a prospector for gold and silver in California. Besides he became notorious for the short story, "The celebrated Frog of Calaveras" (1865). Just like Irving and Haliburton he became a famous writer only after he had sailed for Europe. He had sent back the "Alta Letters" to The Daily Alta Californian newspaper, and a few other reports to the New York Tribune and Herald. He reworked them into a book, which appeared for subscribers only, with the American Publishing Company in Hartford, Connecticut. In this way, The Innocents Abroad appeared eight years before Tom Sawyer and sixteen years before The Adventures of Huckleberry Finn, which was first published in England late in 1884. It is that last book that made him internationally famous and that our generation still likes best of all. By that time he was married to Olivia Langdon, the only woman he said he ever loved, an heiress to a fortune, for fifteen years.[40]

---

[36]Transliterated into German: "*Scheint es dir diese sind Schwalben?*"

[37]Lorne Pierce, *Thomas Chandler Haliburton. Reader*, p. 19.

[38]George H. Brownell "Sam Slick, the Connecticut Clockmaker, Original of Uncle Sam as Source of Inspiration for Dickens, Mark Twain and other Humorists," *Dearborn Independent* (The Ford International Weekly), XXV, October 10, 1925.

[39]Samuel Clemens' folks hailed from Virginia. Were they descended from the Clemen(t)s brothers John and William who arrived in Jamestown in 1624?

[40]Twain met her on the return trip from his cruise to Europe in Dec., 1867. I am basing this subchapter on my research, published in *Northwest Germany in Northeast America*, p. 48 -52.

Twain's innocent "pilgrims" arriving in foreign countries, including the Holy Land, are armed with "moral" superiority to compensate with tall tales and cover up for an abundance of ignorance. His American readers are told what they wanted to hear, just as Haliburton told his readers what they wanted to hear about their unwelcome Yankee neighbours. All three writers are striking a chord by mock exploiting the credulity in a rapid fire delivery of words, – "from sentimentalism to parody," from patriotism toward the US, Canada or England, "from silliness to sober observation."[41] The relationship between the narrated antagonists creates an episodic humour time and again. This comic method reminds of Sam Slick's landing another sale of an overvalued clock. When one comes across Mark Twain's pun on "average" (with the secondary meaning of *Havarie*) "I have been at sea quite enough to know that that was a very good average", when the other had actually sung out of tune, the laughter becomes irresistible. One thinks of the *Ship of Fools*.

Haliburton's and Twain's humour "are on the run", [42] their languages slice up the world differently, whereas Irving's humour digs underneath the surface and is more mock-sinister, but of course ultimately satirical as well. They felt they had to break the rules of conventional grammar once in a while, and substitute it with the grammar of the disadvantaged, the underdog, the victim, the indentured one, while you are running for the main purpose of taking a break from formality and etiquette.

When Twain tosses about the expressions "don't say hain't it", and "it ain't so" – we think that we are let in on a forgotten secret, namely that "hain't, in the Southern Missouri way of speaking, is more closely related to *"haben nicht"* than to "are not (*"sein nicht"*). It is difficult to ascertain how many German dialect ingredients can be found as "arrows" of humor.[43] There is actually not that much, with the exception of *A Tramp Abroad.* The most outrageous example is found in the interlarding of German and English in Twain's German *Meisterschaft* sentences of 1892.The Appendix to this otherwise not that well-known play contains the notorious "The Awful German Language" diatribe, and has become a "classic" in every German Language Department at US. colleges. The often quoted sample, "It's awful undermining to the intellect, German is, you want to take it in small doses" is not very friendly, and its satirical wit is debatable. Almost to compensate for his daring, Twain interlards three versions of Heine's poem *Loreley.* Two other stylistic examples, collected by Holger Kersten,[44] may

---

[41]Henry B. Woham, *Mark Twain and the Art of the Tall Tale.* Oxford University Press N. Y. 1993, Chapter 3, and particularly p. 76-78.

[42]Stuart Hutchinson, *Mark Twain: Humour on the Run.* Amsterdam. Atlanta, Georgia 1994.

[43]John T. Krumpelmann, *Mark Twain and the German Language.* Baton Rouge, LA 1953.Holger Kersten, *Von Hannibal nach Heidelberg. Mark Twain und die Deutschen.* Würzburg 1993, pp. 242ff.

[44]Von *Hannibal nach Heidelberg*, p. 55, 169.

serve as examples of German American dialect anecdotes:

I vos pount to gif ter old vomans ter small pox
Der poots are not quite done, but der heel ish made out.

In our context we need to draw a careful distinction between satire, achieved by means of dialect and the perspective chosen by the narrator. The first overall impression seems to be that Huck speaks almost like a black to his black friend Jim, whereas Jim seems to speak child-like and full of superstition as if he were a Riplet Van Winkle. They both seem to speak "masked." They try to evade the issue (so as not to hurt each other) that a poor Mississippi boy is only slightly better off than Jim. The non-standardness of their speaking taken by itself is not funny.

Hence I disagree with David Sewell[45] that Jim's speech patterns could be termed "romanticized folk speech." Twain did not invent these patterns any more than Haliburton did. The alienation effect (*Verfremdungseffekt*) is committed against the standard English language, not held against underprivileged people. For Sam Slick that might be a secondary aspect. Jim and Huck *both* struggle with standard English. Sub-standard English belongs to English, just as standard Low German is part of the German language, and not just a German northern dialect. Slaves were forbidden to learn reading, so they could only pick up dialect English from the way they were talked to. We do not know how well Huck may have read other than the Bible, which one used to learn more orally including memorization of key passages. Both were better versed in reading the signs of the movements of the mighty Mississippi. Thus I agree with Leonard, Tenney and Davis (1992) when they say:

"Huck Finn, the first person narrator of Adventures of Huckleberry Finn, is a youth from the margins of society who is awkwardly learning to overcome the prejudices of his upbringing – "[46]

But I would not be inclined to credit thematic energy on the part of the narrator with Jim's fear of being sold "downriver":

"I come mighty near being sold down here once & if I had been I wouldn't been here now; been the last of me."

In fact, the two friends teach each other not to go under. We must not forget that

---

[45]Mark Twain's *Languages: Discourse, Dialogue, and Linguistic Variety*. U. P. Berkeley, CA 1987, p. 95.

[46]Ed. by James S. Leonard, Thomas A. Tenney, and Thadious M. Davis, *Satire or Evasion? Black Perspectives on Huckleberry Finn*. Duke U. P. Durham and London 1992, p. 5.

Twain, five years before publishing his masterpiece, became part owner of the Buffalo Express, in which he criticized political abuses of all kinds. He must have been familiar since his small town Missouri boyhood that there was one group of Americans who were in solidarity with black liberation from slavery: the mayor of Germantown, the lawyer F. D. Pastorius, penned the first manifesto against slavery both in German and English as early as 1688. It may be a dangerous jump of six generations up to Twain. But the German Americans of Iowa and Missouri, and probably of Buffalo as well, being on the escape route to freedom in Canada and likely elsewhere were known as "nigger apostles".[47] Germans, if they did not hail from the Northern or Northwestern part of the Old Country had trouble learning English quickly, except, of course, if they brought along a high-class education like Duden.

In the eighteen fifties and sixties of the 19th century it was the rage to learn English "the way a child learns his native language. This method made use of stories and classified ... lists of idioms." Some such "conversation guides" were composed in North America, but sent to Germany for printing. A characteristic example can be picked up from a manual published in 1848 and republished in 1851:[48]

Negro. Read dat letter, Massa, dat tell you my character.
Master. Ah it cannot blacken his reputation. ...

Negro. Iss Massa – me (ich) capital fellow to fill rascal's place. ...
Negro. Massa, me been ebery ting me serve at the bottome of High gate hill, and den dey call me Lily ob de valley – me turn waterman ...

Twain was probably familiar with these wide-spread materials, and may have made use of them in his own contrastive perhaps a trifle haphazard German studies. In any case, he describes a phenomenon often observable: the lowest on the social totem pole is taught a special skill by the second lowest from the margins of society, and the more higher up can afford to satirize the learning process.

This ... "raise[d] the possibility that Twain's emphasis on 'realistic' precision in his use of dialect may conceal an underlying sense that Jim's humanity is significantly compromised by too much reliance on the conventional and inoffensive." [49]

[47]The weekly *National-Demokrat.* Dubuque, Iowa, 10 May 1860.
[48]Heinrich Stedtmann, *Der Kleine Engländer oder die Kunst in kürzester Zeit englisch zu lernen.* p. 90.
[49]*Satire or Evasion*, p. 5.

Missouri, a cross-road between North and South, lay on Ol Man River to Blacks and Germans alike, just as "Father Rhine" (*Vater Rhein*) had been the acculteration center territory of Northwestern and Southwestern Germany, and the Netherlands alike. The river streaming downwards to the old immigration harbor New Orleans from St. Paul, Minnesota, was the acculturation river of North America par excellence. It helped the growing American civilization overcome many hurdles. Just as formerly called "Negro spirituals"[50] created relief from the sorrows of enslavement by "call and response", so these manuals of learning, the language of their contemporaries are based on a similar principle and have a rhythm of their own as well. Nowadays it is called "the direct method". Twain had just as fine-tuned an ear for dialect "calls and responses" and the dialectics between spoken humour and printed satire as had Haliburton.

To summarize, all three writers feared the chaos of incomprehensibility, but particularly Irving and most of the three, Twain.. They were afraid of intellectual or political annexation, "the Babel" of non-tongues. The two, Haliburton and Twain,[51] use regional dialect, Loyalist-Yankee; Missourian with a German and Black ring. This significant linguistic and outstanding satirical line must be more thoroughly researched than is possible here. At least we can say that Haliburton and Twain commanded the power of genuine dialect usage, as well as that of interlarding standard and dialect English.

The mutual incomprehension between speakers in a Connecticut Yankee at King Arthur's Court or in Tom Sawyer Abroad begins to increase. There is no more haven or hiding-place like "Slickville", searched for the sake of former gentility. The satire may have long passed into the realm of "evasion." The time has come and passed again where the WASPS have become ashamed of being Anglo-Saxon, as Twain wondered about in his article, "The Anglo-Saxon Race",[52] written in 1906, four years before his death. The mutual listening to each other's speaking is on the vane. The listening span for satire, except in cabaret form, is not large any longer. The Sam Slicks are no longer "stick in the muds". Slickvilles are no longer lovingly remembered.

---

[50]Ed. John W. Work, *American Negro Songs and Spirituals*. Bonanza New York 1940; my cherished possession.

[51]David R. Sewell, *Mark Twain's Languages*. Berkeley 1987.

[52]Ed. Maxwell Geismar, *Mark Twain and the Three Rs: Race, Religion, Revolution – and Related Matters*. The Bobbs-Merrill Co. Indianapolis/New York 1973.

Chapter 5
Residues of spoken dialect in controlled acculturation literature

Irving, Haliburton and Twain all three went to England as young men first and as grown men again. The two Americans even went to Germany. They became famous writers for telling readers of the English language, be they Americans, Canadians, or Englishmen, what they wanted to hear. Different than the two Americans, Haliburton was born from a distinguished family with a reputation. Irving, on the other hand, was craving for recognition. Twain, after he had moved from the native West to the East (Connecticut), continued to worry about his fame even up to the bestowal with an honorary doctorate from Oxford University very late in life. Both Americans knew bankruptcy. All three practically emigrated to England, Twain for several years, Irving for 17 years, Haliburton for the rest of his life.

All three helped to transform the North American language and established it by their power of humor into an instrument of eloquent prose. Their style was recognized and praised in England first, not only by popular acceptance and enjoyment, but also by the leading English writers of their era. This in turn helped establish American as a legitimate English language of literature, rather than literacy alone. All three had a predilection for the Big Water: Irving for the Hudson, Haliburton for the Bay of Fundy, and Mark Twain for the Mississippi. Nevertheless Hartford, Connecticut, for Mark Twain, New York for Irving, and London for Haliburton, mattered just as much. Writing English was their staff, dialect their crutch, respectability their craved for reward.

All three had a nose for acculturation problems and their adequate depiction. None of them liked the Germanic sounding heavy-handedness in matters of style. They had a scent for fretting out un-English intrusions, be they imported under the guise of "loyalism", "Dutch dynasty" , or Missouri dialect acculturation problems and stylistic intricacies. They made use of dialect, but left no doubt that it had to be exposed as a stick in the mud element. Irving and Haliburton both wanted to keep English "pure". They shared the fear that it needed to be controlled and that German elements required "weeding" as much as possible. In this way their didactic intent was to protect the English language from a foreign linguistic onslaught. Mark Twain was the most ambiguous master of satirical English. He was steeped in organic American English and its various "heeling qualities" as well as educational democratic functions, all wrapped into carefully controlled satire. Their literature contains a wealth of spoken dialect not allowed to intrude into "high" standard American or Canadian pronunciation or to transform written American or Canadian style in their literary canon. But the remnants are clearly visible like a hardened coral reef below the surface of a continent. To follow up in more depth on the sum total of such residues between the ebb of policy and the flood of political practice would require another inquiry outside the scope of this study.

PART FIVE

THE GOING DUTCH:

Balancing the FOUR PARTS debit-credit
Germany-US and Canada: GONE AMERICAN

When millions of residents of consecutive generations leave a country over several centuries, a loss of a considerable amount must be felt in their homeland in the long run. When Bismarck's successor as Imperial Chancellor, the bachelor soldier Count Georg Leo von Caprivi[1] de Caprera de Montecuccoli (1831-1899) made the remark in the *Reichstag* on Dec. 10, 1891: "We must export: either goods *or people*,"[2] he may have echoed the voice of his master, Wilhelm II. At least the chancellor was being rather cynical about imaginary gains made by emigration. On the other hand, one would by common sense alone suspect a gain of *some* kind, achieved by the accepting countries, the US and Canada. But to make up population *and* economic balances are complicated matters to deal with and to resolve.

In the beginning there were no immigration services, and obviously no quotas. But after these two countries were confederated in 1789 and 1867 respectively, the stream of immigrants became funnelled, controlled, and eventually subject to registration. As of 1821 ethnic data were taken in the US. The two North American countries took in the unfree and hungry, the oppressed, in short, the "huddled masses", as the Lady Statue of Liberty pronounces, but also many elite professional people.[3] For a long time all of them were taken in as they arrived.

From the 17th to the 19th century the populations in North America was much smaller than that of the German Empire, which in turn was larger than England's. The US reached the same number of residents as "Germany" in 1882, at the level of 52,000,000 inhabitants each, and permanently surpassed the number of German residents. Today the US have more than 200,000,000 "Caucasian" [=White] inhabitants of which ca. 23% or up to 58 million *could* claim full or part German heritage. Germany has 83 million inhabitants today,

---

[1]Chancellor from 1890-1894. He is best known in Germany for a long, but narrow strip called "Caprivi's finger," situated in Namibia, formerly a German colony. He also withdrew the claim on Sansibar in favor of the island of Helgoland in the North Sea.

[2]*Stenographischer Bericht*, VIII, 1. Session, Band 5. Berlin 1892, p. 3307. Emphasis is mine.

[3]See my "Inter-Colonial Profile Tables" concerning ten territories, about the German immigrants' training and occupations in 17th century North America, *"Those Damn' Dutch,"* p. 68-70.

where several millions *have* to claim a *non*-German heritage. The new German *Zuwanderungsgesetz* (Immigration Law) did not pass the *Bundesrat* (the Senate or Upper House equivalent) with a parliamentary trick of a one vote majority, given by Brandenburg, for nothing today. In the US quotas for nationals erect dikes as questionable means of defense. Our numbers here presented are those of registered or legal immigrants. Complete numbers of others are unknown and hence unavailable.

Chapter 1
German law of emigration background

It may be surprising to many American and most German readers that the German Constitution *(Weimarer Reichsverfassung)* of 1919, valid until 1933, was more specific than even the liberal Basic Law *(Grundgesetz)* of 1949, now in force both in the Federal Republic of Germany and the former German Democratic Republic, is today. The WRV stated in its article 112, I: "Every German is entitled to emigrate to non-German countries. Emigration can only be abridged by federal law." *(Reichsgesetz)*

The layman's opinion that this basic law might have had its roots in the blessings of the French Revolution is erroneous. Historically, the right to leave was a benefit rather than a basic privilege right. It was the other side of the coin, so to speak, in case a ruler did not govern properly so that his subjects were "forced" to leave and conduct a rewarding life elsewhere. A well governing ruler in theory eliminated all sound reasons for his subjects wanting to leave their home country permanently.[4] Indirectly this advantage was related to the spreading of religious freedom. It did not cover those who stayed home, however. The right to staying attached to one's native soil, was much more deep-rooted than giving it up.

By 1780 the right to leave became practically indistinguishable from emigration (based originally on the law of *freier Abzug*),[5] but required the status of a free-born.[6] This kind of regular, high-status emigrant usually had to pay a 10% *Abzug* tax, called *detractus* or in German *Abfahrtsgeld.*[7] They also normally had to have served their time in the army. Suspected draft-dodgers could not get their clearance from the county officials. This status advantage gave regular German immigrants the legal edge over ordinary, on average perhaps slightly younger, English immigrants until the fall of Napoleon, 1815ff. From then on the reform by Stein-Hardenberg, concerning the *Bauernbefreiung* (enfranchisement of the peasants) became law. Emigrants were required to

---

[4]G. v. Berg, *Policey-Recht*, part II (1803) p. 47f. The German Federal Act of 1815, Art. 18 b, guaranteed the "moving off" privilege, provided the other territory or land was willing to accept the migrant's and his family's new residence. By 1817 "unfree" men were no longer excluded and thus could accompany their "masters".

[5]Rotteck-Welcker, *Staatslexikon.* Altona 1,34. vol. 1, p. 14; vol. 2, p. 58; The Prussian *Allgemeine Landrecht* (1794) in second part, seventeenth title § 127, needed 20 rules to regulate "emigration, moving off, and tax". The important stipulation was that one moved off to non-hostile states, so as not to be drafted and dodge the draft at home.

[6]H. G. Scheidemantel, *Repertorium des deutschen Staats- und Lehnrechts*, I. Teil (ed. 1872) p. 50. The guarantee of this privilege to free-borns goes back to the Great German Basic Law, the so-called *Goldene Bulle* of 1356, Kapitel VI § 2.

[7]Abused by the Göring Administration in 1936-1940, regarding propertied Jews "leaving" Germany.

193

notify the administration of their intention to leave (with one's family) until then. Clandestine moving was still to be fined or resulted in a short imprisonment (*ALR* 10 II, 17, § 139). States that were befriended to Prussia and granted reciprocity, were enumerated in the code called *Allgemeines Landrecht* (ALR) . America was not mentioned in this section, although Prussia concluded a treaty opening diplomatic relations with the US in the last year of King Frederick's II reign.

But the right to move was wider and entailed the right to "move through" another non-hostile territory. The hitch consisted in the duty to renounce one's old allegiance *before* leaving. After arrival, the final payment on the passage had to be made, or indenture awaited the newcomer, if he could not pay up. Once the place of settlement in North America was reached, and the oath of allegiance[8] had been sworn, an immigrant was safe.[9] Some statesmen were thinking of emigration as opening a valve against over-population.[10] The new *Staatsangehörigkeitsgesetz* (Law of Citizenship) of 1913, which we touched upon before, made the *jus sanguinis*, the law of blood relationship, prevalent upon the old *jus soli*, the Law of Soil, as in Bavarian, Hessian Pomeranian citizens' ethnicity. In legal terms that meant and still means that German citizenship could be bequeathed even abroad.[11] But the traditional right to emigrate, which is still not abridged, implies no tacit recommendation for unrestricted emigration from Germany.[12] By the beginning of World War One, the "golden" days of emigration freedom were over. The new German passports bundled three legal functions in one state document: one, the inspectability of the bearer, two, the bearer's protection abroad, and three, the protection of a community from a potentially hostile alien in their midst. While in 1867 the passport regulated legal matters concerning *Inländer*, (residents) it switched to regulate *Ausländer* (foreigners) from 1913-16. This switch contained elements of arbitrariness and sometimes hardships as well.

[8]Called "oath of fidelity", because of the Catholics swearing it, in Maryland.

[9]G. Moltmann, *Aufbruch nach Amerika*. Tübingen 1979, p. 85ff.

[10]Freiherr vom Stein, in a private letter, *Korrespondenz*. Vol. 5, p. 325.

[11]Roger Brubaker, *Citizenship and Nationhood in France and Germany*. Harvard U. P. 1992. I am basing parts of this section on my research and sources quoted in *Northwest Germany in Northeast America*, section 1.2.

[12]Ulrich Scheuner, "Die Auswanderungsfreiheit," *Festschrift für Richard Thoma*. Tübingen 1950, p. 223.

Chapter 2
Canada-US acculturation contrasts

It is a fact that 80% of the Canadian population live within 170 km of the US border, while only 10% of the American population live near the Canadian border.[13] Consequently most Canadians have first-hand American experiences. Few Americans look much past the Rainbow or the Peace Bridges, and most Americans take Canada for granted. This proximity implies that quite a few German-Canadians may toy with the idea to try for greener pastures south of the border. And quite a few did until the late sixties, when the draft dodgers went North because of the War in Vietnam.

The degree of denying an over-indulgence in European background history must be different in the US and in Canada. Canada is officially a bilingual country. German is the third largest cultural background in Canada. American and Canadian farms may be similar, but American cities, except a few in Pennsylvania, are by and large incorporated entities. Canadian cities are more traditionally structured with suburbanization features which spread later than in the US.[14] Therefore, it is to be supposed that German Americans, concerning their private life styles – which according to stereotypes include eating dark bread and *Wurst* (salami), and liking to drink beer, can stay identifiably separate from mainstream longer in the US towns or cities than in Canadian ones. The British Canadian life style is so fully preoccupied with the *Francophones,* and their problems in Quebec, that a shorter acculturation and assimilation period is meted out on the third largest immigrant block of the country, and is silently accepted. Ironically the "pull", exerted by the customs of the majority culture, may have shortened the process of Canadianizing on the part of the German-Canadians.

The Americanization of Germans south of the border works at its own pace. It is considered more of a civic obligation than a necessity. American cities with their former German quarters looked more planned. Yet there are more decrepit structures and abandoned houses seen in the US than in Canada nowadays.[15] Not quite half or perhaps only 40% of the Canadian population may be British in an accultured urban sense, whereas in the US the percentage is *much* lower, perhaps around a quarter of the total white population. Therefore, the adjustment for German Americans must have been easier to make in the US than in Canada. There the "linguistic antagonist" is the native French-Canadian speaker. The self-

---

[13]Richard G. Lipsey, eds., C. F. Doran and J. H. Sigler, *Canada and the United States: Enduring Friendship, Persistent Stress.* American Assembly 1985, p. 70.

[14]Michael A. Goldberg and John Mercer, *The Myth of the North American City.* 1986.

[15]Jack Lemon, "Twentieth Century Urban Planning In Canada and the US:" Thoughts on Explaining the Differences. Manuscript circulating at Memorial University of Newfound-land. I thank Chris Sharpe for bringing it to my attention.

assurance of modern Hispanic Americans may be on the upswing today, but it is only beginning to be a rival language in Southern California and in the Sun Belt all the way to Southern Florida. The Canadianization requires probably a more thorough-going effort on the part of the newcomer. You can be a "hyphen-" Canadian, but not a "token" Canadian, as you may be a "token" American all your life in the US.

During the assimilation processes a German settler becomes an American by stages. He *harmonizes* himself to the new country's *mores* (ways and characteristic traits). During the acculturation phase, say, a Westphalian, for instance settling in Missouri, *converts* his personal energy, beginning upon arrival. While this energetic conversion from *landsman* to a Missourian or any new-state settlement is inter-generational and slow, the acculturating experience is more spotty and rather complicated. The assimilative changes from German to American must contain "federal", either harmonizing elements fitting together or rough-hewn remnants staying separate. Since Germans in the Old Country were used to such aspects of federalism, and their homeland's national identity was weak to begin with, their acculturation and assimilation energies fitted particularly well into the new country's and states' requirements. The German settlers were federally and locally "pliable" citizens, and hence less visible than the other groups of foreign immigrants.

Becoming a Canadian, by comparison, seems a less complex task and requires a more direct conversion effort than changing to an American. Since Canada is a confederation, and a centrally organized one at that, its confederated states attach fewer ramifications to the conversion during the acculturation process than the US. Concerning US acculturation ramifications, a former Secretary of State,[16] Carl Schurz, expressed a sense of heightened duties in this way:

> "It should be the job of the Germans, to let reverberate back to Germany the best of what the U. S. have given in thought and deed to the world." [17]

This double-pronged almost tentacled extension to federalism abroad could hardly have been said about Canadian citizenship by choice and its more focussed, new country-centered, expectations under the prevailing circumstances.

It may be surprising for modern Germans of the post-1990 generation to accept that there are other people, namely the Canadians, who are the world's oldest and most continuous anti-Americans and not they the Germans as they

---

[16]Carl Schurz (1829-1906).

[17]Quoted second-hand from Otto Lohr, *The First Germans in America*, New York Stechert 1912, p. 210; rp. in Germany 1962, and again in the US by Don H. Tolzmann in 1992.

may have assumed. Rather, over the long haul, the US has been highly acclaimed by most German travellers and writers.[18] And so has Canada!

Ironically, quite a few new Americans of "recent" German origin may have had the tendency to imitate the moralism of their fellow American citizens. Canadians of German extraction are arguably more used to hierarchically organized British ways of functioning. Ultimately Germans with respect for authority and vertical lines of authority should have been more comfortable settling somewhere in Canada. If they were more assertive, and possessed a matching "frontier" mentality, they probably felt more attracted to the US. These nuances could be registered not only concerning Germans in North America, but in respect to most other immigrant groups also, except for those from Britain settling in Canada. Thus I could not find or identify any outstanding panoramic, commonly shared, German-North American "continentalist" features standing out. "Coping" as an immigrant in either country, assimilating and acculturating north or south of the border, depends on many individual circumstances and on a personality's bendable and dependable strength,[19] or, semi-facetiously expressed, on their "selfish gene," from which the cohortiveness has been detracted during the second part of German immigration history to North America. Perhaps because of the noticeable similarity in outward appearance, ethnicity does not seem to be a watershed barrier for average Germans in either North American country. The question of the relevance of ethnicity, reduced in the way described above, will lead to the following summary.

[18]Wolfgang-Uwe Friedrich, *Die USA und die Deutsche Frage 1945-1990.* Campus Verlag Frankfurt/Main und New York 1991.

[19]John Berry, "Acculturation and Psychological Adaptation," Klaus J. Bade, *Migration – Ethnizität – Konflikt: Systemfragen und Fallstudien.* Osnabrück 1996, p. 171-186.

Chapter 3
The ethno-nationalist American and Canadian models

The ethno-nationalist "tapestry" model implies a woven-in acculturation by the minority immigrant culture in the majority culture. It bases its centripetal power on allowing a certain degree of publicly shown alienation from one's own immediate heritage which is not necessarily shared with every second or third generation immigrant. Inter-generational living is on the wane. This abstract model sponsored as an image by the government grants the runner-up heritage weave an also-run spot and hence a recognizable place on the "tapestry" either reluctantly or voluntarily.

It is understood by everybody that the majority space plus minority images on the tapestry express the majority's permanent hold on power. The majority sets the highlights of its history and its history's interpretation waves. Along with the sense of the times the majority admits an admixture of so many national successes and a few national defeats[20] (e.g. Louis Riel's and John Brown's hangings). According to this model a conflict can only be ended by internal *peace*. It is neither completely reached with respect to Francophones in Canada, nor to Blacks in the US. But it is completely reached with respect to Germans in Canada or the US by the beginning 21st century.

Foreign-born Germans in US America numbered ca. 10% of the population by, say, 1895, while the previous generation of German-derived Americans was at least acculturated, the generation before that fully assimilated, and the earliest generation already fully Americanized and unrecognizabe lfrom the general population on the average. The non-adjusted members in this generational chain were registered as "odd balls" by their families, but benignly left alone by administrations. The problem would naturally "melt away."

The problem of national identity can be traced back to the cohort law and its legal construct of unifying (*Einungsrecht*) of the Hanse.[21] In the final days of the Hanse time when, as we have shown, the leadership ceased to be identical with the cohorts (*Genossen*), representation became dependent on mandate. Until that happened, the municipality itself was the upper crust[22] according to Germanic customary law, and not the chosen representatives as in Roman law. The principle was one of trust, not of mere outward representation. It needs to be stated here with emphasis that the real history of American administrative law, to which the Law of Immigration belongs, has not yet been written This

---

[20]Norbert Ropers, "Ethnopolitische Konflikte und ihre Bearbeitung [why not *Verarbeitung*?] in der Staaten- und Gesellschaftswelt," ed. Klaus J. Bade, *Migration – Ethnizität – Konflikt: Systemfragen und Fallstudien. IMIS – Schriften*. Rasch Osnabrück 1996, p. 171-186.

[21]See PART ONE f. n. 1, Hammel-Kiesow, *Die Hanse*, p. 70.

[22]A rare German Canadianism derived from *krös = Kerbe*, and not from bread crust.

summary is no more than a small hint at a beginning of some light thrown on "this dark continent" (Boorstin).[23]

According to the Canadian "mosaic model", argued by Gerhard P. Bassler,[24] one selectively looks at "multicultural contributions" over a time span of four hundred years, and Canada's third largest group as achievers. The contributions form a variable, the "Germaness" the constant. As soon as one reverses these tags, calling the "Germaness" a variable reverberation, and the "Canadianess" a focussed constant, the picture becomes perhaps a bit more persuasive. From the point of view of Canadian history (and of the foreign German government), contributions made in Canada are Canadian, even if the performers were trained in the Old Country. Historical background elements of the contribution wither away or even fade. So the remembrance of the German roots of contributions is a pedigree-hunting private history. This remark is not made to deprecate the contribution as such, but rather that its "Germaness" is not their outstanding feature. For these achievers, their ethnicity may not have been overly relevant.[25] Was not their common religion and their secondary language a stronger bond holding them temporarily together? The "mosaic" model is just a temporary simile, and is not worth a heated debate, nor has its pattern any more scientific explanatory value than the "tapestry" model. The point is, emigration, a privilege until 1914, upon completion dialectically turns into an administratively controlled immigration measure. These analogies have little value on a scientific scale.

The model netting perhaps some explanatory feature might be one of ethnic "acculturation". Here the result-orientation of the achievement gets emphasized. The mental predisposition seems to matter somewhat more than previously assumed; also the love for honest work and perhaps even punctuality in arriving at one's work place? But these features are found distributed among all people, and therefore lose sharply defined explanatory value. Since there seem to be far fewer unassimilated than assimilated immigrants, the problem of non-rooted Americans or Canadians of the German heritage is manageable. The ultimate perhaps rather banal self-discovery (*anagnorisis*) can be expressed simply: " ... immigrants *were* American history."[26] They spread in both American countries from coast to coast. Measurement other than on the basis of a statistical model is not promising enough. It has been shown in this connection that internal migration measuring methods can, with certain restrictions, also be used for

---

[23]Daniel J. Boorstin, a Rhodes Scholar at Oxford and a J. D. from Yale University, argued that lack of knowledge in his Bancroft Prize winning book, *The Americans: The Colonial Experience*. 1958. 1964, Bibliographical Note, p. 399.

[24]*Das Deutschkanadische Mosaik Gestern und Heute*. Ottawa 1991.

[25]Laverne Rippley, *The German Americans*. 1976.

[26]Oscar Handlin, *The Uprooted*. Little, Brown and Company. Boston, Toronto 1951, p. 3. Emphasis is mine. Second edition, 1973.

gauging emigration and immigration as a continuum. Both form the two sides of the "same coin."[27]

The result oriented, accultural interpretation of a settlement history here attempted in respect to setting some highlights, ultimately ends in stacking up a new little myth of its own. In another four or five years the cohort German co-settlement story of North America will amount to a round quadricentenary in the US. In Canada it has passed without anybody taking notice of it. It all began in Newfoundland, (and if that is not a Germanic name) then not a part of the same colony, by someone essaying for precious metal, which was willing to be melted into coined specie, so badly needed by sellers and purchasers speaking English on both sides of the Atlantic.

---

[27]Wilhelm Winkler, *Demometrie*. Dunker & Humblot. Berlin 1969, p. 238. See also C. H. Hamilton, *Demography*, vol. 2. 1965, p. 429-443.

Chapter 4
The prize of the bargain: who was going Dutch?

An average 19th century immigrant represented a value of productivity estimated at 650 *Thaler*, plus 150 *Thaler* in cash.[28] From 1820-1870 2.4 million Germans emigrated to the US. They represented, according to Friedrich Kapp (1824-1884), 1.75 billion *Thaler* (roughly the same, if measured in dollars) amounting to a daily gain of 1 million dollars for the US [29] during these fifty years.[30] It was not ascertained by Kapp nor could it be reconstructed after such a long time now whether Germany suffered a loss equal to those monetary figures. The German government figured out the payments saved, it had otherwise to recompense the poor with by way of *Armenfürsorge* (dole money comparable to present fwelfare). This should have been deducted, figured Kapp, whom we met as a former immigration official of New York in PART TWO chapter 5, but who was by now a prosperous banker of the *Deutsche Bank* in Berlin. On the other hand, the Bremen and Hamburg shipping lines, the North German Lloyd and the Hapag, prospered and let to an employment boom in Northwestern Germany.

Still on balance the US and Canada both come out way ahead; Germany finds itself heavily on the loser's end. So it remains incomprehensible why the German government did not look into this surreptitious subsidizing of the US and Canadian monetary balances.

Going Dutch, according to the premises here argued, implies that each party is paying his or her own share. If Germans went more often than not as families, each of the life partners paid her or his due. Clandestinely the German government subsidized the export of her people rather than goods. It *went Dutch*, so to speak, all itself. Chancellor Caprivi pointed his finger in more directions than one. By a reversal of the trekking goals the "Wild East" in Europe became the "Wild West" in North America. North America *did not go Dutch* with her German immigrants. Rather she gave her best by going Dutch herself, which means the US provided the framework and the guidelines to immigration at large. The rest was up to them. The single states were probably even more keenly interested in fresh immigrants than the federal government in Washington.

Going Dutch – where? Not the southern direction of the Mississippi, but the up-river Northwest territory of the Missouri pointing toward St. Louis, Kansas City, Omaha and Bismarck, heavily settled by German immigrants, marked the economic expansion of the future. Not the cotton hand picking South, but the

---

[28]V. Senger u. Etterlin, op. cit., p. 47.

[29]*Zur Auswanderungsfrage. Aus und Über Amerika. Thatsachen und Erlebnisse.* vol. 1. Julius Springer Berlin 1876, p. 174f, quoted second hand from Senger u. Etterlin, f. n. 28.

[30]This figure by Kapp did not include the surplus made by the U.S. Treasury.

land machine wheat producing Northwest profited most from these new developments.

Gone American: The reader must be made aware in the end that the "Dutch" symbolism, historically attached to these settlements, wore off over time. These places, from the beginning, were semi-public settlements with semi-private reminiscences. The linking "cohortiveness" was bound to wane. For the most recently raised inhabitants do not speak the old language any longer. Thus the credit for the co-founding effort, resulting in a new development, only indirectly goes to the forbears, but directly to the North American surrounding, their offsprings' new home land.

Germans Settling: Although the "German forbears' " derived percentage in the US population is very high, namely 23% according to the US Census figures, and 11% on the basis of Canadian census figures, historically most "German" North-American immigrants came to live in areas that were not founded or co-founded by members of their strong minorities, but elsewhere. Even a rounded, fluid amount of at least 2,500 co-founded places in the US, and almost 500 in Canada, would at the most make up for no more than 2% of all places founded in the US, and 3% of all places, or a slightly higher percentage, in Canada than in the US.

These comparative figures may contain the beinning of a correction for the thesis that German settlers either "clustered" in the two countries, or co-founded new places. They did both in various degrees, and in so doing, paved the way for their own or their places' assimilation in both Canada and the US. In that sense, generations of people have truly "disappeared" in the American and Canadian populations at large. Thus the ultimate credit for their settling efforts goes to the North American home continent and their inhabitants.

Chapter 5
Americana Teutonicae: E Pluribus Duo; A Mari Usque Ad Mare

North America: No continental superstate developed on the North American Continent. Disregarding the Quebec question for a moment Canada seems secure in her borders. The US is not threatening her Northern neighbor. There has been peace for 190 years between the two.

Both countries are *going Dutch* with each other, that is, pay for their own ways of making government function. Germans, despite their continued arrival in either country, have long become mainstream Americans south of the border, or Canadians north of the border. This demarcation line is mostly a straight one, a signpost. It indicates different political and cultural customs exist and operate separately. Immigration is big business, but it is not subsidized.

It is easy for a Canadian to become an American (although most Canadians would not like to take this step). It is not much harder for a German Canadian to become a US American, and thus a German American in this secondary sense. Many born Canadians and *"hyphenate"* citizens come down to Florida every winter anyhow. You simply hitch up a trailer and go. And some stay for good, German-Canadians among them.

The two countries owe and pay their fellow citizens of German heritage respect, as these citizens owe their respective countries gratitude and tax. The fact that these two separate countries are politically and culturally differently structured , is owed to a small degree also to the silent, but nevertheless active, caring citizens from the Old Countries, in as much as they walked the extra mile in acculturating to a more British style of life in the North, and a less British style of life in the South. The overarching cultural bond is the English language.

Having reached our scientific goal line, we can breathe a sigh of relief. With a good-bye wave from Lancaster County, Pennsylvania, an old *Dutch wagon* rumbles to the horizon, where we observe the sun setting over the roof-top of a Conestoga Museum, its final destination. The journey that was begun out of curiosity, is finished out of reverence for non-typical Pennsylvania, counter-balancing other states: *Just for nice*.

Concerning the assumed dichotomy between native Americans and immigrants, or Anglos and Germans in America, we conclude that it is a superficial one, close to being false. Already during the next generation, the timid encounter has become a vivid amalgamation. Our model of 'going Dutch', that is, immigrating at one's own risk and responsibility, is two-dimensional only at the start. During the next generation the model has to be 'deepened'.

After several immigration waves the German 'pillar' is a strong component of the ever changing American culture. This component carries its weight and helps balance the books on the North American civilizations of Canada and the US. Summed up in a formula: The first generational GOING DUTCH emigration

203

(controlled by family law of blood relationship) has merged in a second or third generational GONE AMERICAN immigration (governed by the law of soil surrounding). Or in Professor F. S. C. Northrop's terminology,[31] the naive realistic American concept, shared by the North German hansards, won over the formal construct of European blood relation law, imported by High German speaking immigrants.

Thus the two-dimensional push-pull model needs to be deepened by onemore settlement dimension, tentatively called private creativity gone public. It was exerted by people joining in action; in our case, by having co-founded and settled places both in Canada and in the US.

In terms of "practical politics" these co-founding processes made the communities in North America *different* from others, but stable. The places co-founded by German craftsmanship were constructed for fulfilling *Canadian* or *American* cultural premises of a new but carefully nurtured heritage of know-how and knowledge. Further enquiry and "epistemological study" (in the sense of F. S. C. Northrop) in terms of practical settlement politics on a state by state basis is encouraged. Perhaps my deliberations can serve as a springboard for further research.

---

[31] *Philosophical Anthropology and Practical Politics*. McMillan N. Y. 1960, with a forerunner in "The Comparative Philosophy of Comparative Law", *Cornell Law Quarterly*, vol. XLV, No. 4, summer 1960. See the dedication of this book.

PART SIX

BIBLIOGRAPHICAL DATA

Chapter 1 Glossary of terms and clichés mentioned or discussed in this book *

Benrath line, phonetically bordering the Northern German speaking manner
Bier, German brewed beer
daller /dollar// *daelder*
Deutsch, "Dutch"
Dutch, in the meaning of Hollandic
Dutch wagon /Conestoga wagon
Forty-Eighters, German immigrants of 1848ff.
frankfurter
Galgenhumor/gallow's humour
"German", an uncertain term if used before 1871
hamburger
Hanse, medieval North German trading association
hanseatic, *Hanse*-like
hometown
Hollandic, in the broad sense of Netherlandic
Hoosier State
hyphenism
Janké, see Yankee
jus sanguinis (law of blood) vs. *jus soli* (law of soil)
kindergarten
Kleinhans, original meaning of Yankee
Kraut, German, derived from *crewt*, not Sauerkraut
musical
nativism
newspaper publishing
Palatinate
Plattdü(ü)tsch , Low[er] German
Plautdietsch, West Prussian Low German dialect
Santa Claus (also patron saint of shipping)
Ship of Fools

   *Famous Germans, according to G. Wilk, *Americans from Germany*, practically hailed in even numbers from the two principal areas south and north of the Benrath Line: 8 Southerners, 8 Hessians, 5 Rhenish/Palatines, 3 Bavarians; 12 Northwesterners, 8 Berliners, 1 Silesian, 1 Thuringian. The seventeen "*Auswanderungsvereine,*" were founded, according to v. Senger u. Etterlin's lists, p. 460f., in near equal numbers, in the North and in the South of Germany, between 1815 and 1860.

205

Staats-Zeitung
Teutonic
Turnerbund
Uncle Sam, abbreviation for US
Yankee/Yänke, see *Kleinhans*
yodel

Chapter 2
German American and German Canadian bibliography

A. Place name sources bibliography

Websters Geographical Dictionary: A Dictionary of Names of Places. B. & C. Merriam Co. Springfield 1967.

Ed. Seltzer, Leon E., eds: *The Columbia Lippincott Gazetteer of the World.* Columbia U. P. 1952.

Corpus Almanac & Canadian Source Book. 31rst ed. Barbara Law. Don Mills Ontario 1996.

Sealock, Richard B. and Seely, Pauline A. *Bibliography of Place Names Literature.* US, Canada, [Alaska, Newfoundland]. 3rd ed. Chicago 1982.

Room, Adrian. *Placenames of the World*: Origins and Meanings of the Names for over 5000 Natural Features, Countries, Capitals, Territories, Cities and Historic Sites. McFarland & Co.

Jefferson, N. C. and London 1997.

Stewart, George R. *American Place Names.* Oxford U. P. 1970.

----------- . *Names on the Land: The Classic Story of American Placenaming.* 4th. ed. San Francisco 1982.

Gannett, Henry. *A Guide to the Origin of Place Names in the United States.* 1971.

Wolk, Allan. *The Naming of America.* Th. Nelson Inc., Nashville/ N. Y. 1977.

Taylor, Isaac. *Words and Places: Illustrations of History, Ethnology and Geography.* Thomas, Edward, reed. E. P. Publications 1978.

Armstrong, George Henry. *The Origin and Meaning of Place Names in Canada.* McMillan Toronto Rp. 1972.

Baker, Ronald L., Ed. *The Study of Place Names* (Hoozier Folklore) Terre Haute, IND 1991.

Shankle, George Earlie. *American Nicknames.* 2nd ed. N. Y. 1955.

Kelsie B. Harder. *Illustrated Dictionary of Place Names in the United States and Canada.* N. Y. 1976.

Zelinsky, Wilbur. *The Cultural Geography of the United States.* Prentice-Hall Englewood Cliffs N. J. 1973.

Benjamin F. Shearer and Barbara S. Shearer. *State Names, Seals, Flags and Symbols.* Revised ed. Westport CT 1994.

Berger, Dieter. *Geographische Namen in Deutschland.* Duden Mannheim 1993.

Geographie der Erde Neue Enzyklopädie.[Index] Eco/Bertelsmann/Octopus 2000.

Small, A., Witherick, Michael. *A Modern Dictionary of Geography. London New York 1995.*

Ed., *Canadian Encyclopedia.* Four volumes. 1985.

B. German American and Canadian bibliography: secondary literature

Adams, Willi Paul. *Die USA im 20. Jahrhundert.* R. Oldenbourg Verlag München 2000.

Adams, Willi Paul/ Peter Lösche. *Länderbericht USA.* Geschichte-Politik. Geographie-Wirtschaft. Gesellschaft-Kultur. 3. aktualisierte Auflage. Campus Verlag 1999.

Bailyn, Bernard. *From Protestant Peasants to Jewish Intellectuals. The Germans in the Peopling of America.* Annual Lecture ... Oxford Berg 1986.

Bade, Klaus, ed. *Deutsche im Ausland. Fremde in Deutschland. Migration in Geschichte und Gegenwart.* C. h. Beck Verlag München 1993.

Bassler, Gerhard. *Das Deutschkanadische Mosaik Heute und Gestern.* Ottawa 1991.

Blume, Helmut. *USA Eine Geographische Landeskunde.* Wissenschaftliche Buchgesellschaft Darmstadt 1987.

Cazden, Robert E. *A Social History of the German Book Trade in America to the Civil War.* Camden House Columbus, S. C. 1984.

Duden, Gottfried. *Europa und Deutschland von Nordamerika aus betrachtet.* 3 Bände. Berlin 1832-1834.

Fuchs, L. H. *The American Kaleidoscope: Race, Ethnicity, and Civic Culture.* Hanover N. H. 1990.

Gehring, Charles T. *The Dutch Language in Colonial New York*: An investigation of a language in decline and its relationship to social change. University Microfilms Diss. Indiana 1973. UMI ProQuest. Printed by xerographic process Ann Arbor, MI 2002.

Gellinek, Christian. *"Those Dam' Dutch": The Beginning of German Immigration in North America during the Thirty Years War.* Campus Verlag Frankfurt/M und New York 1996.

--------------- . *Northwest Germany in Northeast America.* Geschichte Bd. 13. LIT Verlag Münster 1997.

Goldberg, Michael A. and Mercer, John. *The Myth of the North American City.* Vancouver 1986.

Goodfriend, Joyce D. *Before the Melting Pot: Society and Culture in Colonial New York City 1664-1730.* Princeton U. P. 1992.

Helling, Rudolf A. *A Socio-Economic History of German-Canadians.* VjSW Beihefte Nr. 75. Franz Steiner Verlag Wiesbaden 1984.

Jones JR, Henry Z. *The Palatine Families of New York 1710.* vol. s 1 and 2. 1985. (A third vol. *More Palatine Families of New York*).

Just, Michel/Bretting, Agnes/Bickelmann, Hartmut. *Auswanderung und Schifffahrtsinteressen...* Stuttgart 1992.

Kamphoefner, Walter D. *The Westfalians from Germany to Missouri.* Princeton U. P. 1987.

208

Keyser, Erich und Stoob, Heinz, *Deutsche Städtebücher*, five volumes in 11 parts, 1952ff.

Kloss, H. *Atlas der im 19. und frühen 20. Jahrhundert entstandenen deutschen Siedlungen in USA*. Marburg. N. G. Elwert 1974.

Lehmann, Heinz. *The German Canadians 1750-1937. Immigration Settlement and Culture*. Ed. by Gerhard P. Bassler. St. John's Newfoundland 1986.

Lenz, Karl. *Wissenschaftliche Länderkunde Band 30. Kanada. eine Geographische Landeskunde*. Wissenschaftliche Buchgesellschaft Darmstadt 1988.

Meyer, Hildegard. *Nordamerika im Urteil des deutschen Schrifttums bis zur Mitte des 19. Jahrhunderts*. Hamburg 1929.

Moltmann, Günter, ed. *Aufbruch nach Amerika ... 1816/17*. Wunderlich Tübingen 1979.

Och, Joseph. *Der Deutschamerikanische Farmer ...* Columbus, OH 1913.

Olshausen, Theodor. *Die Vereinigten Staaten von Nordamerika im Jahre 1852* . In drei Bänden. Kiel 1853.

Pilz, Thomas, ed. *Die Deutschen und die Amerikaner. The Germans and the Americans*. Moos Verlag München 1977.

Ratzel, Friedrich. *Die Vereinigten Staaten von Amerika*. II Bände. Politische und Wirtschafts-Geographie. München 1893.

Reppmann, Joachim. *"Freiheit, Bildung und Wohlstand für Alle!" ... 1847-1860*. Wyk auf Föhr 1994.

Rippley, La Vern. *The German-Americans*. Twayne Boston 1976.

Rossnagel, Paul. *Die Stadtbevölkerung der Vereinigten Staaten*. Tübingen 1928.

Ruetenik, Julius. *Berühmte Deutsche Vorkämpfer 1626-1901*. Cleveland 1904.

Sachse, Julius Friedrich. *Germany and America 1450-1700*. Re-ed. by Don H. Tolzmann. Heritage Books, Inc. 1897/1991.

Schrader, Frederick Franklin. *The Germans in the Making of America*. Boston 1924.

Senger und Etterlin, von, Stefan. *Neu-Deutschland in Nordamerika*. Nomos Geschichte 1991.

Stedtman, Heinrich. *Der kleine Engländer. Oder die Kunst in kürzester Zeit englisch zu lernen*. Grimma 1848. Reedited 1851.

Trommler, Frank, ed. *Amerika und Die Deutschen*. Bestandsaufnahme einer 300jährigen Geschichte. Westdeutscher Verlag Opladen 1986.

Welmer-Franco, Silke. *Deutsche Dienstmädchen in Amerika. 1850-1914*. Waxmann 1994.

Wilk, Gerard. *Americans from Germany*. 1976 rp. 1995.

Zachrasiewicz, Waldemar, *Das Deutschlandbild in der amerikanischen Literatur*. Wissenschaftliche Buchgesellschaft Darmstadt 1998.

Zelinsky, Wilbur. *Exploring the Beloved Country*. Iowa City w. y.

Zögner, Lothar, *Amerika im Kartenbild*. Berlin 1976.

Zucker, Adolf Eduard von. *The Forty-Eighters. Political Refugees of the German Revolution of 1848*. New York R & R 1967.

C. Further background secondary literature

Behrmann, Walter. *Über die niederdeutschen Seebücher des fünfzehnten und sechzehnten Jahrhunderts.* Hamburg 1906. Rp Meridian Amsterdam 1978.

Boorstin, Daniel J. *The Americans. The Colonial Experience.* 1958. Vintage Books 1964.

Reese, William S. & Miles George A. *Creating America.* An Exhibition of the Beinecke Rare Book Library. New Haven, CT 1992.

Hess, Wolfgang/ Klose, Dietrich, ed.s. *Vom Taler zum Dollar. 1486-1986.* München 1986.

Mossman, Philip L. *Money of the American Colonies and Confederation.* Numismatic Studies Nr. 20. N. Y. 1993.

Nussbaum, Hans. *A History of the Dollar.* 2nd ed. N. Y. 1958.

McKay, George. *Early American Currency.* N. Y. 1944.

Shumway, George. *Conestoga Wagon 1750-1850.* 2nd ed. w.y. w. pl.

Jones, Peter d'A. and Holli, Melvin G. *Ethnic Chicago.* Eerdmans Grand Rapids,MI 1981.

Ricks, Christopher, ed. *The Faber Book of America.* London/Boston 1992.

Trommler, Frank and Shore, Elliott, eds. *The German American Encounter: Conflict and Cooperation between Two Cultures 1800-2000.* Berghahn Books New York Oxford 2001.

Titles added after completion:

Grabbe, Hans-Jürgen. *Vor der großen Flut. Die europäische Migration in die Vereinigten Staaten von Amerika.* USA-Studien 10. Franz Steiner Verlag Stuttgart 2001.

Reichmann, Eberhard. Rippley, La Vern J., and Nagler, Jörg. *Immigration and Settlement Patterns in German Communities in North America.* Publications of the Max Kade German-American Center. Vol. 8. Kansas 1995; reviewed in *Yearbook of German-American Studies.* Vol. 31 (1996) p. 213f.

Epp, Reuben. *The Spelling of Low German and Plautdietsch.* Towards an Official Plautdietsch Orthography. Hillsboro, KS 1996.

Stockman, Robert Lee. *Platt Düütsch/ Low German.* A Brief History of the People and Language. Alto, MI 1998. XIII plus 445 pp.

Bassler, Gerhard, "The Problem of German-Canadian Identity", *Yearbook of German-American Studies.* Vol. 33 (1998) pp. 157-165.

Chapter 3
References on state place names

Before Place Names could be viewed on the internet (1999ff.) the following states, sometimes coinciding with some degree of German American heritage, had reference works:

ARIZONA	William C. Barnes. *Arizona Place Names.* 1935. Rev. Byrd H. Granger. 1960 [7,200 entries]
CALIFORNIA	Erwin G. Gudde. *California Place Names.* 1949. second ed. 1960. Berkeley U. P. 1969. 416 pp.
CONNECTICUT	Arthur H. Hughes & Morse S. Allen. *Connecticut Place Names.* Hartford 1976. 907 pp.
FLORIDA	Allen C. Morris. *Florida Place Names.* University of Miami Press 1974. [14,000 entries]
ILLINOIS	*A List of Illinois Place Names.* Springfield, IL. 1968. 321 pp.
INDIANA	Ronald L. Baker, ed. *The Study of Place Names. Hoosier Folklore Society.* Terre Haute, IN 1991
KANSAS	Richard C. Clark, "Place Names of German Origin in Kansas," *Beiträge zur Namenforschung.* Neue Folge. Heft 4 (1970) 5: 371-404. The Kansas State Historical Society will complete all county histories end of 2002
KENTUCKY	Robert Rennick. *Kentucky Place Names.* Lexington, KY 1984
MINNESOTA	Warren Upham. *Minnesota Geographic Names.* 1920. Rp. St. Paul, MN 1969. 788 pp.
MISSOURI	Robert L. Ramsey. *Introduction to a Survey of Missouri Place Names.* University of Missouri 1934. 124 pp.
NEBRASKA	Lilian L. Fitzpatrick. *Nebraska Place Names.* Lincoln University of Nebraska Press 1960. 227 pp.
NEW YORK	Alexander Clarence Flick. *New York Place Names.* Columbia University Press 1937
OHIO	William D. Overman. *Ohio Town Names.* Akron, OH 1958. 155 pp. [1,200 names]
OKLAHOMA	George H. Shirk. *Oklahoma Place Names.* 1965. Second ed. University of Oklahoma Press 1974. 268 pp, maps
OREGON	Lewis A. McArthur. *Oregon Geographical Names.* 1952. Fourth ed. 1974. 835 pp.
PENNSYLVANIA	Abraham H. Espenshade. *Pennsylvania Place Names.*

211

	Penn State College 1925. Gale Research Rp. 1969, and Baltimore, MD 1970
RHODE ISLAND	Thomas W. Bicknell. *Place Names in Rhode Island.* New York AHS 1920
SOUTH DAKOTA	Edward C. Ehrensperger, ed. *South Dakota Place Names.* Work Project Administration. 1941. 689 pp. Rp. Sioux Falls, S.D. 1973
UTAH	John W. Van Cott and Kimball T. Harper. *Utah Place Names.* A Comprehensive Guide to the Origin of Place Names. University of Utah Press. Salt Lake City 1990
TENNESSEE	TN Place names and post offices on GNIS (see below the first line)
VIRGINIA	Raus McD. Hanson. *Virginia Place Names.* Verona, VA 1969. 253 pp.; VA Geographic Names on GNIS (see below the first line); Thomas H. Biggs, *Geographical and Cultural Names in Virginia.* Information Circular Number 20. Charlottesville, VA 1974
WASHINGTON	Edmond St. Meany. *Origin of Washington Geographic Names.* Seattle 1923. 357 pp. Rp. Gale Research Research Detroit 1968. WA Place Names Database (see below the first line)
WEST VIRGINIA	Hamill Kenney. *West Virginia Place Names.* Piedmont, WV 1945. 768 pp. Rp. WV University Library 1960
WYOMING	Mae B. Urbanek. *Wyoming Place Names.* Third ed. Boulder, CO. Johnson 1974. 236 pp., maps

For the rest of the states

AL, AK, CO, DE, GA, HI, ID, IA, KS, LA, ME, MD, MA, MI, MS, MT, NM, NE, NH, NJ, NC, ND, SC, TN, VT, WI

see either GNIS (Geographic Names Information Service), Local Names directory, US Census Redistricting Data Map, US Geological Survey Geographic Names Infomation Service, Gazetteer and other Place Names Server on the internet; Query by Geographical Names; Getty Thesaurus Geographic Names; the work on the US Gazetteer is still ongoing. For Canadian

server data see: http://geonames.nrcan.gc.ca

TEXAS

The Handbook of Texas Online, the first such in the US, is available on the web, easily handled and a first-rate reference book on place names of Texas. It may owe its existence because Texas as a former republic owns the domain over its territory, not as in other states, the US government

INDIAN RESERVATIONS Burkhard Hofmeister, "Die Grenze von Idianerreservationen in USA." Institut für Geographie, T. U. Berlin, ohne Jahr; W. E. Washburn, *The Indian in America.* New York 1975.

Chapter 4
Statistical data

Table 5 Gn Places

Number State	Year Foundd.	Nr. Counties	Gn Places	North Gn Names
EAST and WEST NORTH CENTRAL				
1 Missouri	1821	114	53	39
2 Iowa	1841	99	52	35
3 Illinois	1818	102	56	38
4 Wisconsin	1840	72	50	34
5 Indiana	1816	92	62	35
6 Ohio	1803	88	53	38
7 Michigan	1837	88	56	36
8 Minnesota	1858	87	56	28
9 Kansas	1861	105	61	41
10 Nebraska	1849	93	46	26
11 N. Dakota	1889	53	49	30
12 S. Dakota	1889	66	35	22
WEST SOUTH CENTRAL				
13 Kentucky	1792	120	37	23
14 Texas	1845	254	101	66
15 Arkansas	1836	75	38	24
16 Lousiana	1812	64	36	24
Irrespective of CENSUS AREA				
17 New Jersey	1787	21	29	17
18 Maryland	1788	23	57	33
19 S. Carolina	1788	46	21	13
20 New York	1788	62	37	25
21 W. Virginia	1863	55	52	29
22 N. Carolina	1789	100	31	21
23 Tennessee	1796	95	43	25
24 Montana	1889	56	17	10
25 Pennsylvania	1787	67	125	82
26 Virginia	1788	95	42	25
27 Oklahoma	1907	77	29	20
28 Georgia	1788	159	32	21
29 Alabama	1819	67	33	19
30 Mississippi	1817	82	24	18
31 Delaware	1787	3	8	4
32 Florida	1845	67	23	16
33 California	1850	58	22	14
34 Colorado	1876	63	28	18
35 Wyoming	1890	23	14	9

36 Idaho	1890	44	21	13	
37 Washington	1889	39	24	14	
38 Oregon	1859	36	28	17	
39 Utah	1896	29	8	6	
40 Nevada	1864	16	7	4	
41 Arizona	1912	14	20	13	
42 New Mexico	1912	33	9	6	
43 Connecticut	1788	8	7	5	
44 Massachusetts	1788	14	5	5	
45 Rhode Island	1790	5	0	0	
46 Vermont	1791	14	3	2	
47 N. Hampshire	1788	10	4	3	
48 Maine	1819	16	14	9	
49 Alaska	1959	none	6	4	
50 Hawaii	1959	none	0	0	South Gn Names:
50 Totals	1990	2840	1.664	1.054	588

1990	statistics	percentage		63%	36%
		non-German	Names 20	or	1%

Table 6 Protocol Sequence

Rank	State	Nr. of Places	co-peopled in
1	Pennsylvania	125	Philadelphia
1			Pittsburgh
2	Texas	101	San Antonio
3	Indiana	62	Indianapolis
4	Kansas	61	Topeka
5	Minnesota	56	St. Paul
6	Illinois	56	Chicago
7	Maryland	57	Baltimore
8	Michigan	56	Detroit
9	Iowa	52	Davenport
10	West Virginia	52	Wheeling
11	Missouri	52	St. Louis
12	Wisconsin	50	Milwaukee
13	Ohio	53	Cleveland
13			Cincinnati
14	N. Dakota	49	
15	Nebraska	46	Omaha
16	Tennessee	43	Memphis
17	Virginia	42	Richmond
18	New York	37	N. Y. C.
18			Buffalo
19	Kentucky	37	Louisville
20	Arkansas	38	x
21	Louisiana	36	New Orleans
22	South Dakota	35	x
23	New Jersey	29	Newark
23			Jersey City

Table 7 Further Statistics

Heinz Kloss, *Atlas der deutschen Siedlung in USA. Atlas of German-American Settlements.* N. G. Elwert Verlag Marburg 1974. Printed with a subsidy by the DFG [First column representing 2,565,707 inhabitants; Second. % column [for 1920] after Rossnagel, (1928)]

Comparative statistics of German immigrants rest on the US Census in 1910 and 1920:

Name	German-American Inhabitants	1910	1920	Rank of %
New York City, NY	606,173	12.7%	12%	29th
Chicago, IL	426,466	19.5%	16%	13th
Milwaukee, WI	166,106	44.4%	35.7%	2nd
Philadelphia, PA	150,654	9.7%	9.5%	34th
St. Louis, MO	138,094	20.2%	21.8%	12th
Buffalo, NY	118,234	27.9%	18.5%	7th
Detroit, MI	113,966	24.5%	12.7%	9th
Cleveland, OH	100,467	18.0%	15%	14th
Cincinnati, OH	88,411	24.4%	25.5%	10th
Pittsburgh, PA	79,283	14.8%	14.2%	21rst
Baltimore, MD	77,009	13.8%	11.8%	25th
Newark, NJ	53,197	15.3%	14%	20th
San Francisco, CA	44,890	11.7%	12%	30th
Jersey City, NJ	38,060	14.4%	13.7%	24th
Saint Paul, MN	37,583	17.5%	20%	15th
Louisville, KY	28,842	15.8%	13.7%	17th
New Orleans, LA	21,969	8.8%	6%	38th
Indianapolis, IN	21,580	9.6%	8.5%	35th
Peoria, IL	20,488	15.7%	16.8%	19th
Boston, MA	19,180	--	2.8%	[40th]
Syracuse,NY	18,272	13.4%	12%	27th
Hoboken, NJ	18,136	26.0%	22%	8th
Dayton, OH	16,934	14.6%	14%	21rst
Marathon county, WI	16,329 farmer	43.0%	----	4th
Albany, NY	13,337	13.3%	12.4%	28th
Washington, D.C.	13,237	5.6%	4%	39th
Fort Wayne, IN	13,176	20.6%	20.4%	11th
Davenport, IO	12,912	30.0%	28.4%	6th
Oshkosh, WI	11,977	36.3%	45.8%	5th

Evansville, IN	11,856	17.0%	16.7%	16th
Omaha, NB	11,711	9.4%	9.3%	36th
Sheboygan, WI	11,479	43.4%	53.9%	3rd
Grand Rapids, MI	11,295	10.0%	7.2%	33th
Elizabeth, NJ	10,676	14.5%	14%	22nd
San Antonio, TX	8,876	10.3%	7.7%	32nd
Washington City, TX	6,823	50.0%	?	1rst
[Galveston, TX]	3,927	13.5%	?	26th
[Leavenworth, KA]	3,069	15.8%	?	18th
[Aberdeen, SD]	1,132	10.6%	?	31rst
Denver, CO	---	9%	9%	37th
Dubuque, IO	[coequal Davenport]	30%	30%	6th

Table 8 Grid immigration Gn/American Settling in almost 400 Years

Period	TU Dresden [1994]	Census [1821-2000]	Zelinsky [1993]	Blume [1987]	Kloss [1974]	own estimate [1996]
1607-1683		none x	none	open	none	---
1683-1743		x	Brinck	300.000	250.000	---
1748-1754		x	[30.000]			---
1755-1820		x	[300.000]	300.000		---
1821 .	Bureau of Immigration starts statistics		:			---
1821-1831		31.000				---
1831-1840		150.000				---
1841-1850		435.000				---
1851-1860		952.000	[1.600.000]			---
Civil War	(til 1890)					
1871-1890	5.000.000	1.900.000				---
1890-1913		1.100.000	[3.000.000]			
W W I						
1921-1940		600.000				---
W W II						
1941-1990		1.237.000				---
Total	7.700.000	6.500.000 bis 1990]	none	7.000.000 [bis 1987]	7.000.000	6.700.000 reg. Immigrts.
1821-1930 [1882]		immigrants inhabitants	to the US: US/Germany	48.000.000 52.000.000	[split even]	

1980 percent.	per census	areas of	Gn American	heritage	density:	
		NC	12 States	40% average	Gn American	heritage
		SC	8 states	14% average	Gn American	heritage
		SATL	7 states	18% average	Gn American	heritage
		MATL	4 states	22% average	Gn American	heritage
		Rest	17 states	13% average	Gn American	heritage
1990-2000		US. Total	48 States	ca.23%GnAm	heritage	2000
			46 States	ca.21%GnAm	heritage	1913
			13 States	ca.11%GnAm	heritage	1790
			13 Colonies	ca. 8%GnAm	heritage	1776
		CAN Total	10 Provinces	ca.11%GCAN	heritage	2000

Chapter 5
Letter by F. S. C. Northrop

YALE UNIVERSITY
LAW SCHOOL
NEW HAVEN, CONNECTICUT

FILMER S. C. NORTHROP
Sterling Professor of Philosophy and Law

20 December 1960

Mr. Christian J. Gellinek
Department of Classics
Pickering College
Newmarket, Ontario, Canada

Dear Mr. Gellinek:

Your letter of December 8th in reply to my questions is at hand. There are two things which I might do because of my interest in epistemological studies of the kind you want to pursue in your thesis for a Ph.D. I gather that you have misgivings about the University of Toronto encouraging or allowing you to do this kind of an investigation in its German Department. The difficulties in admission to a philosophy department which you indicate are also real. In any event, even if you get admitted, you would have to start from scratch and it would take far longer to get a degree in philosophy than either in German or in law. Hence I could take your epistemological type of work up here at Yale with either its German Department or the Law School.

In the former case you could work on your High German, providing they were sympathetic to the epistemological type of investigation which you desire to pursue. Or I could take it up with the Graduate Committee here in the Law School. In the latter case two things have to be considered. First, do you have your law degree from Göttingen? Second, are you proficient in Latin and Greek so that you could do an epistemological study of the creation of Roman law as a science? I take it that in a way the creation of Western law and the creation of the Latin language by people such as Cicero is a single story.

I am taking it for granted that an epistemological study of High German would not be relevant to your doctor's degree in law. One question does, however, interest me about your epistemological study of High German. Could the distinction between High and Low German have anything to do with the distinction between naive realistic folk culture and norms and formal constructs in both mathematical physics and contractual legal science? If there were such a connection, then your research in High German would have relevance to law as well as to the German Department. But even so, it might be necessary to do an epistemological analysis of the Latin language and Roman law in order to make your point with respect to High German.

It should be added that if you chose graduate work in law rather than in the German Department, you would probably be required to take at least a year's work in American law, since my colleagues would want a graduate of this school to know American common law as well as Continental European civil law.

Mr. Christian J. Gellinek   -2-   20 December 1960

        I put all these things before you in order to help you to reach
your own judgment about the best thing to do. May I add also that I do
have a philosophical colleague at the University of Toronto, Professor
John Irving. It might very well be that if I wrote him, he and colleagues
in the German Department might be able to get together so that you could
do there the kind of thing you want to do. It should be said also that
after the next academic year I go into retirement here at Yale.

        Will you let me know what your reflections are on this letter.
I am at your service.

                            Sincerely,

                            F. S. C. Northrop

                            F. S. C. Northrop

The Author

Christian Gellinek was born in Potsdam, the heart of Brandenburg, grew up in neighboring Wannsee, and passed his Abitur in Hamburg-Harburg. He studied law at Göttingen University (OLG Zelle 1957) and emigrated to Toronto, Ontario, Canada. His two highest degrees are the Ph.D. from Yale, and the Habilitation from Basel University. His most important book is a biography of Hugo Grotius, which appeared at Boston in 1983. He is listed in Who's Who in America, 56th and 57th editions and was an American citizen from 1966 to 1988.